S0-AHG-560

Incredible But True!

Kevin McFarland

ILLUSTRATED BY LUIS DOMINGUEZ

Bell Publishing Company • New York

This book was originally published as *Incredible!*
Copyright © MCMLXXVI by Hart Publishing Company, Inc.
All rights reserved.
This edition is published by Bell Publishing Company, Inc.,
a division of Crown Publishers, Inc.,
by arrangement with Hart Publishing Company, Inc.
    b   c   d   e   f   g   h
BELL 1978 EDITION
Manufactured in the United States of America

Library of Congress Cataloging in Publication Data
McFarland, Kevin.
    Incredible but true!
    SUMMARY: A collection of anecdotes about
extraordinary people, unusual plants and animals,
unique structures, and astounding historical
events.
    Edition of 1976 published under title: In-
credible!
    1. Curiosities and wonders.   [1. Curiosities
and wonders]   I. Dominquez, Luis, 1923-
II. Title
AG243.M314   1978   031'.02   78-58693
ISBN 0-517-26321-1

Contents

Garfield could write two languages at the same time

James A. Garfield, 20th President of the United States, was, like Lincoln, born in a log cabin. But by hard work and real ability, he became the head of Hiram Institute, a major general during the Civil War, a leader in Congress, and finally Chief Executive of the United States.

Like many other people, the well-educated former backwoodsman was ambidextrous. That is to say, he was capable of writing with either his left hand or his right. But Garfield was probably unique in being able to write the two classical languages—Latin and Greek—at the *same time*, one with his right hand, the other with his left!

Charles Charlesworth, a seven-year-old, died of old age

Charles Charlesworth first saw the light of day on March 14, 1829. No one in his home town of Straffordshire, England, had any reason to doubt that he would be anything but a happy and healthy child. And indeed, the boy's first years were blissfully ordinary.

At the age of four, however, little Charles sprouted whiskers and reached sexual maturity. Aging rapidly over the next three years, Charles developed conspicuous veins and tendons, white hair, shriveled skin, and the gait and posture of a man ten times his age.

One day in his seventh year, Charles fainted and did not revive. The remarkable child had expired of natural causes, the coroner ruled— merely old age.

The Koutoubiya of Marrakesh is the world's only perfumed minaret

A visitor to Marrakesh, Morocco might believe that his imagination is playing tricks on him when he confronts the Koutoubiya minaret. The tower is a delight to the eye, but of course there is nothing illusory about that. What mystifies tourists is that the minaret seems to give off a delightful smell as well!

The sweet odor visitors detect is quite real. The slender Koutoubiya—a perfect representative of the golden age of Moslem architecture—

has been famous for more than seven centuries for the fragrance emanating from its walls.

The story of the sweet-smelling minaret begins in 1195. In that year, the Sultan Yakub al Mansur defeated Alphonso VIII, the Castilian king, at the battle of Alarcos in Spain. To thank Mohammed for the victory, Yakub ordered that a mosque be built at his capital, Marrakesh. And into the mortar used in the building of the

mosque were mixed some 960 sacks of musk. That fragrance can still be perceived today.

The 220-foot tower affords a magnificent view of Marrakesh. Yet for more than six centuries, only blind muezzins (Moslem priests) were permitted to climb to the top of the tower. For from that height it would have been possible to look into the open courtyards of the harems of Marrakesh — a sight barred to all men!

Giuseppe de Mai had two hearts in his body

When anything pleased Giuseppe de Mai, a resident of Naples, he was doubly excited, for not one but two hearts pounded away inside his chest.

This condition occurs so rarely that scientists throughout Europe became interested in Signor de Mai. In 1894, the London Academy of Medicine offered de Mai $15,000 to obtain his body after Giuseppe died.

Chang and Eng were the original Siamese twins

"Siamese twins" are two separate, identical organisms, each a complete or nearly complete individual. While such births occur with some frequency, only rarely do the twins survive.

Siamese twins may be joined at either the chest, the abdomen, the back, or the top of the head. In cases where the twins share a vital organ, surgical division is not possible, and the twins must go through life together, just as Chang and Eng did in the last century.

Chang and Eng were born in 1811 of Chinese parents in Siam (whence the name for the condition). They were joined at the breastbone, but were otherwise fully developed, independent beings. They toured with P.T. Barnum's circus for years before settling down as farmers in North Carolina. They adopted the last name of Bunker—why, no one knows—and simultaneously married two daughters of a farmer named Yates.

Chang and Eng each ran his own farm one mile from the other's. How, you ask? Chang and Eng would spend three days of each week with one wife and three days with the other wife. What they did on the seventh day, the Lord only knows.

They lived very happily in North Carolina, and between them produced 22 offspring. When one twin died on January 17, 1874, the other survived for only two more hours.

Harbo and Samuelson rowed across the Atlantic Ocean

Only two men in all history have ever crossed the Atlantic Ocean by boat with only their own brawny arms for power. One June 6, 1896, George Harbo and Frank Samuelson rowed out of New York harbor in a boat only 18 feet long, with no sail to push it along nor mast to cling to in a raging storm. But they did take along five pairs of oars, 60 gallons of water, and plenty of canned goods.

And so Harbo and Samuelson, choosing a route just south of that generally plied by steamships, steered for Le Havre, France, 3,250 miles away from New York. Each man put in 18 hours a day at the oars. Five hours a day were allowed for rest, and one hour a day for eating. They generally rested during the daytime, preferring to do their hard labor during the cool hours of the night. They had planned a schedule of 54 miles a day, and they kept to it.

On July 15, a freighter took the men on board for a short respite, gave the two seafarers some fresh food, and sped them on their way. At this time, the rowing mariners decided they would do better if they headed for England. And so they did, shortening their trip by about 200 miles.

On August 1, 56 days after leaving New York, Harbo and Samuelson rowed onto a quiet coast of the Isles of Scilly, England. There were no cheering throngs to greet them, but they had completed one of the most daring voyages ever undertaken by man.

Jahangir owned more jewels than anyone who ever lived

Of the many collectors of glittering jewels down through the ages, Emperor Jahangir, the noble ruler of India who died in 1627, is the most noted who ever lived. It is reported that he owned a total of 2,235,600 carats of pearls, 931,500 carats of emeralds, 376,600 carats of rubies, 279,450 carats of diamonds, and 186,300 carats of jade.

For his time, Jahangir was an enlightened monarch. During his reign, architectural masterpieces rose throughout India.

One of the emperor's hobbies was fishing, but Jahangir never killed a fish he caught. Instead, he would place a string of pearls through the fish's gills and throw it back into the water.

If nothing else, the man was extremely vain, for his name itself, Jahangir, means "Conqueror of the World." In addition, he had other glorious titles such as "Possessor of the Planets," "Mirror of the Glories of God," and "King of Increasing Fortune."

The Venus flytrap can devour a frog

The Venus flytrap is the most well-known member of a group of plants termed "carnivorous," which subsist at least partly on nutrients obtained from the breakdown of animal protoplasm. While most plants receive all the ingredients they need to manufacture food from the atmosphere, soil, sunlight, and water, the carnivorous plants require an additional source of nutrients, chiefly nitrogen, for their survival. These additional nutrients are obtained, for the most part, by digesting insects.

But to digest an insect, a plant must first capture it! To that end, the floral kingdom has produced a number of remarkable species—and perhaps the most remarkable of these is the Venus flytrap.

This bug-baiter can be found only in the coastal marshes of the Carolinas, where the soil is extremely low in nitrogen. The plant consists of a long stem surmounted by a cluster of blossoms, and a dozen or so leaves ending in movable flaps that resemble bear traps. The flaps are hinged at midrib, and edged with sharp spines. In the reddish center of each flap, microscopic glands secrete a sweet liquid that smells much like flower nectar.

Any insect that wanders into one of these sweet-smelling lobes will pay dearly for its curiosity. On each flap are three extremely sensitive trigger hairs. If a visiting insect touches one of these hairs once, nothing happens. But if two hairs are touched, or if the same hair is touched twice, the flaps spring closed and the sharp spines interlock to imprison the catch. This closing motion is extremely rapid: flaps have been observed to close in less than a half second.

When the prey has been snared, glands inside the lobes secrete a digestive fluid which dissolves the edible parts of the insect. After several days the flaps open again, leaving only the skeletal shell of the insect, which is blown away by the wind.

Each lobe is capable of only three or four closings in its life span, after which it is discarded

and replaced by a new trap. But these lobes are spared frequent unnecessary closings by the nature of the trigger hairs. Since two hairs must be touched, or one hair touched twice, a drop of rain or a windblown seed landing in a lobe will not spring the trap. And if the snared insect is very small, the openings between the interlocked spines will permit the catch to crawl out. After such a "false alarm," the flaps will open again within a day or two, without having wasted any digestive fluids.

Actually, the Venus flytrap is misnamed, for it feeds primarily on ants and not flies. But it can digest any insect, or meat in any form. Flytraps have been known to snare creatures as large as a small frog!

The sea elephant can inflate its nose

The male sea elephant, the largest member of the seal family, can claim the largest and most unusual nose of all Antarctic creatures. This three-ton titan has a pendulous snoot that hangs down over his mouth like a short, stubby elephant's trunk. The nose has no special pur- pose, except perhaps to show an enemy when the sea elephant is ready to do battle. For when he gets angry, the sea elephant's nose fills with air and swells like a balloon, forming a proboscis up to twenty inches long!

A hummingbird can fly backwards

Hummingbirds fly in an entirely different manner from most other birds. Whereas you can liken the flying of most birds to the way an airplane flies—straight ahead, with gradual shifts in altitude—a hummingbird's flight is like that of a helicopter. They can move straight up, straight down, or even hover in one spot without falling. And hummingbirds are the only birds that can fly backwards.

This tiny, brilliantly colored bird does not, as you might imagine, owe its name to its song. In flying, the little fellow's wings beat so rapidly that a humming sound is produced—and only a blur is visible!

One species of hummingbird, known as the bee hummingbird, is the tiniest bird in the world. From the tip of the bird's bill to the end of its tail, the diminutive fellow measures only a little more than two inches—it weighs just one-tenth of an ounce!

Queen Kahena had a harem of 400 husbands

Women's lib is nothing new to the Berbers of Northwest Africa. Their famous Queen Kahena of Aurès, Algeria, had a harem of 400 male concubines.

Kahena's Occidental counterpart was an Englishwoman named Theresa Vaughn. On December 19, 1922, Mrs. Theresa Vaughn was brought up before the Police Court of Sheffield, England. The 24-year-old woman had remarried without obtaining a divorce from the disaffected Mr. Vaughn.

It was not until the hearing, however, that the police learned of the scope of the woman's bigamy. A contrite Mrs. Vaughn confessed that since she and her first husband had parted ways five years earlier, she had married 61 men. Traveling widely through the British Isles, Germany, and South Africa, Theresa had accumulated husbands at a rate of better than one a month!

Christian Heinecken was the most astounding child prodigy ever

Christian Friedrich Heinecken was born in Lübeck, Germany, in 1721. Within eight weeks of his birth, Christian was speaking intelligible German. At the age of one, he read the Pentateuch. Next year, between the ages of two and three, he familiarized himself with the entire Bible, both the Old and New Testaments.

In his third year, Christian devoted himself to the study of history and geography, and learned to read both French and Latin.

Word of the boy's prodigious intellect swept Europe, and the King of Denmark invited Christian to demonstrate his acumen at the royal residence in Copenhagen.

Powerful as Christian's intelligence was, his body was amazingly weak. His tiny fingers lacked the strength to even grasp a pen, and he was utterly unable to eat solid food. At the age of four, Little Christian predicted his imminent death. Unfortunately, he was correct.

A luminous moss grows in European caves

Visitors to certain caves in Central Europe are surprised to find the walls, ceiling, and floor gleaming with a gold-green luminescence, as if the rocks were glowing from within. These caves owe their eerie appearance not to luminous rocks, but to a feathery grey-green moss that grows on the surface of the rocks.

This moss, *Schistostega Osmundacea*, produces a series of branching filaments, on the end of which are lens-shaped cells containing grains of the green coloring matter, chlorophyll. Each "lens" concentrates the available light, no matter how faint, on the chloroplast at the bottom of the cell, enabling the plant to carry on photosynthesis in the scant light. Some of this condensed light is reflected out of the cells, and due to the chlorophyll takes on a distinctive gold-green color.

The plover finds its food in the crocodile's mouth

There isn't a person alive who would relish the idea of putting a hand into a crocodile's open mouth, for the jaws of this beast are powerful enough to crush a cow's bones with a single bite. But the daring Egyptian plover regularly places his entire body inside these treacherous jaws —not for a brief instant, but long enough for a whole meal!

The plover and the crocodile have worked out a mutually satisfactory arrangement—the bird gets food, the reptile gets service. When the crocodile has finished a meal, he opens his mouth so that the small bird can hop inside and pick the reptile's teeth clean of uneaten food. The grateful crocodile never shuts his jaws on his welcome guest.

This natural toothbrush also serves the crocodile as a lookout, riding on the reptile's back and giving shrill cries of warning of any approaching danger. And the plover, a tiny valet, digs out parasites from the crocodile's tough hide.

The Cathedral of Florence has a telltale dome

The Cathedral of Florence (Santa Maria del Fiore) features one of the most celebrated domes in architectural history. This octagonal ribbed roof structure was designed in 1420 by the first great architect of the Italian Renaissance, Filippo Brunelleschi—with one interesting peculiarity.

The builder left a small opening in the dome, just large enough to permit the passage of a thin

John Popham, a robber, became Chief Justice of England

When Sir John Popham was a law student in London, he led a wild and spendthrift life. In need of money and in search of adventure, young Popham armed himself with pistols and ventured out into the city after dark to rob the passersby.

Later on, during the reign of Queen Elizabeth I, this same John Popham rose to the highest post in the English judiciary. He became Chief Justice of England in 1592, and held that high office until his death in 1607.

beam of light. A small metal plate was set in the floor of the sanctuary, under the dome. According to the architect's design, the beam of light passing through the opening in the dome should fall exactly on that metal plate each June 21.

This seeming frivolity is not without a purpose, however. Should the beam of light fail to strike the metal plate on June 21, this would constitute a warning that the cathedral had shifted on its foundation. Most likely Brunelleschi himself feared such a shift, for the cathedral was built on a marshy site. Wheeled traffic in the area is prohibited, for fear of disturbing the historic structure.

The Incas built the first highways in America

Today's sprawling superhighways may seem to be the ultimate in road construction, but more than 350 years ago, the Inca Indians of South America built a system of roads through the Andes Mountains that would astound even modern engineers.

At its peak, the Inca Empire extended almost 2,500 miles from Colombia to Chile, and through this mountain country the Incas strung a network of roads to unite their vast domain. As the most important element of the Incas' imperial organization, the road system was built to speed communication and to provide for the efficient movement of men and supplies. The land the Incas ruled was as treacherous as it was vast, and their roads had to cut through marshes, jungles, and soaring mountains. These arteries often climbed heights of over 10,000 feet, and some roads were as long as virtually any modern highway!

Stone retaining walls bordered the roads along much of their length. Enclosed way stations along the route provided for a messenger relay system, and offered protection against sudden mountain storms. Some roads tunneled through mountain cliffs—one such tunnel is almost 750 feet long! At other points, the Incas built causeways over wide marshlands and spanned raging rivers with bridges constructed of twisted rope cables.

The longest of the Inca bridges was immortalized by Thornton Wilder's novel *The Bridge of San Luis Rey*. This 148-foot suspension span crossed a deep ravine of the Apurimac River, swinging precariously in the mountain winds 118 feet above the waters. Until the bridge fell earlier in this century, it was in use longer than any other bridge in America.

All the roads of the Inca Empire met in their mountain capital of Cuzco, Peru, which is today the oldest continually inhabited city in America. Before moving to Cuzco, however, the center of the Inca empire had been another Andes city, but it wasn't until 1911 that this "lost city" was discovered.

Machu Picchu, 50 miles north of Cuzco, is one of the few urban centers of pre-Columbian

America that survives virtually intact. The city straddles a narrow saddle between two peaks, 2,000 feet above a river. Paved stairway streets—stepped because of the slope of the

city—weave between stone houses and military fortifications. Hundreds of agricultural terraces give the city the appearance of a gigantic stairway climbing the side of a mountain.

Even today, archaeologists admit the possibility that other Inca roads and cities may still be lost in the Andes, but to this point Machu Picchu is their greatest find.

31

Sharon Adams sailed alone across the Pacific

On July 26, 1969, Sharon Sites Adams, a 39-year-old California homemaker, sailed her thirty-one-foot ketch into San Diego harbor.

She was given a warm, emotional welcome by her husband, who is a professional sailing instructor, and by hundreds of enthusiastic friends, relatives, and admirers.

Sharon Adams had just become the first woman ever to sail alone across the Pacific Ocean. She had covered the 5,618-mile distance from her starting point, Yokohama, Japan, to San Diego, in 74 days, 17 hours, 15 minutes.

The Church of Monte Cassino accommodates only three people

The church of Monte Cassino, near the city of Covington, Kentucky, is the smallest church in the world.

The church—which from the outside resembles a mausoleum—can accommodate only three people at one time, providing each with a rough wooden bench. The benches face a tiny altar. The walls of the church are only eight feet high, and the church's midget belfry is so tiny that it cannot contain a bell.

The miniature church was built in 1850 by Benedictine monks. They named it after the first Benedictine monastery, Monte Cassino in Italy—which was reduced to rubble by bombs in 1944.

Blondin crossed over Niagara Falls on a tightrope while pushing a wheelbarrow

Jean François Grandet, who performed under the name of Blondin because of his flowing blond hair, was the daredevil supreme. In 1859, he had a three-inch rope strung 1,100 feet across Niagara Falls, 160 feet above the raging waters. Balancing himself with a 40-foot pole, the intrepid Frenchman pedaled over the Falls on a bicycle. Scorning death, he once walked over the tightrope blindfolded. On another day, he pushed a wheelbarrow across the Falls on the tightrope.

On one occasion, he announced he was going to carry a man across the chasm piggy-back style. One hundred thousand curious Americans and Canadians came to Niagara to see that one. The only person he could get to do the stunt with him was his manager, who trembled so violently that Blondin vowed never to do a stunt with a human again.

Always dreaming up new ways to astound the spectators, Blondin would turn somersaults on the rope. He would also have a man below the Falls shoot bullets through a hat he held up as a target. The acrobat even cooked and ate an egg prepared on a frying pan heated on a stove which he had carried out to the middle of the rope himself!

One of his most fantastic feats was to walk halfway out on the brightly lighted rope after dark, and then order the light put out. When this was done, Blondin would continue to the other side in inky blackness.

On September 8, 1860, the Prince of Wales, who was touring North America, showed up in

Canada to watch Blondin's final performance over the Falls. And what a show Blondin gave him!

Blondin attached short stilts to his legs; on each stilt, there was a hook which went around the rope. Halfway across the gorge, Blondin swung by the hooks head-down from the rope. Scores of men and women fainted, believing that he had lost his balance, fallen, and was going to plunge to his death. But Blondin had planned it all as a show-stopper. Hanging by the hooks, he swung gaily in his perilous position, and then nonchalantly got up and continued on to the Canadian shore.

The fronds of some palms are over 70 feet long

In its varied forms, the palm is as important to people of many warm climes as the buffalo was to the American Plains Indian, or the walrus to the Eskimo. Members of the palm family often provide food, clothing, shelter, and other necessities of life to entire populations. The palm is, in effect, a living general store.

There are about 2,500 different species of palm, among them the date, coconut, betel, sago, and Palmyra. Many have dozens of uses. An ancient Hindu song enumerates 801 uses for the Palmyra palm alone!

The African oil palm is one of the largest species, sometimes growing as high as 80 feet. One of these graceful giants can produce as much as 200 pounds of fruit in a year. This tree also provides fiber for crates, furniture, baskets, and rope; the leaf base is used for fuel; the seeds are used for stock feed; vinegar and liquor are made from the fermented fruit. Other palms provide material for sugar, wax, wine, soap, and margarine. And almost all palms produce oil —the total output of palm oil in the world is greater than that of all other nondrying oils combined.

A Brazilian palm species, the *Raphia taedigera*, can claim the largest leaves in the plant kingdom. The feather-like fronds of this short, stout tree are sometimes over 70 feet long and 19 feet broad. Imagine a leaf that could stand on its end to the height of a seven-story building!

Owens established four world's track records in one afternoon

When Jesse Owens graduated from East Technical High School of Cleveland, Ohio, he had established three national high school records in track. At Ohio State University, Jesse ran like the wind and broke a few more world marks. And in the 1936 Olympic games at Berlin the lithe Negro speedster—who had by now acquired the nickname of *The Ebony Express*—built imperishable fame by winning four gold medals!

Nevertheless, the sum total of all this glorious achievement pales beside the performance of Jesse Owens on May 25, 1935, at the Big Ten conference championships held at Ann Arbor, Michigan.

Getting up from a sickbed, Jesse in his first event ran the 100-yard dash in 9.4 seconds, to tie the world's record.

Ten minutes later in the broad jump, Jesse leaped 26 feet eight and one quarter inches *on his first try* to best the world's record.

Nine minutes later, running in the 220-yard dash, Jesse sped down the course in 20.3 seconds to smash another world's record.

And just about 45 minutes after he had participated in the first event, Jesse negotiated the 220-yard hurdles in 22.6 seconds, shattering still another world's record.

In one single afternoon—within the space of three quarters of an hour—Jesse Owens established world records in four events. In this century, no other trackman has ever set more than one world's record in any one day.

Mount Rushmore contains the world's largest sculptures

The largest sculptures in the world are the four busts of American Presidents carved into the side of Mount Rushmore, in the Black Hills of South Dakota. Blasted out of a granite cliff, the busts represent George Washington, Abraham Lincoln, Thomas Jefferson, and Theodore Roosevelt. The faces average 60 feet from the top of the head to the chin—proportionate to men *465 feet tall!*

Most of the work on these colossal figures was performed by Gutzon Borglum, who had to blast away close to a million tons of granite as well as chisel in the delicate features of the likenesses. He labored on the project from 1927 until his death in 1941 without seeing it completed. His son Lincoln Borglum finished the monuments later in that year.

Today, the sculptures comprise the Mount Rushmore National Memorial and are known as the Shrine of Democracy. These immense figures are visible from as far as 60 miles away!

The raccoon washes its food

The raccoon is not very particular about what he eats. This small, black-masked creature can make a meal of almost anything—fruits, vegetables, grain, honey, nuts, eggs, clams, frogs, mice—as long as the food is clean.

Before eating anything, the raccoon first washes the food in the nearest available water. A coon would go hungry rather than eat anything it has not first washed. Sometimes a raccoon will satisfy himself by going through the motions of washing if no water is available.

The desire for cleanliness is so strong in the raccoon that when he's lolling about near fresh-water, the coon will often scrub pebbles until they shine, then pile them up neatly on a rock to dry in the sun!

Lozier and DeVoe planned to turn Manhattan Island around

In the summer of 1824, two retired New Yorkers, named Lozier and DeVoe, perpetrated a wild hoax on their numerous friends. They convinced a crowd that they had obtained the mayor's approval to saw off Manhattan from the mainland, and *turn the island around!*

The purpose of this grand plan was to keep Manhattan's southern end from sinking into the harbor under the weight of the many new buildings. DeVoe and Lozier started immediately to sign up laborers, and to award contracts for food, equipment, and even for a huge anchor to prevent the island from being swept out to sea. After eight weeks of preparation, all those associated with the project were instructed to meet the following Monday morning so they could proceed to the north end of Manhattan where the work was to begin. As instructed, hundreds of workmen plus scores of contractors arrived at the spot. They waited for hours before they learned that Lozier and DeVoe had, for reasons of health, gone on an extended journey.

The passionflower's tendrils are almost continually in motion

Movement is not a characteristic exclusive to the animal kingdom. Many plants are continually in motion; we do not perceive this motion simply because it is too slow. But by taking a number of photographs of a plant over a period of time, and then comparing the photos, this motion can be readily observed. For instance, a series of photos of the passionflower would reveal that the tendrils of this American vine behave much like the tentacles of an octopus, continually coiling and rotating.

A passionflower tendril remains fairly straight, growing outwards with a circular motion, until it contacts another object, such as the stalk of a nearby plant. Then the tendril begins to curl, spiraling around the stalk until the tendril resembles a coiled phone wire.

The passionflower was named by early Spanish settlers in America, who thought that

the structure of the plant was symbolic of the crucifixion of Christ. The passionflower has 10 petals and sepals, five stamens, three styles, a fringed corona, and coiling tentacles. The Spanish settlers saw these as symbols for, respectively, the 10 faithful apostles, the five wounds of Christ, the three nails, the crown of thorns, and the scourges.

O'Higgins won a battle with an army of animals

In 1814, Bernardo O'Higgins headed a small army of Chilean patriots who had been trying to free their country from Spanish rule since 1810. Though they had few arms, the Chileans often managed to give the Spaniards a bad time.

The Spanish king sent boatloads of soldiers to wipe out O'Higgins and his patriot army. But the Chileans fought with such courage and skill that, weak and outnumbered though they were, they could not be vanquished. Nevertheless, under this constant onslaught, O'Higgins' ragged men were being forced to retreat, day by day. It seemed only a matter of time until their backs would be up against a wall.

Just outside the Chilean city of Santiago lay the small town of Rancagua. Here, on October 1 and 2, O'Higgins and his army made a desperate stand. Worn out by days of fighting, tortured by thirst and merciless heat, the Chileans stood surrounded.

Then came a terrible blow. O'Higgins himself was struck by an enemy bullet.

The Chilean patriots seemed doomed to defeat, when the wounded O'Higgins conceived a plan. He ordered his men to round up as many mules, cows, sheep, and dogs as possible. Barns, stables, and pastures were emptied of their livestock, and all the animals were quickly mustered before the commander.

With the vast herd of animals assembled before him, O'Higgins was lifted to his horse. Then, with a shout and a lash of his whip, O'Higgins sent his steed charging ahead. The frightened animals began to run. Soon they became a stampeding, bellowing mass. O'Higgins drove them on and on—straight for the Spanish lines. Maddened by fear, the animals paid little heed to the formidable array of soldiers before them.

The Spanish veterans had never seen such a thundering horde. Terrified, they broke ranks and ran!

Close on the heels of the charging beasts came O'Higgins and his men. They galloped through the path which the animals had made for them. Slashing with their swords, they sped through the Spanish lines.

Helpless and stunned, the Spaniards watched the Chileans escape. Before the Spaniards could reorganize their forces for pursuit. the Chileans were safe in the mountains, There they recuperated, enlisted new recruits, and gathered arms.

Three years later, at the head of an army of 4,000 men, Bernardo O'Higgins returned to destroy the Spanish battalions. In 1818, O'Higgins proudly proclaimed Chile's independence from Spain, and became the first ruler of the new nation.

Mont-St.-Michel is a village in the sea but not an island

In the English Channel, one mile off the coast of Normandy, the rocky islet of Mont-St.-Michel rises from the misty sea like a mirage. In this strangely beautiful village surrounded by medieval walls, ancient houses climb a steep hill towards the towering abbey spire. It is a truly breathtaking sight.

The story of Mont-St.-Michel is as remarkable as its beauty. Hundreds of years ago, the land on which the village rests was part of the mainland of France, a tree-clad granite hill rising 260 feet

Benedictine monks built an abbey on the site of the old chapel, overlooking a rich plain where animals grazed and farmers toiled in the salty air of the distant sea.

One day in the year 725, an earthquake shook the coast. A tidal wave surged inland, devastating the plain. When the waters receded, the farmlands were no more; the hill stood amid a vast stretch of tidal flats. The coastal village of Mont-St.-Michel had become the islet of Mont-St.-Michel.

The monks who had occupied the abbey atop the crag, were convinced that God had spared their holy village from the ravages of the tidal wave, and they remained on the island. Pilgrims from all over France flocked to the village to visit the blessed abbey, and the town of Mont-St.-Michel became rich and powerful through their donations.

The high stone walls of the village and the natural moat formed by the daily rush of the tides made Mont-St.-Michel an invincible stronghold. When all of northern France had fallen into the hands of the English during the Hundred Years War, Mont-St.-Michel remained French. Many times besieged, the village was never captured.

Even in the centuries since the earthquake, Mont-St.-Michel has never truly become an island. Twice each day, a 40-foot tide—one of the highest in the world—rushes in over the tidelands and leaves the village surrounded by water. When the tide recedes, the village is left in the midst of marshy wetland, linked to the shore by a half mile of beach. In 1875, a stone causeway was built to provide access from the mainland in high tide.

Today, 250 people live in tightly packed houses on the tiny enclave. The abbey, as it has for over 1,200 years, lifts its spire 500 feet above the waters around it—the waters that could not conquer Mont-St.-Michel.

above an oak forest. A pagan shrine stood at its summit. The English Channel washed the shore, miles away from the hill.

When the Romans invaded northern Europe, they replaced the old shrine with a temple to Jupiter. Centuries later, early Christians erected a crude chapel atop the rocks. In 708,

Powell walked 50 miles in seven hours

In 1764, Foster Powell set off from London by foot for the town of Bath. The famous seaside resort was 50 miles away, over cobblestone and dirt roads.

It took the 30-year-old barrister from Leeds a mere seven hours to reach his destination. Powell had walked at a rate of better than seven miles an hour!

By comparison, consider that today a good marathon racer requires almost two and one-half hours to run 26 miles over a smoothly paved track.

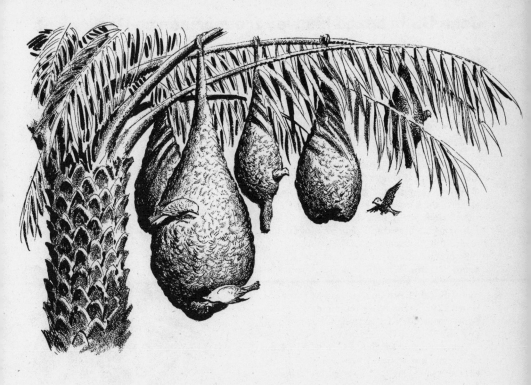

Weaverbirds build colonies of bottle-like nests

The weaverbird, a relative of the sparrow, lives in large nest colonies—with as many as seventy birds populating a single tree. A colony of these African birds can turn a tree into a sort of avian apartment house, with bottle-like nests suspended from every branch!

Weaverbirds build their bottle-shaped quarters by interlacing grass with other vegetation. Openings at the bottom provide access to the nests. The heavy bird traffic that usually surrounds a weaverbird colony also provides protection against enemies.

John Gully boxed his way from prison to Parliament

One day in 1805, Henry Pierce, heavyweight boxing champion of England, came to a debtors' prison to entertain the inmates. For Pierce's victim, the warden chose John Gully. To the warden's surprise, and the howling cheers of his fellow convicts, Gully battered Pierce all around the ring.

The taverns soon were bubbling with the story of Gully's victory. A group of gamblers determined to pay off Gully's debts, and get him out of prison. To repay the gamblers, Gully agreed to fight exhibition bouts for them.

And Gully really fought. He fought so well that he soon amassed sufficient winnings to buy himself out of the clutches of the gamblers.

From 1806 on, Gully managed himself. He signed for an official championship bout with Henry Pierce, and lost the fight in the 59th round. But after that single defeat, he never was beaten again. When Pierce retired in 1807, John Gully was acclaimed heavyweight champion of England.

Unlike many prize fighters, Gully saved his money and knew when it was time to quit. He left the boxing ring, and invested his savings in horse racing. Two of his horses won the famous English Derby.

And then John Gully took a real jump—all the way from the race track to politics. In 1832, he was elected to the House of Commons. Thereafter, he served several terms in Parliament.

When he died in 1863 at the great age of 90, Gully left a substantial fortune and a fine country estate.

And it all began with a roundhouse right...

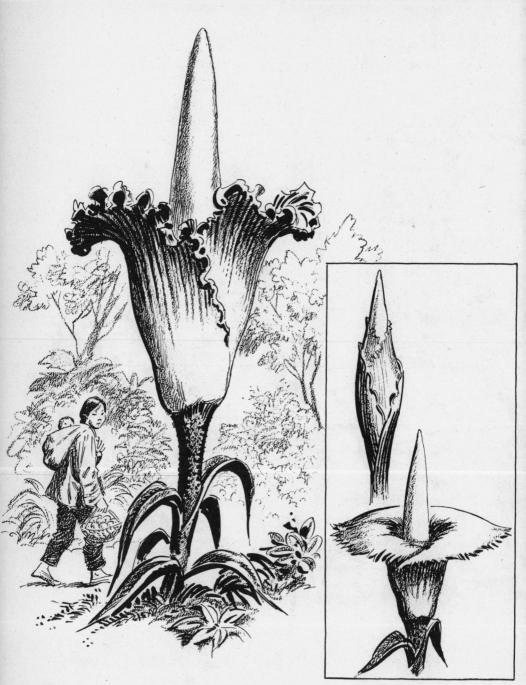

The krubi sometimes grows to a height of 15 feet

If you were to come upon a krubi during a visit to a botanical garden, you might think you were viewing a plant specimen from Jonathan Swift's land of the Brobdingnagians. This flower, a relative of the popular philodendron, is so gigantic that even if you were to stand on another person's shoulder, you would barely be able to reach the top!

The krubi, known commonly as the giant arum and properly as *Amorphophallus titanum*, grows in the jungles of Sumatra, a large Indonesian island. The flowering portion of the plant consists of a mottled green spathe—a modified, folded leaf—wrapped around a yellow spadix (a tall fleshy spike that grows vertically out of the spathe). Specimens of the krubi have been found whose spathe attained the height and upper diameter of eight feet, with a spadix rising another seven feet—for a total height of 15 feet! The leaves of a well-grown specimen, when unfolded, can cover an area 45 feet in circumference.

Actually, the krubi cannot be termed the largest flower in the world, for it is a collection of flowers simulating a single giant flower. Inside the spathe, the spadix bears simple male flowers above and female parts below. But the krubi can definitely claim two superlatives: its spathe and spadix form the largest inflourescence (arrangement of one or more flowers) in the plant kingdom; and its growth rate surpasses that of any other plant.

The krubi may appear to be an ideal plant to grow in your garden to stun your friends, but this exotic colossus will grow only in the hottest, most humid climate—and even there will flourish for just a few days. Besides, the plant exudes such a foul odor it's doubtful you would want it anywhere near your house!

Manley hit two holes-in-one, back to back

Norman L. Manley stepped to the seventh tee at the Del Valle Country Club course at Saugus, California. The date was September 2, 1964. He hit a prodigious drive, and the ball bounced unerringly to the green and into the cup. He had scored an ace, one of the longest ones on record. But the best was yet to come. On the very next hole, the 290-yard eighth, Manley, bubbling with excitement and confidence, hit another mammoth drive. As if directed by radar, that ball landed smack in the hole! Manley had hit two holes-in-one, back to back, scoring six strokes under par for the pair.

The Tacoma Narrows Bridge was the most disastrous structure of this century

In 1940, officials gathered to cut the ribbon on a newly constructed suspension bridge across the Narrows Strait near Tacoma, Washington. The first vehicles routinely crossed the span, and the 2,800-foot Tacoma Narrows Bridge took its place as the third longest suspension bridge in the world.

In high wind conditions, the Tacoma span swayed back and forth between its towers. Sometimes the span buckled, forming undulating hills and valleys in the concrete roadway. Cars used the bridge in decreasing numbers as engineers hastened to discover what was wrong with the sparkling-new structure.

Four months after the completion of the bridge, the roadway blew apart in a 42-mile-per-hour wind and tumbled into the waters below. All the theories of suspension-bridge construction were promptly thrown out the window. The only consolation in the baffling catastrophe was the absence of any cars on the Tacoma Bridge at the time of its collapse.

One year before the opening of the Tacoma span, an almost identical bridge had been built in New York City—the Bronx Whitestone Bridge. In view of the Tacoma calamity, engineers began to fear that this brridge might be less than safe.

Workers in the then fledgling science of aerodynamics ultimately proved that the designers of the Tacoma span had failed to take sufficient account of the effects of high winds on a suspension bridge. Adjustments were quickly made in the Bronx-Whitestone span, which continues in sturdy operation today. In 1952, a second bridge across the Narrows in Tacoma was erected on the still-standing piers of the first bridge. This second bridge stands today as the eighth longest suspension bridge in the world.

By this time, the Golden Gate and George Washington bridges had already been in use for several years, and the principles of suspension-bridge construction were thought to be fully understood. Within weeks of the opening of the Tacoma Bridge, however, it was plain to see that more study was called for.

Mozart wrote a symphony when he was only eight years old

Mozart was the greatest musical genius the world has ever known. His accomplishments were so breathtaking that they are hardly believable; yet the amazing facts given here have all been authenticated.

Wolfgang Amadeus Mozart began playing the harpsichord when he was only three. He seemed to learn everything almost instinctively, and never had to be told twice about anything relating to music. In fact, his ear was so sensitive that it could detect an aberration of even an eighth of a note in the tuning of a violin string.

Wolfgang's father used to play in a string quartet. One day, the quartet was playing at the home of the senior Mozart. The second violinist had failed to come, and young Mozart, then five, took the missing musician's place. He had never seen the music before, but he played it as if he had been practicing it for weeks. His father and the other musicians expressed great amazement, but the child merely shrugged and said, "Surely you don't have to study and practice to play *second* violin, do you?"

Wolfgang started to compose music almost as early in life as he learned to play music. He wrote two minuets for the harpsichord when he was five years old. When he was seven, he wrote a creditable sonata; and, unbelievable as it seems, he was only eight when he wrote a complete symphony.

The elder Mozart knew he had a prodigy on his hands, and he took Wolfgang on a tour of the musical capitals of Europe. The young Mozart played with a mature understanding that electrified the great musicians of Europe. Moreover, the youngster performed feats that were near miracles—tricks of ear and memory that baffled everyone. A melody would be played just once; Mozart would listen and reproduce it faithfully without a flaw. Blindfolded, he would identify all the elements of a chord, no matter on what instrument it was played. He would be given intricate scores to read at sight, and would then play

them with a precision that could be equaled only by a first-rate musician who had practiced for hours, or perhaps days.

In Rome, once a year during Holy Week, the *Miserere* of Gregorio Allegri was performed by the papal choir. The Pope had forbade its performance anywhere else in the world, and the only copy of the score in existence had been jeal-

ously guarded in the papal vaults. A decree issued by the Vatican prohibited anyone from reproducing this holy work in any form. Transgression was to be punished by excommunication.

The *Miserere* was a lengthy, complex contrapuntal composition. Mozart heard it played once. Returning to his room, he transcribed the entire score from memory! The Pope heard about this feat and was so moved by this manifestation of utter genius that instead of anathematizing the boy, he bestowed upon him the Cross of the Order of the Golden Spur.

Before he died in 1791, Wolfgang Amadeus Mozart had produced some 600 operas, operettas, concertos for piano and string quartet, sonatas for the violin, serenades, motets, masses, and many other types of classical music. Perhaps the most astounding fact about this prolific and brilliant production is that Mozart only lived to the age of 35.

The crested grebe carries its young on its back

The crested grebe—like the mute swan, some ducks, and the loon—has a special way of caring for its youngsters. At the first sign of danger, the crested grebe sinks until its back is level with the water. Its young climb onto its back. Then the parent grebe rises to its swimming position and with strong strokes carries the family across the water to safety.

The youngsters must enjoy the ride, for they often hop aboard their parent's back when in no danger at all!

Mosconi beat Moore in pocket billiards by running the entire game in one inning

On April 17, 1956, Willie Mosconi of Philadelphia was matched against Jimmy Moore of Albuquerque, New Mexico, in the world's pocket billiard tournament, held in Kingston, North Carolina. The game, held in front of 350 spectators at the Shamrock Billiard Center, began with Moore taking the table. The game was set at 150 points, which meant the first player to pocket 150 balls won. Moore played a safety on his first shot and never got another chance to show his skill, for the wizard of the green baize just ran out the entire game without a stop.

For those who had followed Willie's career, this wasn't too surprising. In Springfield, Ohio, in an exhibition match played in 1954 against a local hotshot, Mosconi established a world's record by running off 526 balls in a row, a little better than 37 racks. Willie, pitted against Luther Lassiter in San Francisco in March, 1953, in a world's championship match, won in only two innings.

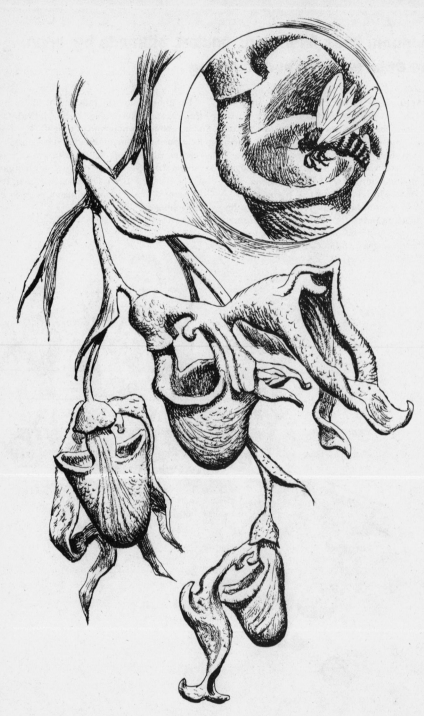

The bucket orchid is pollinated by inebriated bees

Inebriated bees play a part in the pollination of a curious Central American flower known as the bucket orchid. The lip or front petal of this tropical trickster forms a kind of bucket, with a troughlike spout just below the overhanging pollen packets. A fluid secreted by specialized glands collects in the bucket, sparkling invitingly like pools of nectar.

Bees attracted by the flower's strong fragrance are drawn to the lip, where they collect the scented fluid. This bogus "nectar" literally inebriates the bees, and the soused insects tumble into the fluid-filled bucket. Their only course of escape is through the spoutlike opening. As they wriggle to freedom, they cannot avoid brushing against the pollen packets, thereby collecting pollen or depositing previously collected pollen on the stigma.

The bucket orchid operates a kind of shut-off device when a bee takes too long in escaping the bucket trap. After a besotted bee has sloshed around in the bucket for 30 minutes or so, the flower loses its scent. This persuades the bee to make a speedy exit—and thus discourages self-fertilization of the flower. Soon after the laggard bee departs, the scent returns, and the bucket orchid is ready to intoxicate another insect patron.

Waetzel invented a machine with which one man could play 378 musical instruments

A certain Austrian by the name of Karl Waetzel, wo lived during the last century, had a particularly inventive turn of mind. He built a fabulous conglomeration of musical instruments which he called the *panomonico,* an instrument which could be played by a single person. The panomonico included 150 flageolets, 150 flutes, 50 oboes, 18 trumpets, 5 fanfares, three drums, and two kettledrums. The whole thing totaled 378 instruments. Waetzel's fantastic invention was purchased by Archduke Charles of Austria. The irony was that the Duke used the panomonico not to produce beautiful music, but for the purpose of annoying noisy courtiers of his royal household.

Barclay walked 1,000 miles in 1,000 hours—one mile every hour

Captain Allardyce Barclay of Ury, Scotland, was veritably a man with "asbestos feet." At age 17, he could walk six miles an hour. At age 27, he claimed he could walk 1,000 miles in 1,000 hours. A group of Englishmen didn't believe this incredible Scot, and offered odds of 100 to 1 against Barclay's boast.

In June 1, 1809, Barclay lined up ready to go the distance. The terms of the wager called for him to walk one mile within each of the next consecutive 1,000 hours. The mile was to be covered regardless of weather. The hours were to be counted uninterruptedly. He would be obliged to walk one-half mile down a path from his own lodgings in Newmarket and then walk the same half-mile back to his home. Barclay had undertaken a stint that would keep him going without a decent sleep for roughly six weeks. It seemed utterly impossible that any man would have the endurance to do this.

Surprisingly, the lack of rest was not the Captain's major problem. Barclay devised a system of walking the first mile at the very end of a rest period. He then immediately commenced to do a second mile at the very beginning of the following hour. Since each mile took him approximately 15 minutes, this arrangement permitted him to rest for several 1½-hour periods each day. But Barclay began suffering from muscle spasms and blisters. Moreover, there was

grave concern that the wearied contestant might be the victim of foul play on the dark road, for a good deal of money was being bet against him. His brother arranged to have the pathway lit at night.

During those summer days, the road became hot and dusty. Ingeniously, Barclay had a water cart sprinkle the path in front of him. In between times, he cheerfully indulged in solid meals of mutton chops and beefsteaks, washed down by generous drafts of port.

At the start, Barclay required approximately 13 minutes for each mile; but after four weeks of steady perambulating, he was worn to a frazzle. As he plowed through his miles in 20 minutes each, the odds against him grew. But Barclay, half-dead, struggled on.

Strangely enough, as he approached the finish, he actually gained strength. During the last few days, ropes were needed to hold back the crowd, and lords and commoners filled every available room in the Newmarket area. Many were bettors who, in the aggregate, had staked $500,000 on Barclay's trial of endurance.

On July 12, Barclay finished his last mile. The final chore took him a mere 15 minutes, and he wound up 45 minutes ahead of schedule. It was like dashing for a pot of gold, for he had bet a very considerable sum on himself. In winning, Barclay became a wealthy man.

The Great Pyramid of Cheops is the largest tomb ever built

The pyramids of Egypt were the first great structures ever built by man. In the 5,000 years that have elapsed since their completion, countless structures of magnificent beauty and astounding size have been built, admired, and reduced to rubble. Yet the pyramids remain, in age and in scale the apex of human construction.

Over a period of centuries, thousands of pyramids of varying sizes were erected in Egypt. Each was built to serve as the impenetrable tomb of a royal Egyptian, who, buried beneath millions of tons of rock, would be assured peace and continuing wealth in his life after death. Most of the pyramids have been destroyed by the ravages of time and man, but the three greatest—the pyramids at Giza—remain.

The pyramid of Cheops (or Khugu) is the largest of the three Giza pyramids, and the largest tomb ever built. The immensity of this structure is almost beyond comprehension. For an idea of its size, visualize a huge square tract of land—as vast as, say, Shea Stadium—piled high with rocks to the height of a 40-story building! Within this pyramid, St. Peter's and Westminster Cathedral could both be tucked away with room to spare.

The amount of work required to construct this gargantuan tomb is as staggering as its size. The huge stones of the pyramid—each weighing an average of two-and-one-half tons—were quarried miles away from the Giza site, across the Nile River. Each stone had to be cut to size out of solid limestone, ferried across the Nile, and dragged on sledges up to the 100-foot plateau on which the pyramid rests. Then, the stone had to be dragged up a ramp that surrounded the pyramid during construction, and carefully set in place. And this procedure had to be repeated 2½ *million times* for the Cheops pyramid alone!

It is estimated that this pyramid required the work of 100,000 men for a period of 20 to 30 years. In all, 6½ million tons of rock had to be moved to build the pyramid, enough stone to build a wall around all of France. And this work was done without the use of machinery or animals of any kind—not even the wheel!

Despite its immensity, the pyramid constituted only a part of the entire tomb construction project. Dozens of smaller tombs were erected at the base of the pyramid to house the bodies of the king's wives, children and nobles. A long stone causeway was built connecting the pyramid complex to the Nile. The Great Sphinx was itself a part of the Giza complex. Smaller temples, of both pyramidal and other shapes, were constructed around the larger pyramid, and many of these were massive structures in themselves.

Today, little else but the pyramids remains at Giza. Over the course of thousands of years, the burial chambers deep within the pyramids have been plundered of all their treasures. The white limestone wedges that were used to face the tombs have almost completely disappeared. Yet the pyramids still stand in all their superhuman grandeur, and—alone among all of man's constructions—could very well stand forever.

A short distance from the three great pyramids at Giza, Egypt, a curious stone figure of a crouching lion with the head of a man peers solemnly over the ancient Nile Valley. This massive work of carved stone—known as the Great Sphinx—was built almost 5,000 years ago, and is perhaps the oldest monumental statue in existence today.

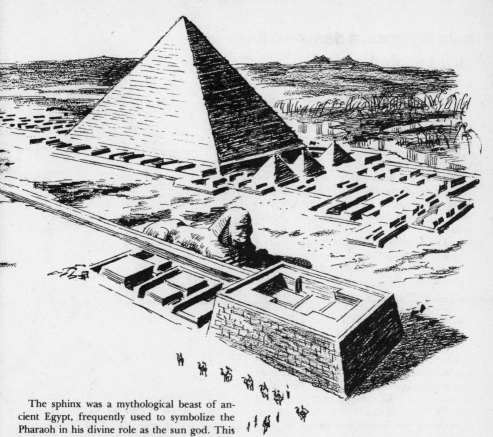

The sphinx was a mythological beast of ancient Egypt, frequently used to symbolize the Pharaoh in his divine role as the sun god. This beast was usually represented in sculpture by the figure of a crouching lion with the head of a man, ram, or hawk. Thousands of sphinxes were built in Egypt, but the Great Sphinx at Giza is one of the few remaining and by far the largest and most famous.

The Great Sphinx was built in conjunction with the pyramid of Chefren, the second largest pyramid of the Giza complex. A long stone causeway led from this pyramid to a temple in the Nile Valley, near which the Sphinx was erected, facing the Nile and the rising sun. The face carved onto this great stone beast is presumably the face of the Pharaoh Chefren, who wished to remind all those who looked upon his pyramid that it was built to the glory of a divine king.

For centuries, the Sphinx lay covered with desert sands, the head alone visible above ground. Age and weather chipped away at the stone head, obliterating the nose and beard and sadly disfiguring the face. But the body lay protected under the sands. When archaeologists recently uncovered the crouching figure, they found the body almost intact.

The entire statue, with the exception of the paws in front, was hewn out of solid rock in one piece. The paws were built of brick. These paws alone could dwarf a man. To appreciate the size of this colossus, imagine a stone figure only slightly shorter in length than a football field, rising almost seven stories off the ground!

And then remember that even this gargantuan figure is dwarfed by those giants of giants, the pyramids.

Lola Montez, a dance-hall girl, toppled a king

Marie Delores Eliza Rosanna Gilbert was born poor in Limerick, Ireland, in 1818. After an unsuccessful marriage to an army officer, she adopted the name Lola Montez, invented a line of ancestors from Seville, and headed for Paris to try her luck on the stage.

Although her singing and dancing were not oustanding, Lola's sultry beauty was. She became a star. Among her numerous stage-door Johnnies were Franz Liszt and Alexandre Dumas pére.

Lola's reputation soon piqued the interest of King Ludwig I of Bavaria. The empassioned 60-year-old ruler despatched agents to France with billets-doux and a casket of jewels.

At the moment, Lola was between lovers. Besides, she had never had a king, so she did not resist the royal summons. Lola soon became not only Ludwig's lover but his chief political advisor as well.

But the burghers of Munich resented the idea that they were being governed by a courtesan, and marched in the streets shouting, "Down with the whore!" In 1848, Lola had the good sense to flee to Switzerland, just in time to miss the revolution she had helped provoke. Her royal paramour was forced to abdicate.

Hedley fell out of his plane and, hundreds of feet below, fell back into it

On January 6, 1918, Captain J.H. Hedley, an American, was flying 15,000 feet over German territory in a plane piloted by a Canadian named Makepeace. Suddenly, their craft was attacked by German fighters. Trying to evade the enemy, Makepeace took his plane into a nearly vertical dive. The suddenness of this maneuver surprised Hedley, who was pulled out of his seat and off into the ozone.

Makepeace gave up his comrade for lost and continued his rapid descent for several hundred feet more before leveling off. Then, incredibly, Hedley alighted on the tail of the airplane! Evidently, the steep dive created a powerful suction in which the American captain was caught.

Hedley hung on to the tail of the plane for dear life. Later, he managed to climb back into his seat. The plane touched down safely behind Allied lines, and Hedley's reprieve from death was complete.

It may take a dozen men to hold a giant python

The largest member of the python family—the reticulated python of southeastern Asia—grows to a length of twenty-five feet. Specimens of this nonvenomous snake have been measured at twenty-eight feet, weighing over 220 pounds! So strong is this gargantuan serpent that, in captivity, the efforts of a dozen zookeepers are sometimes required to hold the snake for forced-feeding.

The stomachs of dead pythons have been examined to determine what the snakes last ate. Incredibly enough, the belly of one medium-sized python contained a full-grown leopard! The claws and teeth of this savage cat had proved insufficient against the terrible strength of the giant serpent.

The chameleon's tongue is as long as its body

The chameleon, a small lizard, is well-known for his ability to change color. The skin of this remarkable reptile can pass through several colors of the rainbow as his mood changes, or as he adapts to surrounding conditions. But equally remarkable is the size and agility of this creature's tongue.

The chameleon's body measures about six inches in length, but his tongue is frequently even longer! The lizard rolls up the oversize tongue inside his mouth, then shoots it out with great speed and suddenness to snare an insect. A chameleon can sometimes catch an insect ten inches away with one quick thrust of his talented tongue!

A saguaro cactus can weigh 10 tons

The saguaro, the giant of the cactus family, is familiar to anyone who has traveled in Mexico or the American Southwest—or ever viewed a Western movie. From a distance, the tall central stem and thick perpendicular branches of the saguaro may resemble a colossal human figure with outstretched arms silhouetted against the sky. Yet despite its prodigious size, the saguaro is one of the slowest-growing specimens in the plant kingdom.

The central stem of this desert titan grows less than one inch during the first 10 years of the plant's life, and does not produce a branch until the stem is about 16 feet high. Later the spiny succulent grows about an inch each year, and can eventually reach a height of 50 feet.

Flowers do not appear until the plant is 50 to 75 years old. The largest saguaro specimens are close to 200 years old, and weigh over 10 tons!

Cecil Nixon built a robot which could play 3,000 tunes

An ingenious Californian by the name of Dr. Cecil Nixon constructed a robot in 1940 with uncommon abilities. The doctor, who named his creation Isis, fashioned the instrument in the form of the ancient Egyptian goddess. Isis rested on a couch with a zither on her lap.

The instrument could play any of about 3,000 tunes if asked to do so by anyone within a 12-foot radius. This came about because Isis was constructed so that voice vibrations touched off her complicated mechanism. Isis' right hand picked out the melody on the zither, while her left hand performed the accompaniment.

The machinery inside of Isis included 1,187 wheels and 370 electromagnets. There were numerous other parts. As a crowning touch, Dr. Nixon made Isis react to a warm temperature. When she got hot, she would remove the veil from her face all by herself.

It is not known what has happened to Isis in the 30-odd years since she was built. Apparently, she is not on exhibition anymore.

An elephant eats almost around-the-clock

The elephant is the largest land mammal ever to grace the earth. The African species—which is larger than its Asiatic counterpart—often weighs more than five tons. Yet this jungle giant is completely vegetarian, subsisting on nothing but leaves, grass, and fruit.

To satisfy his understandably huge appetite, an elephant can spend up to *eighteen hours* a day feeding! Even in the zoo, where the pachyderms are given more concentrated food, a large elephant will consume one hundred pounds of hay and large portions of fruits and vegetables daily!

Aside from his voracious appetite, the most remarkable feature of this thick-skinned colossus is undoubtedly his trunk. No other animal can brag of a proboscis so long—or so versatile. For the elephant's trunk is the best all-purpose tool in the jungle. The pachyderm uses it to breathe, to smell, and to feel. He also uses his trunk as a tube to suck up food and water, as a derrick to lift enormous weights, and as a trumpet to blare out his anger. The elephant even uses his trunk to give himself a shower, blowing water over his back in a fine spray, and to cover his back with dirt or mud to shield his skin against the sun's rays. And, of course, this trunk is a deadly weapon.

An elephant's trunk contains more than forty thousand separate muscles—more than a man has in his entire body! These muscles make the big nose agile as well as strong: with his trunk an elephant can kill a man with the pressure of one squeeze, or pick up a piece of thread from a polished floor!

The Taj Mahal is the most beautiful building in the world

On the bank of a placid river deep in the heartland of India rests the building many people consider the most beautiful in the world—the Taj Mahal. Although in size and grandeur it is the equal of any palace or temple, the Taj Mahal was built as neither a royal residence nor a place of worship. It is the tomb of one woman, a monument to love.

About 300 years ago, Shah Jehan ruled a vast Moslem empire in India. The Emperor's wealth was enormous, his coffers filled with gold and precious jewels. His capital, Agra, was one of the most magnificent cities in the East, resplendent with marble palaces and fragrant gardens. Yet of all his treasures, the Emperor most prized his wife, Mumtaz Mahal.

When she died in 1629, the grief-stricken monarch decided to build a monument of unmatched beauty and splendor to serve as a resting place for his beloved. From all over the world, Jehan summoned architects, sculptors, and jewelers to his marble city. From Persia came boatloads of silver; from Arabia, pearls by the thousands. For 18 years, 20,000 men worked on the glorious tomb. When it was completed in 1648, the mausoleum—called the Taj Mahal—was the most beautiful building in one of the most beautiful of cities.

In size alone, the Taj Mahal is a wondrous architectural achievement. The octagonal building extends for 186 feet on its longest side, and rests on a vast marble platform 313 feet square. In each corner of the platform stands a white marble minaret, 138 feet tall. The walls of the mausoleum are 70 feet high and are topped by a massive bulb-shaped dome. From the platform to the tip of the dome's pinnacle, there looms a distance of 243 feet—the height of a 20-story building.

But the true splendor of the Taj Mahal lies not in its size, but in its breathtakingly sinuous forms. The exterior is entirely of white marble, inlaid with semi-precious stones which form Arabic inscriptions, floral designs, and arabesques. The burial room itself is surrounded by a marble screen whose intricate carvings give it the appearance of lace rather than stone. And surrounding the building on three sides is an elaborate walled garden with marble pavements, fountains, and pools that reflect the Taj in all its dream-like brilliance. The tableaux of the milk-white Taj, the emerald-green gardens, and the blue of sky and water are dazzling beyond words.

Shah Jehan had planned to build another mausoleum to house his own sarcophagus. This tomb was to be an exact duplicate of the Taj, but constructed of black marble rather than white. The twin structure would sit on the opposite bank of the Jumna River, directly across from the Taj, with a silver bridge connecting the two tombs.

However, before his plans could be carried out, Jehan was dethroned by a rebellious son. After his death, the Emperor was laid to rest beside his wife, under the dome of the Taj. Perhaps it is just as well that construction of Jehan's second tomb was never attempted, for the perfect beauty of the Taj Mahal could hardly have been equalled.

Claude Seurat was the skinniest man who ever lived

Claude Ambroise Seurat, better known as "The Living Skeleton," was born at Troyes, France on April 10, 1797. His parents were poor but robust people, and their infant son seemed destined to follow in their footsteps—Claude was an apparently normal child of average size. But as he grew in stature, his weight did not increase correspondingly. Indeed, what little flesh he possessed as an infant seemed to wither away. At full maturity, Claude had a back-to-chest thickness of only *three inches,* one inch less than the measurement of his puny biceps.

In 1825, at the age of 28, Seurat agreed to exhibit himself in London. On the way northeast from his native Troyes, he stopped at Rouen, where no less than 1,500 people crowded around him in one day. A contemporary account of Seurat's London premiere on August 9, 1825, is given by a Mr. Hone in the *Every Day Book.* Hone was "instantly riveted by [Seurat's] amazing emaciation; he seemed another 'Lazarus come forth' without his grave-clothes.... My eye, then, first caught the arm as the most remarkable limb; from the shoulder to the elbow it is like an ivory German flute ... not having a trace of muscle, it is as perfect a cylinder as a writing rule."

Seurat's head was the only part of his body that was not shrunken. Accordingly, neither were his faculties in any way diminished. Seurat was smart enough to extract a small fortune from this London exhibition, though he did not live long enough to enjoy it.

The tailorbird sews its nest together with threads

The Indian tailorbird builds a most peculiar nest. The male of the species first finds two leaves close together near the end of a branch. Then, using his bill as a needle, he punches holes along the edges of the leaves and sews them together with thin vegetable fibers. The swinging, pocketlike nest is lined with cottony down, and the female tailorbird has a snug home for her eggs!

Franks swung an Indian club 17,280 times an hour

On August 2, 1934, working out in a gymnasium in Newcastle, Australia, William Franks picked up a heavy club and began swinging it around his head at an amazing speed. It was the typical Indian club, shaped like a bowling pin, popularly used by gymnasts until the early 1950's.

But Franks wasn't just out for exercise. Twirling the club at a rate of about 300 times a minute, Franks kept up his performance for a full hour. When he was done, the scorekeepers and timekeepers had recorded 17,280 twirls of the wooden pin—a record for sure!

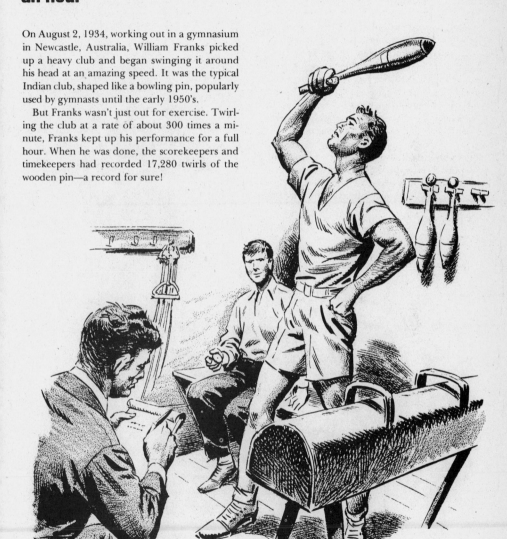

The giant clam weighs five hundred pounds

If you've ever enjoyed the treat of a dozen juicy clams, your mouth is sure to water at the thought of a clam so large you couldn't even lift it! Deep among the coral reefs of the South Pacific there actually exists such a monster—the giant clam, or *Tridacna gigas,* which often weighs as much as five hundred pounds. This huge mollusk has a deeply ridged shell two feet long, so large that halves of the shell have been used in French churches as fonts for holy water. And the fleshy portion of the giant sometimes weighs twenty pounds—every ounce firm, delicious meat!

This extraordinary creature—the largest known bivalve—is also quite treacherous. South Sea pearl divers swimming close to the clam have been caught by a hand or foot between the mighty valves—and held until they drowned!

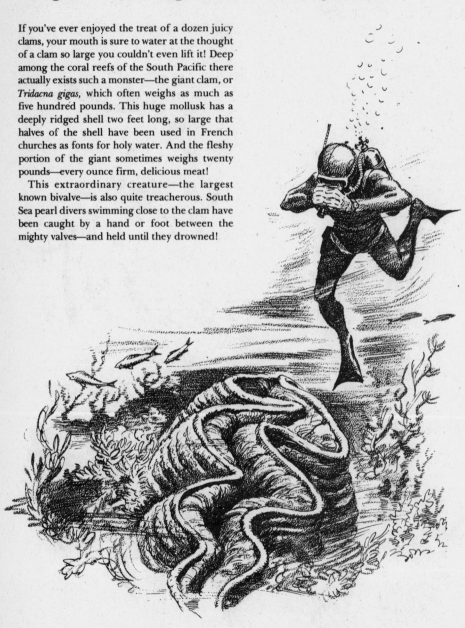

Young ran a mile in 8:30 with a man on his back

In 1915, the world's record for the mile run was four minutes 14.4 seconds. On April 12th of that year, Noah Young, an Australian, ran around a Melbourne track for the length of a mile in eight minutes 30 seconds, and established a world's record. How come?

Well, Young was carrying a man on his back. The runner weighed 198 pounds. The lad he was lugging along weighed 150. It was quite a performance.

The Leaning Tower of Pisa is beautiful for its imperfection

One of the best-known towers in the world owes its fame neither to beauty nor to size, but to imperfection. Hovering on the apparent brink of collapse, the campanile of the Cathedral of Pisa—better known as the Leaning Tower of Pisa—attracts thousands of visitors each year to its precarious galleries.

Apart from its obvious tilt, the tower is an exquisite work of architecture, a free-standing bell tower in the Italian Romanesque style. The tower's cylindrical core is surrounded by six galleries of marble columns, crowned with a multi-colored belfry. Visitors can climb the tower and step out onto the deck encircling the belfry for a dizzying look at the cathedral and streets below.

Construction of the tower began in 1174. A stone-bed foundation was laid 62 feet deep in the marshy ground. Tree trunks were used as piles. Nonetheless, a tilt to the south soon became apparent. To compensate, the builders increased the height of the galleries on the south side of the tower. Further adjustments were made during the 13th century, but the tower only leaned further towards the south.

Actually, not only does the tower lean to the south, but—due to the extra height added to the south side—it curves towards the north as well. The 179-foot tower is now *14 feet* off perpendicular!

The famed astronomer and physicist Galileo is believed to have put the tower's tilt to good use. As the story comes down to us, in 1589 he conducted an experiment by dropping objects from the upper galleries. The tower's lean assured Galileo that the falling objects would not strike the side of the structure on their way down. These experiments helped the physicist to formulate his laws of motion, which maintain that objects fall at the same speed and with uniform acceleration, regardless of their weight.

Various proposals to save the tower have been put forth through the years. One of these proposals must work if the tower is to survive; otherwise, collapse is only a matter of time.

A similar leaning tower in Saragossa, Spain, fell in 1887. But even if the Tower of Pisa is saved by eengineers, one thing is certain: with its southward tilt and its northward curve, the tower will never stand straight.

The deer botfly is the fastest creature alive

A tiny insect known as the deer botfly is easily the speed champion of the world. This marvelous mite can fly at the rate of *818 miles per hour*—faster than a jet plane! In fact, if we could fly a plane at the speed of the tiny botfly, we would circle the globe without ever seeing the sun set—for we'd be traveling at a speed close to that of the earth's rotation!

A two-day-old gazelle can outrun a full-grown horse

The gazelle, a small African antelope, has been called both the most graceful and most alert of all mammals. But the wary gazelle is also one of the world's swiftest creatures, capable of sprinting at close to sixty miles an hour!

So important is speed to the survival of the gazelle that nature has endowed it with swiftness from the moment it is born. Many animals are weak and barely able to stand up during their first days of life, but a young gazelle can run a few moments after birth. And within a few days, a fawn can outrace a full-grown horse!

Gazelles race only when chased. The rest of the time they spend nibbling leaves and grass and keeping their eyes peeled for lurking predators. But the gazelle never takes a drink of water! Like prairie dogs, kangaroo rats, and a few other animals, gazelles have a digestive system capable of extracting enough water from the food they eat to live healthily.

The macrozamias are the oldest living plants

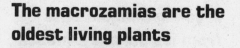

—more than three times as old as the California giants.

The macrozamia is a palmlike tree which commonly grows to a height of 60 feet. Its gigantic cones are sometimes two feet long, and can weigh up to 80 pounds each! There is controversy concerning the exact age of these Australian trees—counting their concentric rings is a very difficult task—but it is generally agreed that certain macrozamias are the oldest living things on earth.

Contrary to a popular notion, the giant sequoias of California are not the oldest living trees. That honor belongs to a group of macrozamia trees in Queensland, Australia, which are estimated to be anywhere from 12,000 to 15,000 years old

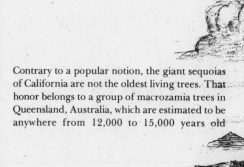

For pollination, almost all figs depend upon the same species of wasp

The fig genus boasts a number of remarkable plants among its over 600 species of shrubs, vines, and trees. The banyan tree, for example, is a fig. Another fig species produces a trunk only six feet high and a projecting canopy of branches over 150 feet across! A certain Malayan fig sends stems into the soil from the base of its trunk, and actually bears its fruit underground. Still another species displays a pagoda-like canopy of branches which provides easy access for the plant's pollinator, the bat. But almost all other figs have one thing in common: for pollination, each is dependent upon one, and only one, species of wasp!

The Smyrna fig, one of the most popular of the edible varieties, is among those pollinated by wasps. As in the case of the yucca, the plant and the insect are mutually dependent—the insect cannot reproduce without the fig, and the plant cannot bear fruit without the help of the wasp.

The female flowers of the Smyrna fig are borne on the inside wall of hollow receptacles we later eat as fruit. Male and neuter flowers are produced within inedible receptacles called "gall figs." Female wasps pass through a tiny orifice at the end of the gall figs, and lay eggs in the neuter flowers.

These eggs hatch when the fruit is ripe. The newborn wasps mate within the fig, and the females exit via the orifice, picking up pollen from the male plants on their way out. These wasps then visit other figs, and the female flowers they pollinate later ripen into seed-bearing, edible fruits.

The process may seem complicated, but it prevents self-pollination of the fig, and offers a fine example of the interdependence of nature.

A young penguin eats from its parent's mouth

Living in the rigorous climate of the Antarctic is not easy, and the few creatures that do reside there have evolved in some very peculiar ways. The penguin is a good example. The penguin is a bird, but it cannot fly, and its feathers are more like fur. The wings of this black-and-white fellow are used as flippers, making the penguin better suited for the sea than land. And the penguin is the only bird that can walk upright on its own two feet!

In the frozen Antarctic, even a simple task like eating becomes complicated. A penguin parent does not give the food it catches directly to its young. Instead, the parents swallow the food first. Then, when the meal is partly digested, it opens its bill wide. The baby penguin then thrusts its bill inside the parent's mouth and feeds on the predigested food!

The penguin's walk is awkward. But if a penguin wants to move fast over land, it rolls on its stomach, pushes with its wing flippers, and belly-whops across the ice and snow!

Bogardus shot 1,000 glass balls in 102 minutes

In the late 1800's, American shooting contests drew crowds of as high as 100,000. Captain A.H. Bogardus, New York born, moved to the Midwest in 1856. The lad found his new home to be great bird country, and he soon learned that a youngster could make a name for himself if he was considered to be the best shot around. Within the next dozen years, Bogardus became the finest trap shooter the Midwest had ever known.

As the nation's bird supply diminished, shooters turned to clay pigeons, and later to glass balls. In the early 1890's, when Bogardus was at his peak, the marksman put on a memorable performance before a crowd in New York's Gilmore Garden. While timers kept the score, Bogardus started shooting away at glass balls which were catapulted about 30 feet or so into the air. He shoved shells quickly into his breechloader, and ping! ping! ping! he banged down the balls one after another at record speed. He missed very few.

As Bogardus popped his 1,000th target, the official timer stopped his watch. The man had

been shooting but one hour and 42 minutes, and had hit his targets on the average of 10 a minute. For almost two hours steady, Bogardus hit a glass ball every six seconds!

A slime mold can crawl like an amoeba

Probably the most bizarre shapes to be found in all the plant kingdom belong to a group of minute fungus-like plants known as slime molds. In their reproductive state, a slime mold can take the form of a birdcage, a doughnut, an umbrella, a cattail, or one of many other peculiar shapes. A slime mold may also appear in almost any color of the rainbow. Unfortunately, few slime molds can be seen without at least a magnifying glass.

At one time, slime molds were thought to be animals, for they are sometimes capable of locomotion. For a time they were also considered to be fungi. Today, slime molds are recognized as plants of a distinct phylum, with their own unique properties.

Each slime mold progresses through two stages of life. In the first, it resembles the shapeless one-celled animal known as the amoeba; in the second, it becomes intricately organized and possesses many fungal properties. It's easy to see why scientists were puzzled for so long in categorizing the slime mold.

When a slime mold spore germinates, it produces a number of protoplasmic bodies called swarm cells, which move with the use of flagella, whip-like appendages. These cells fuse sexually to form a large amoeba-like mass, usually an inch or so in diameter—but in some cases more than several feet across!

It is during this stage of life that the slime mold is capable of locomotion. The jellylike mass—called plasmodium—crawls by a contractile process over rotted vegetable matter; it feeds by engulfing bacteria, molds, and fungi.

In this state, the slime mold is more like a blob of protoplasm than a plant. Each mass of plasmodium is not an individual organism: if it is divided, each smaller mass will display all the properties of life the larger mass had exhibited. And smaller blobs can be joined to form a larger mass of plasmodium!

The blue whale is the largest animal that ever lived

You may be surprised to learn that the largest creature ever to grace the earth is still flourishing. Contrary to a popular assumption, the dinosaur can't lay claim to that title. The largest of those reptiles—the brontosaurus—rarely grew to a length of more than ninety feet, and averaged well under fifty tons. These measurements seem modest compared to those of that famous leviathan—the blue whale. Specimens of this seagoing giant have been reported as long as 120 feet—longer than a city block—and many weigh close to *120 tons!*

Almost everything about this creature is colossal. The blue whale has the biggest nose and the biggest tongue of anything alive, and a mouth so large that a full-grown man can stand erect inside the enormous cavern, and still have to stretch his arms to touch the roof of the whale's mouth!

Despite its size and enormous appetite, the blue whale can swallow nothing larger than a shrimp! Most of its food consists of tiny fish and sea animals bigger than the head of a pin. The whale doesn't have to hunt for this food—it merely swims slowly through the water with its huge mouth open. Small sea creatures enter the cavernous mouth and get caught in a brushlike growth of bony hairs that hang from the roof of the whale's mouth. Every so often, the whale closes its jaws, expels the water inside, licks the food off the roof of its mouth with a gargantuan tongue, and swallows thousands of tiny morsels.

Although the whale spends its entire life in the ocean, it is not a fish. Rather, it is a warm-blooded mammal that breathes air—just like seals, beavers, otters, and other sea animals. The longest a whale can stay submerged is about half an hour. But this feat is astonishing when we realize that a man, holding his breath to the utmost of his endurance, can stay under water for only two or three minutes!

When one of these mammoth mammals comes to the surface of the ocean for a breath of fresh air, it shoots a fountain of vapor into the air that can be seen from miles away. Most people believe that the whale is spouting water from its

nostrils, but this is not the case. A whale never deliberately takes water into its breathing passages; if it did, the creature would drown just as surely as a human being would.

Before a whale dives underwater it fills its lungs with air, and, when it resurfaces, expels this air with great force. This breath, warmed

and moistened by the whale's lungs, condenses upon contact with the colder outside air and forms streams of vapor resembling water. And if the whale happens to exhale—or "blow"—a short distance below the surface, a considerable amount of water may be carried upward with the escaping air.

There is a great deal of evidence to suggest that some whales are capable of a form of "speech." A humpback whale, for instance, emits a series of very low sound waves that travel great distances through water to inform other members of its species of its whereabouts. Some scientists believe that two humpback whales can communicate with each other across the breadth of an entire ocean!

Osbaldeston rode horseback for 200 miles in eight hours and 42 minutes

George Osbaldeston was a 155-pound jockey who operated the Newmarket Inn. He was known as "The Squire." On November 5, 1831, George announced that he would ride horseback for 200 miles in less than 10 hours over a Newmarket track. To back his words, Osbaldeston put up 1,000 guineas in cash, a considerable sum in those days.

The terms of the bet were that the rider could change horses (he would ride one horse for four miles and then switch to another horse), that he could use the same horse two or more times, that all elapsed time—whether used for riding, mounting, or resting—would be counted, and that if a horse failed to last a distance for any cause whatsoever, that would just be too bad and Osbaldeston would lose.

The race would take place on a set Saturday, regardless of the weather.

Days before the race, Newmarket was crowded with racing fans. On Saturday, November 5, 1831, as per agreement, the ground was measured at Newmarket's Round Course. George would mount at Duke's Stand, where many celebrities had gathered to watch, and he would go the four-mile distance around the track, ending up at Duke's Stand to mount another horse. "The Squire" would do 50 laps.

A fresh lamb-skin-covered saddle would be ready for George every time he arrived for a new mount. So would refreshments, including porridge, warm jelly, and weak brandy. A change of clothing was also laid out, but Osbaldeston did not require it.

The hazards were many: a lame horse could slow him down; an injured horse could ruin the day; an accident to himself would be the supreme disaster. Thundershowers threatened to turn the track into a quagmire; and in fact, it did rain all day long. But the dauntless jockey, clad in a purple silk jacket and doeskin breeches, was off and running at 7:12 a.m. He made it around the first four miles in the good time of nine minutes flat. *Clasher*, his 10th horse, broke down near Duke's Stand, but Osbaldeston nursed it home. His 13th mount, *Coroner*, used for a second time, turned in an 8:40 clocking. His 21st mount, *Fury*, negotiated the track in 8:10. Without question, "The Squire" was running well as the race neared the halfway point.

After a six-minute rest period, on round No. 31, the jockey ran into his first setback. *Ikie Solomons* tripped and threw him, but Osbaldeston held onto the reins and managed to avoid serious mishap. Still, the accident cost him about four minutes' time.

Now the rain began to fall faster. By the 48th round, horse and rider were both mercilessly drenched by a driving torrent. One of "The Squire's" mounts actually did turn around on the track and try to run back to shelter. But George braved on.

As he crossed the finish line, Osbaldeston drew a mighty cheer. He had spent seven hours, 19 minutes, four seconds on his horses, and another one hour, 22 minutes and 56 seconds mounting and resting. His total elapsed time —eight hours and 42 minutes—was well under the allowed 10 hours of his bet.

However, "The Squire" hadn't had enough. After he rode home on his favorite horse, he penned a letter to *The Times of London* offering to make the same 200-mile trip in eight hours! There were no takers.

The Temple of Borobudar depicts the life of Buddha in sculpture

The Temple of Siva at Borobudar, Java, is one of the largest and, to Western eyes, most peculiar Buddhist shrines in the world. By following a circular route to the top of the pyramidal structure, a visitor can study the life of Buddha and an elaboration of Buddhist religious doctrine—all told in finely carved relief sculpture!

This reliquary mound was built during the ninth century but lay overgrown with dense jungle for 900 years until its restoration early in this century. The monument consists of seven square terraces of gradating size, surrounded by a high wall and surmounted by three circular terraces or platforms. On these platforms rest 72 small bell-shaped stupas, or reliquary housings; each contains a sculptured Buddha visible through the stupa's perforated stonework. At the pinnacle, one large stupa encloses a large, unfinished Buddha.

Although four stairways—one on each side—rise across the terraces and platforms toward the topmost stupa, the builders of the Temple of Borobudar did not intend that pilgrims climb to the top of the shrine so simply. Rather, they planned a circuitous route lined with teeming relief sculpture. A pilgrim began his visit by walking around the high outer walls, examining the story in sculpture of the Buddha and the various moral doctrines of Buddhism. As he rose from terrace to terrace, the pilgrim inspected the pavilions, the statue-crammed niches, the carved waterspouts, and the relief sculpture that filled the terrace walls.

When read in a circular ascent to the shrine, these reliefs demonstrate, in progressive fashion, ever more profound moral doctrines. The high walls of the terraces prevent a pilgrim from viewing a higher level than the one he is on.

The pilgrim's winding route does not stop when he reaches the circular platforms. Only after he has passed the 72 small stupas is he ready to view the great Buddha that crowns this marvelously ingenious structure.

Huang Erh-nan painted with his tongue

A celebrated Chinese artist of the 1920's, Huang Erh-nan, painted lotus flowers and butterflies on silk. But it was not the subject matter of his art that made Huang so unbelievable; it was his technique. Huang Erh-nan used his tongue as a paint brush, and his mouth as the receptacle for black ink.

The Peking artist first filled his maw with the thick ink Oriental artists prefer for their finest work. Then he leaned over the fine silk cloth he had stretched out on a table, and brushed in his paintings—paintings noted for their delicacy and charm.

El Oued is the city of a thousand domes

The city of El Oued, Algeria, is nestled in a large oasis deep in the Sahara Desert. Surrounded by the Great Eastern Erg—the most barren region of the entire Sahara—El Oued basks in the fierce desert sun for 365 days a year, almost untouched by rainfall.

The residents of this age-old caravan trading center have constructed their one-story homes with thick mud walls for protection against the scorching sun. To further reduce the heat within these structures, almost every *room* in the city is roofed by its own mud dome. While some homes are topped with a single oblong dome, others sport clusters of small circular domes which give the densely packed city a truly bizarre appearance. From the air, El Oued looks like a bunch of egg cartons turned upside down!

Lope de Vega wrote more than 1,500 plays

Félix Lope de Vega Carpio, the renowned Spanish dramatic poet born in 1562, wrote an estimated 1,500 plays—not to speak of countless poems, epics, and prose works. Of these 1,500 plays, about 500 survive.

De Vega penned his first drama at the age of 11, while a student at a Jesuit school. From that moment on, he poured out a torrent of theatrical works the like of which has never been equaled.

Ever since the 13th century B.C., men have marveled at the mammoth stone statues outside the temple of Amon Re, hewn out of the side of a steep cliff at Abu Simbel, Egypt. Each of four gigantic sculptures—the largest is close to 70 feet high—depicts the great Pharaoh Ramses II seated on a massive stone chair, facing eastward over the Nile.

During Ramses' 67-year reign, Egypt acquired unprecedented wealth and power, and the Pharaoh left monuments throughout his empire. Among these were the temples at Luxor, Karnak, and Abu Simbel, three of the greatest works of ancient Egyptian architecture.

After Ramses' reign, no one could sail up the Nile without coming under the gaze of the four watchful statues on the western bank—and the large figures before another temple slightly to the north.

At the foot of the four seated figures stand a number of smaller statues. One is set directly in the wall behind the colossi. Entrance to the temple is gained by stairs between the two center statues, which lead to a narrow hall passing between two rows of standing figures inside the temple.

In the 1960's, it appeared that these age-old monuments would be lost forever. The Egyptians were constructing the Aswan High Dam upriver from the temple site, and the water that would flood the Nile Valley for 310 miles behind the dam threatened to submerge many archaeological treasures—among them Abu Simbel.

International negotiations aimed at preserving the statues resulted in the adoption of an Italian plan for moving the entire temple complex to higher ground. Money for the conservation project was alloted by UNESCO, an agency of the UN. An international team of archaeologists and engineers set to work, sawing the statues into massive blocks and reassembling them 200 feet above the original site.

In 1970, the Aswan High Dam was completed. The original Abu Simbel site is now submerged under Lake Nasser. But the statues of Ramses—after 32 centuries at one site—still gaze stoically over the Nile Valley.

The colossal sculptures of Abu Simbel have stood for 32 centuries

Saunders ran 120 miles in less than 24 hours

One of the most unusual competitions that ever took place was the track race held in the American Institute's indoor arena in New York City on February 21, 1882, under the auspices of the Williamsburg Athletic Club. The rules stipulated that the race would be 24 hours long. The athlete who did the most mileage around the track in that time would be declared the winner.

At 10:00 p.m., 14 competitors lined up for the race. After 23 hours had elapsed, only seven remained on the track. James Saunders was so far ahead it seemed impossible for anyone to beat him.

By common consent, the race was halted a few minutes later—almost an hour before the stipulated finish. At this point, Saunders had run 120 miles. He had won $100 in cash, and the cheers of a crowd of 800 fans.

The shrew is the world's smallest—and most ferocious—mammal

"Shrewish" is a word often used to describe a brawling, scolding woman, and the term is apt. For the shrew, a tiny mouselike mammal, is ounce for ounce the most ferocious creature in the world.

This pugnacious fellow is only two inches long and weighs about as much as a nickel. And it's a good thing that the shrew is the smallest mammal on earth, for his appetite and aggressiveness make a lion seem tame by comparison. This little package of dynamite has a bite like a cobra, eats twice his own weight in meat every day, and can whip an animal three times his size. If he's hungry enough, he'll even eat another shrew!

In addition to a set of needlelike teeth, this two-inch tiger has a mouth full of poison to help him bring down larger prey. The shrew's saliva contains a strange, virulent poison that can kill a mouse within three minutes. And the poison gland in the shrew's mouth can produce enough doses of venom to kill two hundred mice! The pint-sized shrew is a tough customer indeed!

The carrion flower comes well by its name. This African plant, known properly as *Stapelia grandiflora*, so resembles carrion in appearance and odor that it can fool carrion flies into laying their eggs in the petals.

This malodorous mimic is generally about one foot across, with the mottled reddish color—and the stench—of a piece of partially decomposed meat. Tiny flies which normally lay their eggs in decaying meat alight on the flower, and as they wander over the stamens their bodies pick up grains of pollen. The next time one of the flies is fooled by a carrion flower, these grains will be inadvertently deposited on the second flower's stigma—thereby fertilizing the plant.

Abertondo swam the English Channel round trip

The English Channel has been licked by such a legion of athletes that today the feat of swimming its treacherous 22 miles is old hat. But the particular Channel feat of Antonio Abertondo, though dreamed of for decades by swimmers, had never been achieved before.

When on September 21, 1961, Abertondo waded into the chilly sea off Dover, he had set himself an unprecedented challenge: he would swim not only from Dover to Calais, France, but—without a break—from Calais back to Dover—a round trip, without rest, of 44 miles!

The Argentine, then 42 years old and a hefty man with a trace of middle-age spread, and greased from head to toe to protect himself against the cold, entered the water in the morning. Abertondo negotiated the first half of the trip in 18 hours and 50 minutes. Ashore in France, he paused for two minutes—only long enough to sip a hot drink. Then he plunged once again into the tide-tossed waters.

After a few miles, weariness set in—extreme weariness. On the return trip, the waves hit harder, belting his face until it swelled. Even under the goggles his eyes grew sore. Hallucinations followed, the swimmer imagining that huge sharks were in his path.

But Abertondo pumped on, arm over arm and kick after kick; and yard by yard he put the miles behind him.

It was more than a day since he had last touched land—a full 24 hours and 25 minutes after he had left Calais—and 43 hours and 15 minutes after he entered the water at Dover —that Antonio Abertondo writhed out of the surf onto the English shore. The last mile had taken a full two hours. Then, like an agonized shipwreck, he collapsed in the arms of his astounded observers.

Azzar lay on a bed of nails for 25½ hours

The fakirs of the mysterious East claim to have performed fantastic feats of endurance. But many fakirs are no more than common fakers, and upon investigation it usually turns out that their purported feats took place under circumstances that render their claims dubious.

In Sydney, Australia, there is a fakir who backed up his claims by performing in the presence of newsmen and numerous other spectators, outside Walton's on Park Street, one of Sydney's leading department stores.

On the morning of November 20, 1969, bearded Zjane Azzar, clad only in turban and loincloth, gingerly lowered himself into a prone position on a bed of razor-sharp six-inch nails, spaced two inches apart from each other. Throughout that day, the following night, and into the next morning, Azzar remained on his bed of nails, refreshing himself from time to time by smoking a cigarette or by eating a hamburger and some ice cream. During much of this period, he clearly suffered considerable pain. Once his pulse reading was so weak that the attending nurse had to use hot and cold compresses to revive him, and wanted to call the whole thing off.

Azzar refused. He remained stretched out on his bed of nails for a total of twenty five and one half hours, surpassing all previously recorded feats. As Azzar tried to raise himself at the end of his ordeal, he said, "My body has been dead for fourteen hours," and then fainted. He was later examined by a doctor who found him weak but despite the pattern of deep indentations in his back, the fakir was little damaged physically.

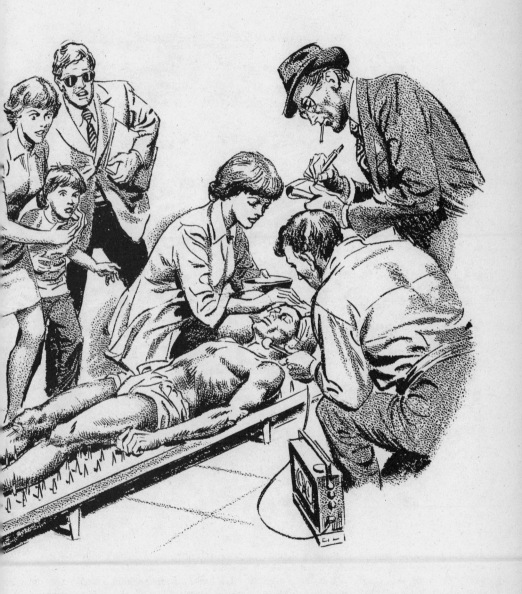

The Panama Canal connects two oceans

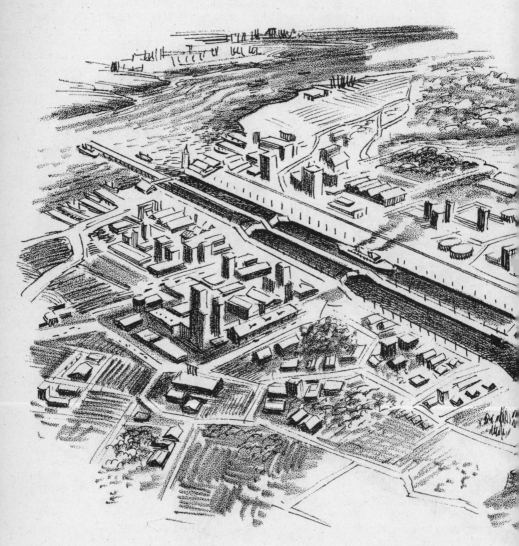

The Panama Canal is neither the longest, the widest, the deepest, nor the oldest canal in the world. Yet, as the only canal which connects two oceans, and the canal whose construction presented the most difficult challenges, the Panama Canal is the greatest man-made waterway in the world.

The initial attempt to build a canal across the narrow isthmus of Panama in Central America resulted in one of the most tragic engineering failures in history. In 1881, a French firm headed by Ferdinand de Lesseps—who had earlier constructed the Suez Canal—began to dig a canal across the isthmus. While de Lesseps was able to conquer the desert of Suez, he could not overcome the mosquito of Panama. Within eight years, close to 20,000 men died of malaria while working on the ill-fated project. The French company went bankrupt after suffering losses totaling $325 million, and de Lesseps left Panama.

In 1907, an American construction crew headed by G.W. Goethals journeyed to Panama to try their luck where the French had failed. Panama leased the U.S. a strip of land 10 miles wide for the canal. A massive project to wipe out the malaria-carrying mosquito was successful, and work proceeded without the hazard of disease that doomed the French venture.

Construction began at both ends of the projected canal and progressed inland through a dense tropical jungle. An artificial lake was formed; locks were constructed; the famed Gaillard Cut, for years the largest ditch in the world, was dug through 660-foot Gold Hill. At the peak of construction, 300 railroad cars—each carrying 400 tons of dirt—left the site daily. A total of 10 billion tons of earth were moved for the canal—a figure greater than the total weight of the Great Pyramid of Cheops! In 1914, the canal was completed.

To navigate the canal, a ship must rise or fall a total of 85 feet. To accomplish this, massive locks were constructed which raise a westbound ship first to the level of the artificial lake—Lake Gatun—then to the level of a second lake —Miraflores—and, at the Pacific end of the canal, lower the ship back to sea level. For eastbound ships, the procedure is reversed.

The locks at Miraflores comprise the largest lock system in the world. The largest Miraflores lock is over 1,000 feet long, with gates seven feet thick and as high as a seven-story building. Electric cars, or "mules," on the side of the canal pull the ship through the locks, and water empties in and out of the lock through tubes as large as railroad tunnels.

The St. Lawrence Seaway between Canada and the U.S. extends over 2,300 miles from Duluth, Minnesota, to Belle Isle, Quebec, and hence is more than 45 times as long as the Panama Canal. But the St. Lawrence waterway was built by deepening and widening rivers, and utilizes the Great Lakes for much of its length. The Panama Canal, on the other hand, was carved out of virgin jungle. In addition, the time saved by a seven-hour trip through the canal is a saving unmatched by any other canal in the world, with the possible exception of the Suez (a 9,000-mile journey around South America requires at least two weeks). Each year, over 15,000 ships take advantage of the Panama shortcut.

An interesting footnote to the Panama Canal story: due to the curve of the isthmus, the Pacific end of the canal actually lies 27 miles *east* of the Atlantic end! Also, the canal has provided the world with perhaps its most clever palindrome (a line that can be read in either direction):

A man, a plan, a canal–Panama!

Countess Rosa Branicka operated on herself

In the mid-19th century, the wealthiest noble in Poland was the Countess Rosa Branicka. Her assets were valued at some 20 million dollars and her lands were worked by 125,000 serfs.

In 1843, the health of the 63-year-old Countess began to fail, and she went to Germany to receive expert diagnosis of her ailment. There she learned that she was suffering from cancer of the breast. The doctors recommended immediate surgery.

But the Countess, perhaps not willing to frighten her family, would not agree to an operation. Instead, she traveled through Germany, Switzerland, and France, buying various surgical instruments in various towns. She would buy a scalpel in one place, a lancet in the other—but never more than one item in any one place, so that no one might guess her intentions.

When she had finally assembled all the instruments that she thought were necessary, Countess Branicka secluded herself in a Paris hotel. There she removed the cancer from her breast. Her recuperation was swift, and she soon returned to Poland where she lived to the ripe age of 82.

The Purandhar Gate is built on a foundation of solid gold

For sheer extravagance, the Fortress of Purandhar near Poona, India, may be without equal in the world. While the fortress itself is less than luxurious, the gateway to this ancient structure was built upon a foundation of *solid gold!*

The Rajah of Bedar ordered the construction of the fortress in 1290. However, his engineers soon informed him that the site for the planned gateway was so marshy that any structure built

Engineers dug two large cavities in the earth, each 12 feet deep. Into these pits they laid 50,000 14-karat gold bricks, weighing a total of some 27,000 pounds. At current prices, the cost of the foundation alone—which emptied the Rajah's treasury—would be over *$40 million!*

It might be added that the foundation did achieve its aim: the gate of Purandhar still stands today, almost 700 years later!

there would soon sink into the ground. According to legend, the Rajah followed the advice he received in a dream and decided to construct the gateway on a foundation of solid gold.

Prince Randion was known as "The Caterpillar Man"

Prince Randion was born in British Guiana in 1871 without arms or legs. At the age of 18, he was brought to America by P.T. Barnum. Though a medical man would label the Prince a human torso, Randion was known in the circus as "The Caterpillar Man" or "The Snake Man."

Despite his handicap, Prince Randion could write by holding a pencil between his lips, could roll a cigarette, and could shave himself. These last two talents were exhibited in Tod Browning's 1933 movie *Freaks*. Moreover, Prince Randion married and fathered five children.

An eagle's nest may weigh a ton

Most birds build a new nest for their eggs each year, and some birds even construct two or three new homes in one season. But the bald eagle uses the same nest year after year. This mighty creature chooses only one mate for its whole lifetime, and builds a single nest, or aerie, high up in a tall tree. Each year the eagle keeps this massive nest in repair by adding more material, so that, after a few years, the aerie may weigh as much as two thousand pounds!

Beamon broad jumped more than 29 feet

For many years, the long-jump record hovered in the area of 27 feet, with each new mark besting the previous one by only an inch or two. Just as many sports observers had once held that running the mile in less than four minutes was a physical impossibility, many claimed that 27 to 28 feet was the human limit for long jumping.

Then came the 1968 Olympic Games in Mexico City, where Bob Beamon did to the long-jump pundits what Roger Bannister had done to the brahmins of the mile run.

As a member of the United States Olympic team, Beamon was, of course, an outstanding jumper. In fact, he had set an indoor record of 27 feet, 1 inch, and had made an outdoor jump of 27 feet, 2-¾ inches.

Despite this, none of the 45,000 spectators at Olympic Stadium were prepared for what they were about to witness on October 18, 1968. Beamon began his running start to the take-off board, and flew off like a shot. Apparently, aided by the thin air of Mexico City, which is situated at an altitude of 7,350 feet above sea level, Beamon soared across the long-jump area with his knees pulled up to his chest and his arms extended sideways.

The onlookers watched in amazement, then broke into wild applause as the stadium's scoreboard flashed confirmation of what they had seen—a jump of 6.90 meters, or 29 feet, 2-½ inches. Beamon had surpassed the previous record by nerly two feet!

The Mexican jumping bean searches for shade

The name of that familiar curiosity, the Mexican jumping bean, is actually a misnomer on two counts. First, the jumping bean is not a true bean, but a simple seed. Second, the bean does not "jump"; its rolling and tumbling movements are due to the presence of a tiny moth larva!

The jumping bean is the seed of the *yerba de flecha*, a chiefly Mexican shrub related to the rubber tree. A certain species of moth frequently visits the plant and deposits eggs in the blossoms. When an egg hatches, the caterpillar bores into a seed and spins a silklike thread with which it lines the walls of its one-room apartment. After nourishing itself on the inner tissue of the seed, the insect enters the sleeping pupa stage, and later gnaws its way through the outside of the seed to emerge as a moth.

The movement of the bean results from the larva's attempts to escape direct sunlight, which would render the inside of the seed too hot for comfort. The larva shifts about inside its temporary home, turning and tumbling the seed until it finds a patch of shady ground. No one has determined how far a single jumping bean can travel, but the distance is thought to be considerable.

The Great Wall of China took 1,700 years to complete

It has been said that of all the man-made structures on the face of the earth, the only one that could conceivably be visible from the moon is the Great Wall of China. Wending its way over more than one-twentieth of the earth's circumference, the Wall is an unparalleled feat of engineering and human determination. In size, materials, and human labor, it is the largest construction project ever undertaken by man. Enough stone was used in the entire project to build an eight-foot wall girdling the globe at the equator!

From its eastern end at Shanhaikuan on the Yellow Sea to its western end at Chaiyukuan in the Gobi Desert, the Wall stretches over mountains, deserts, and plains a distance of 1,500 miles. If the Wall were picked up and moved to the United States, it would stretch from New

York to Topeka, Kansas! But with its numerous twists and turns, the Great Wall is actually 1,700 miles long—and including all its peripheral extensions and offshoots, the length is 2,500 miles. More than 24,000 gates and towers dot the Wall over its serpentine course.

In the eastern regions of China, the Wall is built of stone faced with brick, to an average height of 25 feet. Here the wall is generally 20 to 30 feet wide at the base, tapering to 15 feet at the top. Most portions of the eastern Wall are wide enough to permit six horsemen to ride abreast along the top.

In the west, however, the Wall is constructed largely of earth faced with stone, or simply of earth piled into mounds. Today this section of the Wall has fallen into ruin, and at points is almost obscured by drifting sands.

As the Wall stands today, it is an amalgamation of many walls built over a period of 1,700 years—making the Wall the longest continuous construction project in human history. The first emperor of China, Ch'in Shih Hwang-ti, from

whose name the word *China* is derived, began building the Wall in the 3rd century B.C. Large portions of the eastern Wall were constructed during this 11-year reign. From all over the newly unified China, laborers were conscripted for the project; many died during the construction. The wall was continually augmented and improved over the centuries, with the major work being done during the Ming Dynasty (1368-1644).

Why such a gargantuan project was undertaken is not known for certain. Originally, the Wall was thought to have been built to provide a defense against Mongolian tribesmen to the north, but authorities point out that the height and the extent of the Wall made it undefendable against any army determined to invade China. Indeed, armies were successful in breaching the Wall many times throughout Chinese history. The Wall itself may have been a prime motive for some of the Mongolian invasions, for by enclosing many of the water sources in the outlying regions, the Chinese made it necessary for the tribesmen on the Mongolian plains to cross the Wall in search of water.

Some authorities maintain that the Wall was constructed solely to define the limits of Chinese sovereignty. (The Chinese penchant for walls is well demonstrated by the fortifications built around all old Chinese cities.) All land within the Wall was considered China; everything beyond, the wilderness. In fact, the Wall did serve for hundreds of years as the boundary between the Orient and the Occident.

Others maintain that the Wall was undertaken to provide employment for the Chinese masses in times of hardship and unrest. Whatever the reason for its construction, the Wall stands as one of the most incredible, and certainly the largest, construction feats ever accomplished by man.

Fakir Agastiya held his arm upraised for 10 years

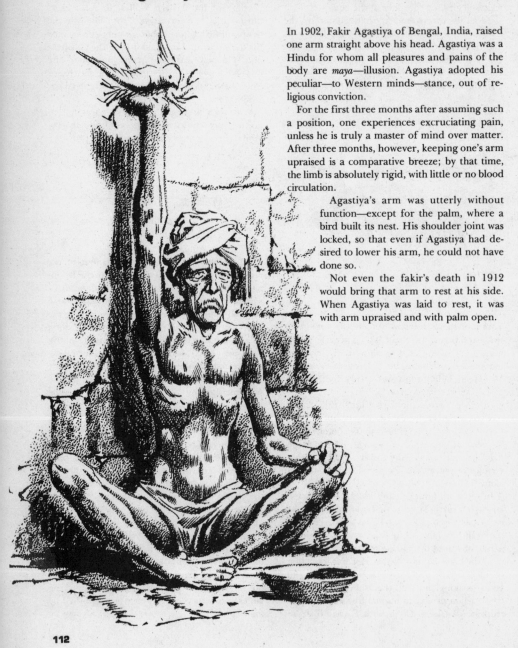

In 1902, Fakir Agastiya of Bengal, India, raised one arm straight above his head. Agastiya was a Hindu for whom all pleasures and pains of the body are *maya*—illusion. Agastiya adopted his peculiar—to Western minds—stance, out of religious conviction.

For the first three months after assuming such a position, one experiences excruciating pain, unless he is truly a master of mind over matter. After three months, however, keeping one's arm upraised is a comparative breeze; by that time, the limb is absolutely rigid, with little or no blood circulation.

Agastiya's arm was utterly without function—except for the palm, where a bird built its nest. His shoulder joint was locked, so that even if Agastiya had desired to lower his arm, he could not have done so.

Not even the fakir's death in 1912 would bring that arm to rest at his side. When Agastiya was laid to rest, it was with arm upraised and with palm open.

The Clément girl was
born with only one eye

In 1793, the Clément family of Tourcoing,
France, was stunned at the first sight of their
new child, a daughter. The girl was born with
one eye in the center of her forehead.

She was indeed a replica of the giant Cyclops
of Homer's *Odyssey*. Otherwise normal, the girl
lived until the age of 15.

An African girl was a grandmother at 17

At the age of seven, Mum-zi joined the harem of Chief Akkiri, ruler of the estuary of Calabar, Nigeria. Shortly after her betrothal, Mum-zi became pregnant. At the age of eight years and four months, she gave birth to a perfectly normal, well-developed child.

When the daughter of Mum-zi and Akkiri also gave birth at the age of eight, Mum-zi became a grandma at age 17—the youngest grandmother on record.

The Hoover Dam is over 70 stories high

In the northwestern corner of Arizona, a road emerges from a bleak, dusty landscape and passes over a concrete wall stretched across a dizzyingly deep canyon. On one side of the wall, the Colorado River twists southward through the barren hills; on the other side, a blue lake extends far back along the Arizona-Nevada border. This lake is Lake Mead, formed by the massive concrete wall of the Hoover Dam—the first of the giant concrete dams.

The Hoover Dam is no longer the highest dam in the world. During the last 17 years, eleven higher dams have been built or are under construction. But the Hoover Dam, begun in 1931, pioneered the techniques of modern dam building and remains one of the true structural wonders of the world.

Before the construction of this concrete colossus, the basin now filled by Lake Mead was a canyon cut through the desert plateau by the Colorado River. More than 500 square miles of this canyon were cleared in anticipation of the waters that would soon begin to flood it. Upriver from the Hoover Dam site, a temporary earthen dam was erected to hold back the river, and four tunnels 50 feet in diameter were cut through the earth to channel the water around the construction site.

The concrete had to be poured without interruption for two years, workers toiling day and night. In 1936, the concrete wall was finally completed, and the four tunnels were sealed. Water began to pile up behind the dam, eventually filling in the canyon and forming the 115-mile long Lake Mead—which until 1955 was the world's largest man-made lake. At the dam, this lake is over 600 feet deep!

To hold back such a massive weight of water, the Hoover Dam had to be built to a thickness of 600 feet at the base—the length of two football fields—tapering to 45 feet at the top. The dam stretches 1,300 feet from one rim of the canyon to the other, and rises 726 feet above the floor of the gorge. In all, over 7,000,000 tons of concrete were used—a weight greater than the Great Pyramid of Egypt.

The benefits of Hoover Dam? A hydroelectric plant at the base of the dam has a capacity of over 1.3 million kilowatts of power, enough to light a good-sized city. And water from Lake Mead is used to irrigate over 1 million acres of land in the U.S. and Mexico.

For a time, the name of the dam was changed to Boulder Dam, but reverted to Hoover Dam in 1947. Today the dam and lake not only provide electricity, water, and flood control for millions of people, but they also comprise a National Recreation Area visited by thousands every year.

**The elephant tree
discharges a scented fog**

You may have been unfortunate enough to sample first-hand the malodorous defense mechanism of the skunk. Would you have guessed that a member of the plant kingdom makes use of a similar mechanism to ward off dangerous intruders? Well, it's true: the elephant tree, a small shrub tree indigenous to northern Mexico, discharges a cloud of fetid-smelling oil to protect its leaves from hungry herbivores.

The elephant tree, *Bursera microphylla,* owes its popular name to the swollen form of its trunk and branches. The base of this short tree especially resembles the thick, puffy legs of an elephant. Aside from its few branches, the tree sports only a few thin leaves and occasionally a number of apricot-colored fruits.

Any animal that tries to nibble on one of these fruits or leaves is in for an unpleasant surprise. With the slightest tug on one of the elephant tree's leaves, the animal is inundated by a mist of oil as foul as a skunk's spray.

The mist actually consists of tiny particles shot in a jet from openings in the bark; the jet can reach up to three feet from the tree. Any bothersome animal disturbing this arboreal wonder will advertise its mistake for weeks to come!

Chamberlain scored 100 points in a professional basketball game

It figured to be a no account game in a no account place. Neither the New York Knickerbockers nor the Philadelphia Warriors were going anywhere in the National Basketball Association standings in 1962, and the neutral site where they played, the little Hershey Arena in Hershey, Pennsylvania, was well off the major league road map.

But on the night of March 2, Wilt Chamberlain made basketball history. Standing 7-feet, 1-inch, Wilt the Stilt heaved 100 points into the basket! In compiling his score, the perfectly coordinated giant scored on 36 field goals in 63 tries, and sank 28 out of 32 free throws. Since that day, no one has come close to Chamberlain's record—not even Wilt himself.

Needless to say, his team won, 169 to 147.

Lemmings commit suicide by the millions

The instinct of self-preservation is perhaps the most basic drive in all living things. Yet lemmings, small mouselike creatures that live in the icy northern regions of Scandinavia, frequently commit mass suicide—and no one has been able to discover why!

High in the Scandinavian mountains, the furry lemmings abound, eating reindeer moss and roots and building cozy underground nests. When food is plentiful these tiny rodents lead quiet, peaceful lives.

But every few years the lemming population grows so large that their food supply can no longer sustain them. Then all the lemmings leave their burrows at the same time and gather together in mighty hordes. Like an army heading for a great battle, they swarm out of the highlands and rush downward over the sloping plains.

Normally, lemmings fear and avoid water. But during their mass march they brave streams and lakes, devouring everything in their path and leaving a swath of devastation behind them as they draw ever closer to the sea.

After running for weeks the lemmings finally reach the seashore, and then, row upon row, plunge headlong into the water! For a short time the frantic rodents remain afloat, breasting the rough tide like millions of tiny rowboats cutting into the surf. But soon the creatures tire, and one by one sink to their doom.

During a lemming migration, the bodies of the animals can completely cover the surface of the water. One steamer off the Norwegian coast reported that for a full hour the ship had to cut its way through a thick shoal of lemmings swimming out to sea—swimming out to die!

Many theories have been offered about this mass suicide. Some zoologists argue that the fatal plunge of the lemmings is just an error of judgment, that the creatures think the ocean is just one more wide river to cross on the way to a nesting ground with a larger food supply. But all explanations remain only guesses, and the suicidal lemming remains one of the most baffling mysteries of the animal kingdom.

119

Louis Cyr was the strongest man in the world

He stood only five feet, ten and one half inches, but his huge chest, which bulged 60 inches in circumference, seemed like a barrel that had popped out of his 300-pound frame. His legs and his biceps were tremendous. The strength of the farm boy from St. Cyprein, Quebec, is the stuff that legends are made of.

But Louis Cyr was no legend. He really could lift a full barrel of cement with one arm, and he

once pushed a freight car on the railroad tracks up an incline. On another occasion, 18 men who in the aggregate weighed 4,300 pounds stood on a platform. Louis Cyr lifted the platform. And to get tongues wagging, Cyr lifted 588 pounds off the floor—with one finger!

But undoubtedly, Cyr's most dramatic feat occurred on the day he was pitted against four workhorses. On December 20, 1891, standing

before a crowd of 10,000, in Sohmer Park, Montreal, Louis Cyr was fitted with a special harness. Four draft horses were lined up opposite Cyr, a pair of them to his left, and a second pair to his right. Heavy leather straps encased his upper arms; sturdy hooks at the end of these straps were attached to whiffletrees which led to harnesses strapped to four horses.

Cyr stood with his feet planted wide and placed his arms on his chest. As Louis gave the word, the grooms urged their horses to pull. The regulations of the contest ruled out any sudden jerk. The four horses pulled with all their might and main on the strong man, trying to dislodge Louis' arms from his chest. If Cyr lost his footing or either arm left his chest, he would lose the contest.

The grooms whipped the horses, and urged them in every way to pull harder and harder. But the horses slipped and slid, while Cyr didn't budge an inch. After a few minutes of tugging, it was obvious that Cyr was stronger than all four horses put together.

Foster stayed under water for over 13 minutes

On March 15, 1959, Robert Foster entered the swimming pool of the Bermuda Palms Hotel in San Rafael, California. Before entering the pool, Foster had primed himself for his ordeal by breathing in oxygen from a tank for a half hour.

As Foster lowered himself into the pool, members of the Marine Skin Divers Club prepared to time him. A doctor was present and an expert in first aid stood by, for Foster intended to stay at the bottom of that pool longer than any other man had ever been under water.

This he did. When he emerged, the clockers stopped their watches at 13 minutes, 42.5 seconds.

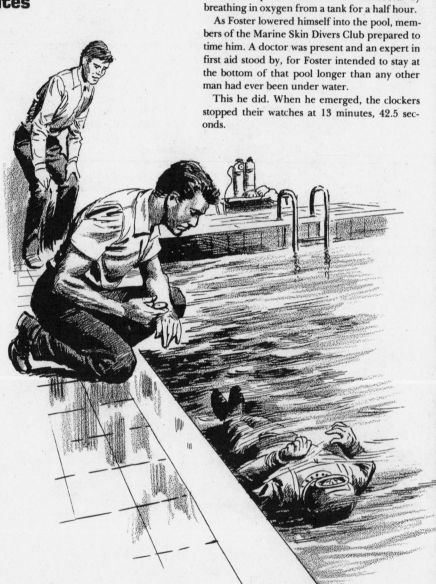

The koala lives entirely on eucalyptus leaves

The koala, a small Australian marsupial, looks just like a toy teddy bear. He gets his name from an aboriginal term meaning "no water," for this cute creature never drinks water in his entire life. But the koala is a fussy eater: He'll eat only the leaf of the eucalyptus tree! And he spends almost all his time in one of these trees, continually munching the tasty leaves.

The Mosque of Omar was built to house a rock

The Mosque of Omar in Jerusalem was the first mosque erected with a dome. But this holy structure is more noted for the object it was built to house—a large granite rock sacred to the followers of Islam. Today, the mosque is best known as the Dome of the Rock.

Christians as well as Moslems hold this rock sacred. It is upon this massive stone that —according to Judeo-Christian tradition—

Abraham agreed to sacrifice his son Isaac as proof of his obedience to God. In the 10th century B.C., the Hebrew King Solomon constructed his great temple on this site, with the most sacred area of the temple—the Ark of the Torah—directly over the rock. Solomon's temple was subsequently destroyed by the Babylonians, but another temple was constructed on the site by King Herod. This temple was destroyed by the Romans in 70 A.D.

According to Moslem belief, the prophet Mohammed was carried from Mecca to Jerusalem on a winged horse, and set down atop this long-revered rock. Shortly after the Mos-

lems captured the city of Jerusalem in 637, they began to construct a mosque to enclose the sacred stone, preserving it for the followers of Islam.

This mosque, an eight-sided structure topped by a wooden dome almost 100 feet high, was completed in the year 691 and named for the caliph Omar. The courtyard surrounding the mosque occupies almost one-sixth of the entire area of the old walled city.

The rock itself—a massive chunk of granite 60 feet long and 40 feet wide—contains a number of deep hollows, which Moslems hold to be the footprints of the giant horse that brought Mohammed to the sacred city.

A banyan tree can have 320 trunks

If you believe that all trees take root in the soil and grow upward, you've overlooked a peculiar Indian giant known as the banyan. This curious tree, also known as the Indian fig, actually grows downward from a rooting place high above the ground!

The seeds of the banyan are dropped by birds into the branches of a suitable host tree, where they germinate. Ropelike shoots descend from the sprouting seed and take root in the soil at the foot of the tree. These shoots gradually thicken until they form trunks, which in turn sprout and send more shoots into the soil to support the heavy horizontal limbs. Eventually the banyan becomes a tangled mass of trunks and branches which completely obfuscate the host tree.

A banyan tree may develop as many as 320 trunks and well over 3,000 smaller branches, covering a total ground area of 2,000 square feet. Alexander the Great is said to have camped under a banyan tree that was large enough to shelter his entire army of 7,000 men!

Anderson lifted 6,270 pounds of dead weight with his back

In his early 20's, Paul Anderson of Toccoa, Georgia ranged in weight from 300 pounds to 360 pounds. Not only was he one of the biggest men around, but he was unquestionably the strongest man on earth. The powerful 5-foot, 10-inch Georgian had wrists that measured nine inches around. His neck was a burly 23 inches in circumference.

Anderson was the first man in history who could press, as the weight lifters say it (that is, lift from the floor to above his head), a barbell of 400 pounds. Among other feats, Paul could do three knee bends in succession while he carried a 900-pound barbell across his shoulders. He powered his way to an Olympic championship as an amateur.

On June 12, 1957, Paul Anderson, then a professional weight lifter, established himself as the superman of the age. He placed a steel safe full of lead on a specially-made table, and then loaded the remaining surface with bars of heavy auto parts. He then crawled under the table and placed his hands on a stool to support himself. Then, elevating his back, he lifted the table inches off the floor—a weight of 6,270 pounds!

Three tons is just about the weight of two good-sized automobiles. Or to put it another way, Anderson lifted the combined weight of all the players on a 33-man college football team.

Vidocq, a jailbird, became the world's greatest detective

Eugène Francois Vidocq was a clever criminal as well as the outstanding detective of his day. His mysterious and romantic life on both sides of the law have established him as the model of the mastermind sleuth.

Born in 1775, the son of a baker, Vidocq grew up to become a soldier, deserter, hardened criminal, master of escapes and disguises, and last of all, in 1809, a police spy for the *Service de Sureté*. Later, as head of that detective branch, he was one of the first to investigate crime and criminals through an established procedure, as opposed to the catch-as-catch-can ways of his time. As both the scourge and friend of many criminals, he often understood them better than they understood themselves. Indeed, outlaws often discovered that their "trusted accomplice" turned out to be Vidocq himself, in a completely convincing disguise.

After serving for 23 years in the *Sureté*, the famed sleuth was removed as its head in 1832, charged with instigating a crime so that he might gain praise for uncovering it. For the remaining 25 years of his life, Vidocq ran a paper mill, employing ex-criminals for his work force.

Banvard painted a canvas three miles long

In 1840, a 25-year-old New Yorker by the name of John Banvard set out on the Mississippi River in a skiff. For the next 400 days, he rowed and poled his craft along the river, busily sketching the scenery. Thus began the most monumental journey in the history of painting.

Over the next five years, Banvard worked diligently on "The Panorama of the Mississippi," as he named his work. Depicting 1,200 miles of landscape from the mouth of the great river to New Orleans, Banvard labored on an equally grand canvas: 16,000 feet long and 12 feet wide.

The enormous painting was exhibited on two upright revolving cylinders. Despite the fact that it took two hours to view the entire "Panorama," thousands gladly paid to see this sensation. Banvard's colossus earned $200,000 in its tours of leading cities in the United States and Europe. Subsequently, it was sold to an Englishman. Then it vanished.

Beavers build dams, canals, and lodges

Busy as a beaver is one catchword that's really based on fact. Almost from the day he is born until the day he dies, the beaver simply never stops working!

The beaver's ingenuity and industry are astounding. This buck-toothed rodent spends his life constructing lodges, dams, and canals that are marvels of animal engineering. And his only tools are a set of powerful front teeth and a broad, flat tail!

When a young beaver has learned how to use these tools, he leaves his parents' lodge and begins constructing a home of his own. His first step is to select a good location for his dam. When he has found a quiet waterway where no other beaver has staked a claim, he sets to work at once, gnawing down trees and carrying the lumber back to his dam site. In one night, this bark-happy vegetarian can cut down an aspen six inches thick, chop it neatly into six-foot lengths, and drag the logs to the bank of the stream where he plans to build his dam.

If there are not enough trees near the site, the beaver will go further into the forest in search of lumber. But as eager as he is, the beaver doesn't believe in doing an ounce of unnecessary work. So, if the distance from the trees to the dam site becomes too great for him to drag the lumber, the beaver simply digs a canal! He then uses this canal—which may be over one thousand feet long—to float the lumber down to the construction site!

To build his dam, the beaver first lays a foundation of branches and leaves packed together with mud, then piles layer upon layer until a pond is formed on one side of the levee. While working, the beaver uses his flat tail like a trowel, slinging mud and packing it tightly to waterproof his construction.

Next, the hardworking rodent gets busy building his house, a lodge constructed of wood and mud in the middle of the newly formed pond. This house is actually a two-story log cabin, most of it below the surface of the water. This underwater fortress contains many rooms and passageways, and the only entrance is under the surface of the pond. The beaver's snug and comfortable living quarters are in a penthouse above the water.

By the time the dam and house are completed, summer has arrived. The young beaver then takes a break from his busy schedule to find a wife. And he's choosy, for once two beavers have mated, they stay mated for life!

Once mated, the beaver continues to work. He and his partner must chop down more trees to make the dam higher, so the pond behind the dam will grow bigger. They must also hurry to store up twigs and branches and pieces of bark for the coming winter. Year after year, Mr. and Mrs. Beaver continue their work.

Why does this clever creature insist on living in the middle of a pond? To make sure that no other animal can reach his lodge during the long periods the beaver spends inside his house. And there's another reason the beaver keeps so busy: His front teeth keep growing as long as he lives. If he doesn't grind them down with constant gnawing, those teeth will grow so large that the beaver won't be able to chew his food!

The great industry of this animal benefits other woodland creatures, too. The ponds and lakes that result from beaver dams provide perfect nurseries for fish and wild fowl. The beaver-made reservoirs make life possible for animals that might otherwise die of thirst in the dry summer months. And in parts of the country where beavers are left to build their dams unmolested, floods and soil erosion are practically unknown!

The Geodesic Dome becomes structurally stronger as it increases in size

The geodesic dome, designed by the American architect, engineer, and inventor R. Buckminster Fuller, may turn out to be the most important structural innovation of the 20th century. This dome is built with a frame of interlocking tetrahedronal shapes copied from nature, as in the structure of crystals or plant cells. Fuller's dome is the only structure yet devised whose strength actually *increases* with its size!

Because of this fortunate peculiarity, a geodesic dome could be built to enclose an area of any size. Theoretically, entire cities could be covered with such a dome to form a climatic environment which would be completely controllable by man. Even more intriguing is the possibility of enclosing a currently nonarable expanse of land, such as the Sahara or the Antarctic, and thus rendering it fertile!

Mihailo Tolotos never saw a woman

Mihailo Tolotos, a Greek monk who died in 1938 at the age of 82, was perhaps the only man never to have laid eyes on a woman. Mihailo's mother died when he was born, and the infant was whisked away the following day to a monastery atop Mount Athos. Tolotos spent the remainder of his life among the monks—completely isolated from female society. Women and *even female animals* were prohibited from entering the monastery, a tradition dating back to the founding of the retreat more than nine centuries earlier.

The idea of bubble-topped cities may seem to be more in the realm of science fiction than engineering fact, but thousands of geodesic domes have already been constructed throughout the world. To date, the largest is the Union Tank Car Company in Baton Rouge, Louisiana. Completed in 1958, this dome is 384 feet in diameter and 116 feet high. However, many larger domed projects have been proposed, among them a shopping center in East St. Louis, Illinois, that calls for the construction of a geodesic dome close to a *half mile* in diameter!

Linster did 6,006 consecutive push-ups without pause

On October 7, 1965, 16-year-old Charles Linster of Wilmette, Illinois, got his coaches at New Trier High School to act as his witnesses. The young man, then five feet six and one-half in-ches tall and weighing 153 pounds, was going to attempt an endurance feat that would put his name into the record books.

Chick Linster, an accomplished gymnast, had done an awful lot of practicing doing push-ups. The push-up, a simple enough exercise in itself, consists of stretching out one's full length, chest down on the floor, and then, keeping a straight back, lifting one's self off the floor by pressing on the palms of the hands. The descent is made by simply bending the elbows until the chest touches the floor once again. This common exercise is seen in almost all gymnastic classes. A dozen push-ups is considered a fairly good workout for the average man who is in good physical condition.

On that day, performing for three hours and 54 minutes, Chick Linster executed 6,006 push-ups without stopping.

A baby puffin soon outweighs its mother

The young puffin has perhaps the most doting mother of any bird in the world. The mother puffin, or sea parrot, gorges its single offspring until the youngster has grown large and fat enough to outweigh its mother!

But then the mother flies away. The youngster is too fat and too young to start searching for food on its own. For days it lives off its fat, gradually slimming down until it is light enough to fly, and then sets out on its own.

Who was the man in the "iron" mask?

In 17th-century France, when Louis XIV proclaimed, *"L'etat c'est moi!"* — "I am the State!" — the glutted prisons were France's busiest institutions. Louis could ruin a life with a carefree flourish of the royal quill. But though the "Sun King" chose his victims indiscriminately, there were at least *apparent* reasons why a poor wretch might have incurred the King's displeasure.

But not so for The Man in the Mask. Why he lingered "in durance vile" no one knew. No one knew *then*—no one knows *now!*

In 1669, a tall, well-dressed man of courtly bearing was turned over to Monsieur Saint-Mars, Governor of the fortress of Piguerol. Monsieur Saint-Mars treated his prisoner with great respect, permitting him such privileges as books and the comfort of a priest. But there was one thing Monsieur Saint-Mars would *not* allow: the prisoner was never permitted to show his face. For 34 long years, the prisoner wore a mask of black velvet—wore it because to take it off meant death; wore it, perhaps, to hide a face whose agony might shame the King.

Alexander Dumas romanticized this story in his great novel *The Man in the Iron Mask.* But it is a well-authenticated fact that the mask was fastened to the prisoner's face not by rivets of steel, but by rivets of fear.

Why did Louis XIV condemn this man to a living death? Why did he go to such extremes to hide this man's identity? Why did he spare this man at all? These are questions which historians, after centuries of research, have been powerless to answer.

Some have suggested that the prisoner was an illegitimate son of Louis XIV, and was jailed because he represented a threat to his half-brother, the Dauphin, heir to the throne.

Others maintain that the prisoner was Eustache d'Auger, a young participant in the Black Masses conducted by the notorious poisoner, Madame de Brinvilliers. Supposedly, of the several participating ladies who later became royal mistresses, one saved d'Auger from the guillotine by begging mercy from Louis XIV.

Still another view is that the prisoner was a twin brother of Louis XIV, imprisoned to avoid a contest for the throne. Because of his royal blood, he was treated with the dignity due his station. His face was covered to avoid identification.

Intriguing possibilities, all—but whether any of these postulations are true, no one can say with certainty.

Huey Long made the longest speech in history

At 12:30 p.m. on June 12, 1935, Senator Huey Long of Louisiana began a filibuster in the Senate. When Long finally dropped into his seat from physical exhaustion at 4 a.m. the following day, he had been speaking continually for 15½ hours—the longest speech on record. The speech was 150,000 words long and included such irrelevancies as cooking recipes and humorless anecdotes. Long's marathon monologue filled 100 pages in the *Congressional Record,* and cost the Government $5,000 to print.

The pitcher plant snares insects with a narcotic drug

The carnivorous Venus flytrap and bladderwort rely on lightning-quick movements to catch their prey. But there is another kind of carnivorous plant that does not move at all, and instead relies solely on its ingenious design to lure and snare its insect dinner. These plants are called pitcher plants. There are many species, whose forms vary greatly, but all pitcher plants have one thing in common—hollow leaves that can be death chambers for any invading insect.

The American species of pitcher plant are almost all native to the southeastern United States. Each plant consists of a flower at the end of a long drooping stem, surrounded by a rosette of hollow leaves shaped like slender pitchers or horns. Each pitcher, or leaf, is topped by an overhanging canopy which prevent rainwater from filling the chamber. Gland cells near the top of each pitcher secrete a honeylike substance which smells much like nectar.

The insect that wanders into a pitcher in search of sweet nectar is not likely to make the mistake twice. The inside walls of the slender chamber are covered with thin hairs which make the leaf surface extremely slippery. An insect entering at the top of the pitcher slowly begins to slip further into the funnel-like tube. The sharp, downward-pointing bristles prevent the struggling insect from moving in any direction but down. And if the victim tries to fly away, it bumps into the canopy at the top—which is usually transparent—and tumbles back into the trap.

The unfortunate guest is forced further and further into the pitcher, until it reaches a pool of fluid at the bottom. This fluid contains a narcotic drug which incapacitates the doomed creature, which soon drowns. Bacteria present in the fluid then begin to digest the catch, and the plant absorbs vital nutrients. The skeletal remains that can be found at the bottom of most pitchers are mute testimony to the prodigious appetite of these harmless-looking plants.

The Verrazano-Narrows Bridge is the longest span in the world

For many years, the entrance to New York Harbor through the Narrows Strait was considered too wide to be spanned with a bridge. Due to the depth of the Strait and its heavy ocean-going traffic—all ships entering the port of New York must pass through this channel—the use of a causeway, cantilever, or any other kind of bridge calling for the placing of pillars in the Strait was ruled out.

The construction of the Brooklyn Bridge in 1883 demonstrated that a suspension bridge could span a sizable distance without pillars obstructing the passage underneath. But the Brooklyn Bridge spanned only 486 feet, a distance hardly comparable to the 4,000-foot-plus width of the Narrows. Then, in 1937, came the completion of the Golden Gate Bridge in San Francisco, with its unbroken span of 4,200 feet. This achievement confirmed the capabilities of the suspension bridge, and plans for a bridge across the Narrows were begun in earnest.

A visitor to New York sailing through the Narrows in 1959 would have observed the bridge taking shape on the shores of Brooklyn and Staten Island. In that year, two steel towers began rising near the sites of Fort Hamilton and Fort Wadsworth, the old fortresses that had guarded the entrance to New York Harbor.

Two years later, a visitor would have found the tall gray towers completed, and thick steel cables strung above him across the busy Strait. By early 1962, a small segment of the roadway structure was suspended from the cables in the very middle of the Strait—for the construction of the roadway began in the center of the span and proceeded toward the two towers.

In 1964, after five years of work and $325 million in construction costs, the longest span in the world was opened to traffic. The bridge was named the Verrazano-Narrows after the Strait it spanned and the Italian explorer who was the first European to sail into the harbor.

From tower to tower, the span extends 4,260 feet, 60 feet more than the Golden Gate span. The two towers—as tall as 70-story buildings—are so far apart that they were constructed five inches out of parallel to allow for the curvature of the earth! The highest point of the roadway is 228 feet above the water and extends between its two anchorages a distance of 6,690 feet!

One year after the opening of the Verrazano-Narrows Bridge, a second roadway level—which had been almost completely constructed but had not been intended for use for at least another ten years—was quickly put into operation as traffic on the bridge far surpassed all expectations. The two roadways provide for 12 lanes of traffic and weigh more than 60,000 tons!

Emperor Sutoku penned a book with his own blood

During the twelfth century, Sutoku, Emperor of Japan, was sent into exile for three years. He passed this long period copying the *Lankauarn Sutra*, a Buddist religious work, in red ink—his own blood!

The emperor's book totaled 135 pages containing 10,500 words. Sutoku hoped that his patient efforts would not go unrewarded—that Buddha, his diety, would return him to the Japanese throne. History records that Sutoku *did* return to power again in 1144 and ruled Japan for two more decades.

Sanson was Chief Executioner at the age of seven

In France during the early eighteenth century, the job of Chief Executioner was handed down from father to son. Thus, when the elder Charles-Jean-Baptiste Sanson passed away in 1726, his son Charles automatically assumed the post—even though he was only seven years old.

At that time, prisoners condemned to death were decapitated. Since young Charles was not yet strong enough to handle the heavy executioner's sword, he was permitted to employ a "helper" named Prudhomme who actually wielded the blade. But little Charles had to be present at every execution, for he was the only one authorized to put the official seal to the grim act.

Finally, at the age of 12, the Chief Executioner took on the full responsibility of his job by chopping off the heads of the condemned himself.

The anglerfish catches its prey with luminous bait

Miles below the surface of the ocean, where pressure is a thousand times greater than at sea level and no glimmer of light pierces the cold darkness, creatures take on appearances more bizarre than the strangest land animals. One of the oddest of all deep-sea creatures is the female anglerfish, a large, grotesque fish that uses a luminous appendage to catch her prey.

Affixed to the top of the anglerfish's body is a thin strand of flesh, up to four inches long, that floats in the water like a fishing line. The strand is tipped with a wad of fleshy bait that glows in the inky blackness of the deep. Smaller fish attracted to the dangling light are quickly gobbled up by the waiting angler as they approach.

The glow of the angler's lure is due to a phenomenon known as bioluminescence, which also accounts for the firefly's glow. A chemical reaction takes place at the end of the angler's lure—as well as in any of the other luminous appendages the fish may have on her body—which releases radiant energy in the form of a glow.

This luminous property belongs only to the female angler. The male is much smaller, and completely parasitic to the female. Early in its life the male bites into the skin of a female and hangs on. The site selected appears to be haphazard, and occasionally more than one male becomes affixed to a female. Soon the lips and tongue of the male fuse with the flesh of its host, and the blood-streams of the two creatures connect. Almost all the organs of the male then degenerate, except the reproductive organs, and the male gets its nourishment directly from the blood of the female!

It has been suggested that this unusual relationship has evolved because anglerfish are slow-moving, live in almost total darkness, and are solitary, so that their chances of finding a mate would otherwise be remote.

**Robert Wadlow was
8 feet 11 inches tall**

When Robert Wadlow was born in 1918 in Alton, Illinois, no one paid special attention to his arrival except his parents and relatives. For Robert was an ordinary baby, tipping the scales at a healthy eight and a half pounds.

But young Robert began to grow and grow. At the age of five, he was 5'4"; at 10 he was 6'5"; at 14, 7'5"; at 18, he soared by three inches—and he still kept on growing! This spectacular growth caused Robert to have difficulty with one foot, on which he had to wear a heavy metal brace.

Eventually, the brace led to an infection of the ankle. The fever caused by the infection claimed Wadlow's life in Manistee, Michigan, at the age of 22. At his death, Robert Wadlow was the tallest man in recorded medical history, at a fraction more than 8'11".

George Psalmanazar perpetrated the greatest literary hoax of all time

"George Psalmanazar" is the pseudonym adopted by a Frenchman who, in the first years of the 18th century, bamboozled the whole of Europe.

His facility with several languages enabled Psalmanazar—his real name is not known—to travel through Europe posing as a Japanese convert to Christianity. This fraud was quite lucrative, for few Europeans had ever seen a Japanese, and they were willing to pay to do so.

While in Holland in 1702, Psalmanazar's ruse was penetrated by an English army chaplain named William Innes. Innes, however, did not expose the Frenchman. He agreed to keep his discovery to himself, provided that Psalmanazar go to England as a "Formosan" convert to Christianity giving credit for the exotic conversion to Chaplain Innes.

Since the isle of Formosa (now generally known as Taiwan) was even more mysterious than Japan, Psalmanazar was able to make up his own "Formosan" language. Anglican churchmen, impressed with Psalmanazar's piety and erudition, paid him to instruct missionaries in this unknown tongue. The church also commissioned him to translate the Bible into "Formosan!"

In 1704, he even published a book entitled *An Historical and Geographical Description of Formosa,* which enjoyed much popular success. Psalmanazar provided such juicy tidbits as the fact that Formosans sacrificed 18,000 babies to their gods each New Year's Day, and that they ate raw meat. To make the latter point more graphically, Psalmanazar himself ate uncooked meat in public. To make Formosans seem a more palatable people, Psalmanazar declared that classical Greek was taught in all the island's colleges!

Psalmanazar's hilarious hoax ended in 1706, when increasing suspicions and accusations from abroad forced him to repudiate his assertions.

The banana "tree" is actually a giant shoot

Banana stalks are commonly referred to as "trees," but they are not trees in the correct sense of the term. Actually, banana "trees" are large perennial herbs that reach their full growth in one season. Frequently attaining a height of 30 feet or more, bananas are thus one of the world's largest plants without a woody stem or trunk.

The banana's "trunk" is actually a gigantic shoot; what appears to be a solid bark is in fact only a hollow sheaf of leaves. As the plant reaches maturity, the true stem pushes up through this sheaf and emerges at the top of the plant, bearing the female flowers that will develop into the plant's familiar yellow-green fruit. When the fruit is ripe the entire plant is cut down, for the "tree" will not bear fruit again.

Originally, all varieties of banana produced seeds. But now, after thousands of years of cultivation, the seeds are either sterile or completely absent from the plant. Banana planters must use pieces of rootstalk to generate a new plant.

Jeremy Bentham, 140 years dead, still sits in his favorite chair

Jeremy Bentham (1748-1832) was one of England's greatest philosophers, jurists, and political theorists. He is principally known for his theory of Utilitarianism, which held that the guiding morality of both men and nations should be the greatest happiness for the greatest number of people.

Few men ever lived—or died—in greater harmony with their principles. Utilitarian to the last, Bentham willed his body to the University College Hospital in London, which he had founded in 1827. His expressed intent was that "mankind may reap some small benefit on and by my decease, [my] having hitherto had small opportunities to contribute thereto while living."

Bentham was far too modest in his last testament. His life had been dedicated to the reform of English law, and to the extension of voting rights to the poor and landless. He traveled widely, and his ideas had a profound impact throughout the Western world.

Yet for all his palpable success, Bentham's later years saw him gripped with melancholy. Alone and without a family, he seems to have become obsessed with the idea of self-perpetuation. In bequeathing his remains for dissection, the philosopher stipulated that after the medical school had obtained all possible use from his corpse, the skeleton be placed on display at University College Hospital.

In accordance with Bentham's specific directions, his head was severed from his body, and replaced with a wax model of his head, topped with a beaver hat. The rest of the skeleton was padded and dressed in one of Bentham's own suits, and the philosopher was seated in his favorite chair, his actual skull at his feet.

And there Jeremy Bentham sits today, in the hospital he founded, more than 140 years after his death.

Lewis chinned the bar 78 consecutive times

Anton Lewis was a professional strong man. He traveled throughout the world giving exhibitions and shows.

In 1913, the Englishman, on stage before an audience in Brockton, Massachusetts, grabbed a high bar with both hands and hoisted his chin up alongside it. This in itself is an exercise common enough to be seen in any gymnasium. But Lewis' performance was extraordinary.

Generally speaking, a fairly good athlete can chin the bar between 10 and 16 times; chinning two dozen times is a standout performance. Before Lewis stopped that night in April, he had chinned the bar 78 times—a world's record that still holds!

The lyrebird's plumage resembles a lyre

The lyrebird, an Australian resident with a body much like a pheasant's in size and shape, has unusually large tail feathers that closely resemble a lyre—the harp-like musical instrument played by the ancient Greeks. Only the male lyrebird possesses these odd feathers, which he fans out over his back while wooing the female.

The male builds a sort of "stage" for these colorful performances, a circular mound made of twigs on which the bird sings and displays his finery.

The lyrebird is a skilled mimic, too. The male can not only imitate the song of other birds, but the sounds made by many mammals—including some sounds made by dogs and man!

Javier Pereira lived to be 169

In 1956, a Colombian Indian named Javier Pereira was brought to the Cornell Medical Center of New York Hospital to undergo a battery of tests to determine his age. Pereira had caused quite a stir with his claim that he had been born in 1789—the year of George Washington's inauguration as President. Author Doug Storer had discovered this ancient Indian, and Storer determined to show Pereira to the world.

The doctors at New York Hospital could make no exact determination of Pereira's age, but they went on record as saying that he was certainly "over 150 years old."

Shortly after Pereira died in April, 1958, at the age of 169, the Colombian government issued a postage stamp commemorating this modern Methuselah.

The fabulous stupas of Anuradhapura are unmatched in the world

A stupa is a Buddhist monumental mound built to house a sacred relic. Usually constructed of earth faced with stone, these often massive reliquaries can be found in all the nations in which Buddhism is practiced, and many stupas are over a thousand years old. One of the greatest and oldest collections of stupas in the world is

found in Anuradhapura, on the island of Sri Lanka, or Ceylon.

This ancient city served as the capital of Ceylon for 12 centuries and was a center of pilgrimage for many Buddhists. Today, the ruins of Anuradhapura include several colossal stupas (some larger than the great pyramids of Egypt), a temple hewn from solid rock, and the Brazen Palace, so named for its roof of brass.

But the most marvelous of all the sacred structures in Anuradhapura is the Ruwanweli Pagoda. This stupa, built in 144 B.C., is constructed on a base of *solid silver*, over 500 square feet in area and seven inches thick. The value of the metal used in the foundation alone has been estimated at close to 3 million dollars!

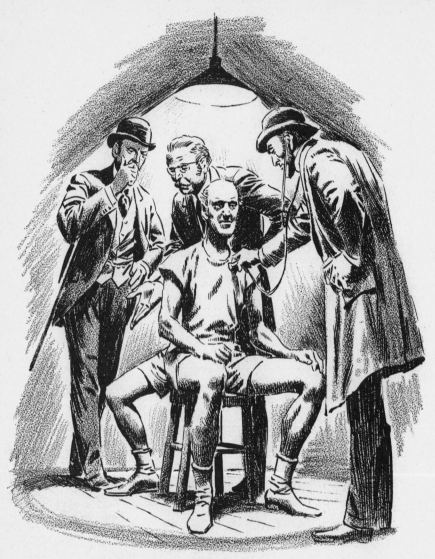

Francesco Lentini had three legs

Francesco A. Lentini was that rare medical phenomenon, the pygoméle—a person born with an extra limb growing from the buttocks. Born in Sicily in 1889, Lentini was able to walk and run on all three legs until the age of six, at which time his two normally positioned legs began to outgrow the third.

When Lentini was a mature adult, his extra leg was three inches short of the ground. Nevertheless, Lentini could still move it independently of the other legs, and it was sufficiently strong and coordinated to kick a football.

Wandering John Chapman planted apple trees for 44 years

John Chapman—better known as Johnny Appleseed—was born in Springfield, Massachusetts, in 1774. Little is known for certain about his early years, except that he was in Pennsylvania in the mid 1790's, distributing apple seeds and saplings to families bound for the West.

In 1801, Johnny appeared in Licking County, Ohio, with a sack of apple seeds he'd collected from cider mills in Pennsylvania and New York. From then until his death in 1845, Johnny Appleseed covered more than 100,000 square miles with apple trees. He retraced his paths over and over again to cultivate and prune the trees he'd planted.

Along the way, Johnny drew attention with his eccentric garb—a coffee sack for a shirt and a tin pot for a hat, in which he would cook his meals. This was fine with him—he distributed Bibles as well as seeds.

Johnny Appleseed was a folk hero in his own day, and his legend seems to have grown with the passage of time. The orchards which dot the Eastern United States today are a memorial to his love for the land and for his fellowman.

The duckbill platypus has fangs on its feet

Is it a bird? Well, it lays eggs, and has the bill and webbed feet of a duck. Is it a mammal? Could be. It nurses its young as a dog or cat suckles its offspring. But it burrows tunnels like a rodent. And it has fangs with which it can squirt poisonous venom into an enemy, just like a snake. Then what *is* this strange concoction of a creature? It's a duckbill platypus, one of the oddest specimens in the animal kingdom.

The platypus is usually placed in the mammal family because it nurses its young with milk, but in fact this singular fellow belongs in a class all its own. And the platypus can be found only in that fabulous land of queer and mysterious creatures—Australia.

Since the duckbill lives half in the water and half on land, nature has given it some of the best features of a bird, a reptile, and a mammal. Take the platypus's feet, for instance. Not only are its toes webbed so that it can swim under water like a turtle or otter, but they are also equipped with hard, sharp claws for digging tunnels in the mud. And on the inside of each short leg, the platypus has a needle-sharp "fang" made of bone. This dagger is hollow, like a rattlesnake's tooth, and through it the platypus can shoot a deadly poison! If an animal is jabbed with one of these poison needles, he's as good as dead.

Like a duck, a platypus uses its paddlelike snout to poke about in the mud of a river bottom, uncovering worms, snails, and tiny shellfish. Also like a duck, and unlike every other mammal but the spiny anteater, the platypus lays eggs. To give birth, a female platypus deposits two crisp white eggs in her tunnel-nest under the river bank, and then sits on them, just like a bird! When the eggs hatch, out pop two peculiar little creatures that look like hairless squirrels.

Naturally, an improbable-looking specimen like the duckbill platypus would be a popular attraction at any zoo. But these creatures have proved very difficult to capture. What is worse, they have not thrived in captivity. If you'd like to catch a glimpse of the strangest of all mammals, you just might have to go to Australia!

The sequoia is the tallest living tree

Even if you've never been to California to view the sequoia trees, ou've probably seen a picture of one of these giant evergreens straddling a road, a dwarfed automobile making its way into the tunnel cut through the tree's thick trunk. The sequoias are indeed the colossi of the plant kingdom: they are the tallest trees in existence and are among the oldest living things on earth.

Trees of the genus *sequoia* were flourishing on earth as long as 100 million years ago, and once grew throughout much of the Northern hemisphere. But the sequoia was almost exterminated by the ice sheets of the glacial ages, and today only two species survive. Both are found only on a narrow strip of land on the U.S. Pacific Coast.

The members of one species of sequoia, known as the big trees, sometimes grow as high as 325 feet, with trunks up to 30 feet thick. Some of these trees are believed to be 4,000 years old. But the real giants of the genus are the redwoods, which can achieve a height of 340 feet —as high as a 30-story building—and a girth of 25 feet. The big trees are the bulkiest, the redwoods the tallest living things on our planet.

The wood of these American titans is extremely valuable as outdoor building material, for sequoia bark is largely resistant to fire, fungus, decay, and insect devastation—which may explain why these old-timers have been around for so long!

The secretary bird kills and eats poisonous snakes

The secretary bird, a long-legged African relative of the hawk family, lives almost exclusively on lizards and snakes—even *poisonous* snakes. When battling the venomous reptile, the secretary bird uses its wings as a shield and strikes at the snake's head with blunt, powerful claws, at the same time jumping out of reach of the poisonous bite with incredible speed.

When the snake becomes completely exhausted, the secretary bird seizes its catch and hurls it in the air several times, then crushes the dazed reptile's head. A dangerous bird indeed!

Angkor Wat is the world's largest religious structure

From the 9th century to the 14th, the city of Angkor was the capital of the Khmer Empire in present-day Cambodia. The home of close to 2 million people, Angkor stretched over 40 square miles in the midst of a jungle. Prosperous Khmer kings constructed immense temples, palaces, and monuments, until Angkor was the largest and most magnificent city in all the Orient.

Sometime in the 14th century, the Khmers were routed and their capital sacked. For the next five centuries, Angkor was deserted. Dense jungle growth covered the streets and buildings. Monkeys, bats, and panthers roamed the empty halls. To all the world, Angkor was no more than a legend.

Then, in 1861, Henri Mouhot, a French naturalist, accidentally discovered the jungle city while searching for butterflies. And to the world's amazement, almost every stone in the lost capital was still in place! Travelers and scholars rushed to Angkor to view one of the most marvelous constructions in history—Angkor Wat.

The main temple at Angkor—known as Angkor Wat—is the largest building in all Asia, and the most gigantic religious structure in the world. The temple's vast network of galleries, colonnades, courts, and stairways is crowned by five acorn-shaped towers, the tallest over 250 feet high. Elaborate stone carvings cover thousands of feet of wall space throughout the enormous temple. Images of gods and goddesses, cobras, kings, and Khmer dancers line the rooms and halls, as intricately carved as the most delicate cameo.

Angkor Wat is approached by a 1,200-foot stone causeway passing over the moat which surrounds the temple. Each side of the causeway is bordered by 54 stone genii—eight feet tall—who support the body of a seven-headed stone cobra, the divine serpent of the Khmers. At the end of the causeway, a 65-foot entrance tower leads into the temple.

The central temple is only one of many grand structures in this vast jungle city. Libraries, baths, gateways, palaces, and temples are spread over an area so large that a visitor could not hope to see all of Angkor in a week's time. The task of clearing away the jungle that chokes the ancient capital is so great that it has never been completed!

In size alone, Angkor is a breathtaking sight, and its temple is a marvel of construction and artistry. That such a magnificent city could remain lost for so long is truly one of the wonders of the world.

Yogi Haridas was buried alive for 40 days

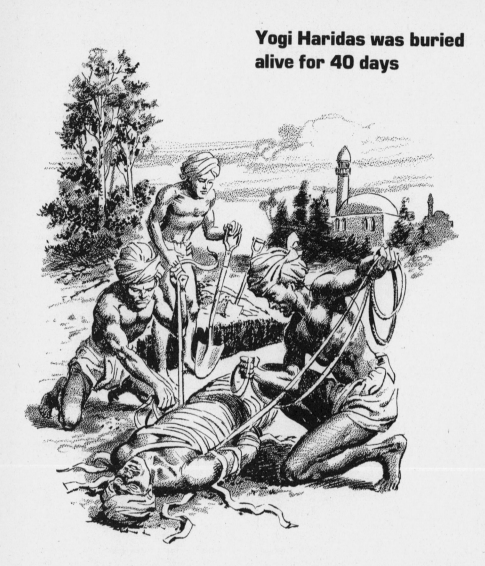

The world's record for the longest live burial is 101 days. But when Mrs. Emma Smith of England attained that mark in 1968, she had air, food, and drink piped into her eight-foot coffin, and she was able to chat with those above ground by means of a closed-circuit television hookup.

By constrast, when Yogi Haridas was buried in Lahore, Punjab, in 1837, he was left *completely* *unattended* for 40 days. He did not eat, he did not drink, he did not breathe. The Yogi had attained a catatonic trance known as *samadai*—suspended animation. When he was dug up after 40 days, his assistants revived him, with little difficulty, and Yogi Haridas went on to live for many more years.

Wickham plunged into the sea from a height of 205 feet

"I'll dive from anywhere!" Alex Wickham was fond of saying. "You supply the board and the water, and I'll do the jumping!"

And jump he did, even when his friends set the board atop a cliff overlooking the Yarra River near Melbourne, Australia. On March 22, 1918, Wickham climbed onto the diving board and plunged off in perfect diving form. Halfway down, he lost consciousness, and he hit the water with such force that his bathing suit was ripped from his body. Fortunately, he regained consciousness upon impact.

After Wickham came to the surface and swam to shore, his stunned admirers measured the height of the cliff. It was 205 feet 9 inches high. Wickham had leaped from a perch as high as a 15-story building—and lived!

The murre swims underwater

There are but few birds that can swim underwater. The murre is one of them. Moving its stubby, powerful wings like oars, the murre slices through the frigid Arctic waters to catch the small fish that comprise its dinner.

The murre is an Eskimo favorite both as food and as a provider of soft skin for comfortable slippers. Murre eggs, when fried, are highly colorful. Unlike hen's eggs, they are azure blue with blood red yolks!

Mohammed III began his reign by killing 19 brothers

In 1595, Mohammed III of Turkey (1567-1603) became sultan of the Ottoman Empire. Under his father, Murad III, the Turkish grasp on the empire had begun to slip as the sultan was dominated by his harem. Even though Murad's generals managed to win some decisive battles before his death, his son Mohammed recognized that for him, the throne would be a very precarious perch.

With a ruthlessness spurred by stark terror, Mohammed tried to solidify his hold on the empire through fratricide. One of his first acts as sultan was to order the execution of 19 of his brothers, thus serving a warning to anyone else who might have had visions of a coup. For all his bloodthirsty machinations, Mohammed III ruled only eight years before joining his 19 brothers in death.

The World Trade Center, which stands on just two acres, can accommodate 130,000 people

The skyscraper is the symbol of the modern city. Today, cities of even modest size boast 20- or 30-story buildings, and almost every large city in the country is characterized by the contours of its 30- and 40-story skyline. Yet as late as 90 years ago, a building of 10 or more floors was considered a giant!

Until the 1870's, the need for thick masonry walls and the lack of a sophisticated elevator limited most office buildings to a height of five or six stories. In 1870, the Equitable Life Insurance Company Building in New York broke new ground by rising to a height of 130 feet. But, like earlier structures, the Equitable Building was supported by masonry walls. The first building to employ a steel skeleton for support, and thus the first true skyscraper, was the Home Insurance Company Building, erected in Chicago in 1885.

After the invention of the electric elevator in 1887, the title of the world's tallest building passed in rapid succession to a number of structures. The 612-foot Singer Building in New York claimed the title upon its completion in 1908, but this height was surpassed just a few months later by the 700-foot Metropolitan Life Building, also in New York. In 1913, the Woolworth Building in New York took over as the world's tallest, at an altitude of 792 feet. Then in 1931, came the first building to rise over 100 stories—102, to be exact; this 1,250-foot tower was New York's Empire State Building.

During the 1940's and 50's, the advent of the curtain-wall building (a building almost entirely walled with steel and glass) brought a new shape to the skyscraper. Office buildings tended to be larger in base area but shorter in height, and it began to seem that the Empire State Building would retain its crown forever. In the late 1960's, however, the plan for a new office complex in New York was announced: the World Trade Center, a project that called for the construction of *two* 110-story towers side by side!

By 1974, the Center was virtually complete on its 16-acre site in Lower Manhattan. The two 1,350-foot towers had been topped off, and many tenants were conducting their business in what had become the tallest buildings in the world.

The two towers are striking in scale and in simplicity of design, and stand out boldly even from the colossal skyline of Manhattan. The steel-and-glass-faced structures are oblong in shape, flat-roofed, and 209 feet square at the base. Although the two towers occupy only slightly more than two acres of ground area, they can accommodate 50,000 workers and 80,000 visitors daily!

Naturally, the designers of such a gigantic complex were confronted with numerous problems, each of which they solved with innovation and daring. For example, more than 1.2 million cubic yards of earth and rock had to be excavated from the site, and the job of transporting such a massive load from Manhattan to a distant land-fill site seemed overwhelming. So, the builders decided to dump the fill at the adjoining Hudson River shoreline, thus creating 23.5 acres of new land to be deeded to the City of New York. Another problem—how to wash 43,600 windows—was solved with automatic window-washing machines that slide up and down the facades of the buildings in stainless-steel tracks.

To provide sufficient elevator service for so large a building would seemingly require that close to half the floor area of each tower be devoted to elevator shafts. The solution to this problem was the "sky lobby." The towers contain lobbies on the 44th and 78th floors as well as the first. Passengers bound for the upper two-thirds of the building board large express elevators which speed them to a sky lobby, where they board a second, local elevator that takes them to their floor. The system assures that no passenger will have to stop at more than six floors before reaching his own. More importantly, since the local elevators run only between one lobby and another, three elevators actually use the same shaft! Thus, the 104 elevators in each tower take up only 13 percent of the floor area, as compared to the 23 percent required for shafts in most office buildings.

The World Trade Center was not to reign for long as the world's tallest structure. At 1,450 feet, the Sears Tower recently constructed in Chicago tops the New York towers by 100 feet. How long the Chicago giant will be the highest in the world is anyone's guess. Engineers claim that it is now structurally feasible to construct skyscrapers over a mile high!

Ferdinand Waldo Demera was the greatest imposter of the 20th century

Ferdinand Waldo Demera saw no reason why his lack of a high-school diploma should stand between him and a professional career. So, through ingenious deceptions and a lot of *chutzpah,* Demera opened the doors that society had closed in his face.

Knowing he would need an impressive résumé and references, Demera compiled a fanciful history of previous jobs, and wrote his own references under fictitious or forged signatures.

During the Korean War, Demera somehow found his way onto a Royal Canadian ship as Surgeon Lieutenant. He had had no previous training in medicine. Nevertheless, when he was called upon to operate—and he operated on 19 soldiers during his stay—he acquitted himself well, as Canadian military records indicate.

Another highlight of Demera's career was the time he spent as a professor of applied psychology at several colleges. Passing himself off as a Ph.D., he was academically respected and well-liked by students, faculty, and administration at each school he fooled.

When Demera's academic con game was exposed, he dipped out of sight for a few years before turning up as a guidance counselor for inmates at a Texas prison. Once again, he performed admirably while thumbing his nose at the professional requirements for training.

No institution ever brought criminal proceedings against Demera, knowing that its own reputation would suffer more than Demera's. A Hollywood movie was made of Demera's life more than a decade ago, and since then he has dropped out of sight. But no one knows for sure that he will not strike again—or that he is not out there at this moment, poking fun at some pillar of the Establishment.

The rafflesia is the world's largest flower

The mammoth *Amorphophallus titanum* (krubi or giant arum) is commonly referred to as the world's largest flower, but in fact this plant is a collection of flowers simulating one huge flower. The real giant among flowers is the rafflesia, a parasitic plant found in the same Sumatran rain forests as the *Amorphophallus titanum.*

The rafflesia plant is unique in that it has no stem and no leaves, simply one enormous, fetid-smelling flower. The mottled, thick-petaled growth often reaches a diameter of three feet and a weight of 15 pounds. And the nectary in the center of this giant is capable of holding as much as 12 pints of liquid!

As a parasite, the rafflesia grows on the exposed roots of other plants, and sucks its nourishment directly from its host. It especially likes to grow on the root of the cissus vine. How do rafflesia seeds find their way to these cissus vines? Strange as it may seem, it is strongly suspected that the seeds are dispersed by elephants!

After a rafflesia dies, the flower decays into a mass of pulpy liquid, in which the seeds float. When an elephant (or perhaps rhinoceros) steps into the putrid mess, the sticky fluid adheres to its foot. As the animal walks, the gluey substance picks up leaves and twigs which begin to annoy the animal.

It so happens that the cissus root is a perfect tool for the elephant to use to wipe the irksome mess from its feet. The animal rubs its foot against the roots, which protrude through the soil, and thereby leaves a deposit of rafflesia seeds on the vine. Soon one or more of these seeds will sprout into a new rafflesia plant, at home on its favorite host!

Somerset Bridge is the smallest drawbridge in the world

The world's smallest drawbridge is located at Ely's Harbor on the island of Bermuda. This tiny span—known as Somerset Bridge—consists of two masonry embankments connected by two tiny wooden draws.

The entire bridge is less than 20 feet from one bank of the waterway to the other. The two draws in the center are each shorter than the width of the bridge. When the draws are pulled up, the opening in the bridge is barely wide enough to permit the passage of one sailboat!

Elijah ben Solomon, Head Rabbi of Lithuania, memorized 2,500 volumes

Elijah ben Solomon (1720-1797) was the Head Rabbi of Lithuania, and the leader of the large Jewish community in Vilna. While he was revered for his piety, his mental powers were such that he was universally known as Elijah the Gaon (the Genius).

Elijah's brain was a library in itself; once he read a book, it was committed to his memory. This required no special effort on his part—it just happened! The Gaon is said to have memorized 2,500 volumes, including all the important Hebrew religious works. From these, he could quote any passage at will.

Da Vinci was a genius in art, mathematics, astronomy, and invention

Given a choice, which would you prefer to be —painter, sculptor, architect, musician, poet or philosopher? Or perhaps you'd prefer to be an inventor, a biologist, an astronomer, a geologist, or a mathematician? Imagine a man whose genius permitted him to become all these things, and a master in every one of these disciplines! Such was the incredible Leonardo da Vinci.

Born near Florence, Italy, in 1452, Leonardo—while still a schoolboy—solved complicated mathematical problems that stumped his teachers. In his teens, he was apprenticed to the noted painter, Andrea del Verrocchio. By the age of 20, the student had equaled his master!

While still in his early 30's, Leonardo painted the famed "Last Supper," the giant tableau which, though its colors have faded with time, ranks as one of the world's supreme art masterpieces. Not long after, he painted another immortal, the "Mona Lisa," perhaps the most famous painting in the world.

In middle age, Leonardo created many of the beautiful decorations in the Pope's Palaces of the Vatican and in St. Peter's Basilica in Rome.

During his lifetime, Leonardo won renown almost exclusively as an artist; yet his notebooks contain scores of sketches of fantastic inventions, anticipating scientific creations that were not to be accepted for centuries to come. Indeed, most of Leonardo's brainchildren—such as the airplane, the helicopter, and the submarine—were laughed at during his lifetime, and were forgotten until modern science rediscovered them.

The Chesapeake Bay Bridge-Tunnel is the longest deep-water bridge in the world

At the mouth of the Chesapeake Bay there is a narrow causeway which stretches as far as the eye can see. When you cross the bridge and reach the middle of the bay, you are completely out of sight of all land.

When engineers began planning the Chesapeake Bay crossing, they knew that the channel's width—over 17 miles at the narrowest point—called for the construction of a low causeway. Yet through this channel would pass some of the largest ships in the world, bound for Baltimore, Norfolk, and other cities that make up the largest single port area in the United States. These deep-water vessels could not pass under a causeway. A tunnel under the ship channels seemed to be in order, yet the cost of a 17-mile long tunnel—five miles longer than the longest tunnel ever built—was prohibitive. So the engineers decided to build both—a combination causeway and tunnel that would carry vehicles across the bay yet permit ships of any size to pass over the roadway tunnels.

Construction of the Chesapeake Bay Bridge-Tunnel began in 1961. Four man-made islands were built in the bay to anchor two tunnels—each over a mile long—directly under two ship channels. Close to 15 miles of causeway was constructed on pillars rising 30 feet over the bay, with a 28-foot-wide roadway on top. Higher trestle bridges were built near both shores.

In 1964, after 37 months of work and over $210 million in construction costs, the bridge-tunnel was completed, stretching 17.6 miles between Cape Henry and Cape Charles, both in Virginia. Today, for a toll in excess of $5, drivers can save hundreds of miles of travel around Chesapeake Bay.

The Chesapeake Bay Bridge-Tunnel is not the longest bridge in the world. That title belongs to the bridge across Lake Pontchartrain, a 24-mile causeway connecting New Orleans and Lewisburg, Louisiana. But the Louisiana bridge crosses a shallow lake. The Chesapeake Bay Bridge-Tunnel traverses a deep ocean bay, and its com-

bination of bridge, tunnel, and causeway makes the Chesapeake, if not the longest, at least the most unusual water crossing in the world.

Mohammed II disemboweled 14 attendants to find a watermelon seed

Mohammed II was Sultan of Turkey from 1451 to 1481. His fabulous conquests made the Ottoman Empire the power it was to be for four centuries.

One day, his dinner was interrupted by some pressing affair of state. When he returned to the table, he was much put out to discover that his dessert, a juicy melon, had vanished.

Mohammed was incensed. Immediately, he interrogated fourteen of his royal attendants. Each denied any knowledge of the theft. Determined to reach the bottom of this larceny, Mohammed then ordered his court doctor to slit open the stomach of each of the pages—which the doctor did!

Mohammed's hunch was ill-founded. None of the stomachs bore any trace of melon.

What did the sultan do next?

He apologized, and contented himself with another dessert.

Vergil spent $100,000 on the burial of a fly

The Roman poet Vergil (70 B.C.-19 B.C.) is universally recognized as one of the greatest literary artists the world has ever known. He wrote the masterful *Eclogues* and *Georgics*, but his fame rests principally upon the *Aeneid*.

Besides being a supreme poet, Vergil was a fascinating man, with an incredible flair for the bizarre. For example, read of this incident reported by Suetonius Tranquillis in his *Life of Augustus*.

When Rome was placed under the rule of the Second Triumvirate (Augustus, Marc Antony, and Lepidus) in 43 B.C., the lands of the idle rich were ordered confiscated and allotted to war veterans. Certain grounds were exempted from this ordinance, such as cemetery plots and mausoleums.

Fearing that his manor on the Esquiline Hill in Rome would be taken from him, Vergil conceived a brilliant ploy. In his house, he staged an elaborate funeral for a fly which he claimed to be his dearly beloved pet. Various Roman dignitaries delivered mournful orations, as did Vergil, and the fly was interred amid splendid trappings which cost more than 800,000 sesterces—the equivalent of well over $100,000 today.

Vergil's outlandish rites for his "pet" fly transformed his home into a "mausoleum," thus saving it from the hands of the government.

Two women each gave birth to 69 children

Actually, there are two such women: Mrs. Fyodor Vassilet of Russia and Mrs. Bernard Scheinberg of Austria.

Mrs. Vassilet achieved her prodigious total of 69 in 27 confinements. She gave birth to four sets of quadruplets, seven sets of triplets, and 16 pairs of twins. If you add up these figures, you'll see that not one confinement produced a single birth. Mrs. Vassilet enjoyed considerable renown, and appeared at the court of Czar Alexander II. She died in 1872.

Mrs. Scheinberg's story is remarkably similar to that of Mrs. Vassilet. She, too, gave birth in 27 confinements; none of these produced less than two children; and miraculously, she likewise gave birth to fours sets of quadruplets, seven sets of triplets, and 16 pairs of twins!

When Mrs. Scheinberg died at the age of 56 in 1911, her husband Bernard remarried, and had 18 children by his second wife. Bernard Scheinberg had sired a grand total of 87 progeny.

The Trans-Siberian oil pipeline is the longest man-made object in the world

While the Great Wall of China can lay claim to many superlatives, it is not the longest structure in the world. That title goes to a much more modern construction—the fuel pipeline. Because at most points it is buried two feet below ground, a pipeline is certainly not as impressive a sight as the Great Wall, but as an engineering feat it is far more important to our civilization than the Wall was to the ancient Chinese.

Exclusive of highways and railroads, no man-made object can compare with the great pipelines in length. These steel tubes, usually one to two feet in diameter, are most commonly used to carry oil or natural gas from outlying wells to the refineries near big cities.

The longest oil pipeline in the world—owned by the Interprovincial Pipe Line Company of Canada—extends 1,775 miles from wells in Alberta to refineries in Sarnia, Ontario. Along its route, 13 pumping stations move 7 million gallons of oil daily, pumping the oil from three to

six miles an hour through the subterranean tubes. However, the world's largest oil pipeline will soon be the Trans-Siberian oil pipeline in the Soviet Union; when it is completed, it will stretch almost 2,860 miles.

An already completed natural gas pipeline between Texas and New York City stretches 1,840 miles, and an incomplete Russian pipeline will extend 2,100 miles. On the drawing boards now are a gas pipeline across Canada with a planned length of 2,200 miles, and a Russian pipeline that would stretch close to 5,700 miles—more than three times the length of the Great Wall!

Kamala and Amala, Indian girls, were raised by wolves

Throughout history, there have been many reports of human babies brought up by animals—wolves, apes, lions, and so on. But upon investigation, very few of such stories have turned out to be true. One case that has been authenticated is that of the Indian "wolf-girls."

In October, 1920, the Reverend J.L. Singh, who headed an orphanage in Midnapore, India, was asked by his neighbors to get rid of a "man ghost" which supposedly inhabited a large ant-hill nearby. Singh organized a party to keep close watch over the anthill. When darkness fell, he saw three full-grown wolves come out of a tunnel within the hill, followed by two cubs. Then, close behind, emerged two horrible-looking creatures with what appeared to be human bodies.

The following morning, the den was dug up. Huddled together were two wolf cubs and two young children, both girls—one about eight years old, the other about one and a half. When captured, the children were even more ferocious than the cubs.

The task of weaning these "wolf children" back to human ways was formidable. The Reverend and his wife gave the girls the names of Amala and Kamala. The children refused to wear any clothing; long matted hair fell below their shoulders; their teeth were sharp and pointed. The girls refused all vegetable food—but could scent the odor of raw meat at a considerable distance. Though they were not able to stand erect, the girls could move along on all fours at an astounding speed. They slept through most of the day, but liked to prowl about at night. They avoided humans, while seeking the society of dogs and goats.

Little by little, however, the wolf-girls came to accept the kindness of the missionary and his wife. Then, after almost a year in the orphanage, Amala, the younger child, died. Kamala wept—the first time she had ever shown human emotion.

For weeks, Kamala lingered over the places where Amala had sat and slept, sniffing anxiously like a dog, and uttering strange cries.

After a while, Kamala drew closer to the missionary's wife and began to take greater interest in the other children. She stopped gulping down her food in wolf fashion. She learned to drink out of a cup instead of lapping up her liquids. She even mastered some 40 words and began to wear clothing.

After some time had passed, Kamala learned to walk upright, but she still proceeded slowly

and unstably. When she wanted to run, she reverted to moving along on all fours.

After nine years in a human environment, Kamala had lost most of her animal characteristics and had become a lovable, obedient child. Then, on November 14, 1929, she died.

One reason for her early death was explained by the physician attending her. He stated, "There was great difficulty in feeding the poor wolf-girls anything but meat and milk. If they could have been induced to take a balanced diet, they could have returned to an ordinary human condition from the state of an animal."

The flea is the world's champion high jumper

Anyone who owns a pet is likely to be all too familiar with a bothersome little insect called the flea. These hard-boiled, bloodsucking pests live in the hair of warm-blooded animals, and can pass from one host to another quite easily. But did you know that fleas do not have wings? Their mobility depends entirely on their extraordinary leaping ability. These meddlesome mites can jump one hundred times their own height—a feat comparable to a man's jumping as high as a forty-story building!

Fleas can be not only irksome, but dangerous as well. Adult fleas feed on the blood of their host—dog, cat, man, rodent, or whatever, depending upon the species—which they suck after piercing the skin with their specialized mouthparts. For this reason, several species of flea can transmit disease-causing micro-organisms from one host to another. The bubonic plague or "black death" of medieval times, an example of a disease transmitted by fleas, was estimated to have killed as much as three-quarters of the population of Europe within twenty years.

The bizarre fruit of the sausage tree can weigh 15 pounds

If you've ever walked into a butcher shop where sausage links and salamis dangled from the ceiling, you have an idea of what it might be like to stand under a spreading sausage tree. Surely one of the oddest looking plants on earth, this African native grows to a height of 30 to 40 feet. Its large hanging flowers bloom at night, giving off a mouselike odor that is appealing to the tree's favorite pollinator, the bat. But it is the fruit that gives this tropical wonder its remarkable appearance, and its name.

Cordlike stalks hanging from the branches end in long, slender fruits which greatly resemble sausages. These wiener-shaped marvels are usually about one to two feet long, but can grow to three feet and can weigh up to 15 pounds each! Some grow in bunches like bananas, others dangle alone at the end of their stalks. The sight of these gigantic "sausages" dangling from the rain forest canopy is truly one of the most unusual in nature!

Otto Witte impersonated a king and fooled an entire country

In 1913, Albanian revolutionaries threw off the yoke of the Ottoman Empire and established their nation as an independent state. For a nominal ruler, the little Moslem nation on the Adriatic naturally looked to Turkey, and chose Prince Helim Eddine.

The capital city of Durazzo was decorated colorfully and the people crowded together to welcome the prince's carriage. The first to emerge was a seven-foot man in an ornate military costume, with a saber at his side and a fez atop his head. "Stand back," he cried. "Make way for the new Prince of Albania!" The second man out of the carriage was not so tall, but exceedingly broad in the chest and shoulders.

After these two, the Prince stepped forward, to the cheers of the masses. After a few words of greeting, helim Eddine offered his first official decree: that he was now a citizen of Albania, not Turkey, and that there would be a week of general celebration and an amnesty for all prisoners. The people responded wildly to this magnanimous gesture. The new nation had a new national hero.

That night, at a feast, Helim Eddine was presented with a 25-woman harem. As befit a Moslem ruler, he gratefully accepted this gift. The next day, he further endeared himself to the natives of Durazzo by appointing the city's councilmen to be his cabinet. The councilmen

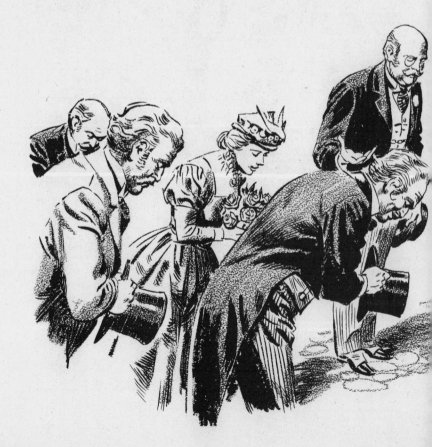

were so honored that they moved to promote the Prince to King. The Prince graciously acceded to their wishes, suggesting that as King he be known as King Otto. This puzzled the cabinet members, since Otto was a distinctly non-Moslem name. Nevertheless, they had no reason to stand in his way.

It was not until the fifth day of King Otto's reign that the general gaiety waned. A wire arrived in the prime minister's office. It was signed by the real Eddine who was still in Turkey, and who was quite puzzled by reports that he had arrived in Durazzo.

The picture started to become clear. The prime minister rushed to the imperial chambers, but "King Otto" and his two aides-de-camp were gone.

A long investigation into the matter revealed that King Otto was, in fact, one Otto Witte, a circus performer. His two aides had been the circus giant and the circus strong man.

Albania had lost a king, but Otto Witte had enjoyed the best four days of his life.

Day bowled 33 consecutive strikes

In bowling, knocking down all the pins with one ball is called a *strike*. To bowl a perfect game, player must throw 12 strikes in a row. Such a perfect performance has been accomplished now and then, but the bowling of a perfect game is a rarity. It is estimated that perfect games occur just about once in every 450,000 tries.

During an exhibition at Price Hall in Cincinnati, Ohio, in 1937, Ned Day of West Allis, Wisconsin, bowled 33 strikes in a row! This was equivalent to bowling almost three perfect games in succession.

The African titmouse builds a bag-like nest

The African penduline titmouse—a big name for such a small creature—has a nest unlike any other bird. The male of this species constructs an intricately woven nest, ingeniously hung from the end of a branch, that looks exactly like a neat bag with an overlapping flap. A convenient opening in the flap is just large enough to let the titmouse slip in and out.

The goliath beetle can peel bananas

The goliath beetle of West Africa is the world's largest insect, measuring up to *six inches* in length. This awesome creature is magnificently colored with a deep red, velvety body and a black-and-white striped head and neck. But the giant's most fearsome characteristic is a pair of black horns, each close to a quarter of an inch long—larger than the bodies of many insects!

Ordinarily, the beetle uses these horns to dig into the bark of a tree for its favorite meal of juicy sap. But when one of these mammoth insects was placed in a museum and fed a diet of bananas, it used the horns to slowly peel the fruit!

Sepalla averaged 11 miles per hour by dog sled for more than 133 miles

For a quarter of a century, Leonhard Sepalla was considered to be the best dog-sled racer in Alaska. During his long career, he had possessed and trained 1,000 sled dogs, and he had made a name for himself in the frozen north by rushing the sick to hospitals and rushing medical supplies to the sick by dog sled over the trackless wastes.

In February of 1927, Sepalla, then aged 50, came down to the United States and entered the New England Point-to-Point race, which initiated in the town of North Conway, New Hampshire. It was to be a run of 133½ miles

down to Wolfeboro, New Hampshire. Oldtimers who were supposed to know, predicted that Sepalla's little Siberian malamutes would never be able to hold up on the jagged, icy trails and mountainous terrain of New England; it would take crossbred huskies to negotiate the steep inclines. But Sepalla thought otherwise.

In order to avoid congestion on the trail, the starting teams were staggered, departing on the race a few minutes apart. When the signal for him to leave was given, Sepalla pulled the green shade down over his eyes and began talking to his little Siberians. The man chattered to his dogs all the way, and one onlooker said that it

seemed that Sepalla's constant talk lulled the dogs into a hypnotic state. But be that as it may, his faithful animals obeyed his every word.

As he checked into Wolfeboro, 2,000 fans found out what Alaskans had known for years: that Leonhard Sepalla was the best man who ever drove a dog sled over ice and snow. The champion had traversed more than 133 miles in a little over 12 hours, an average speed of better than 11 miles per hour.

A flatfish has both its eyes on one side of its head

When flatfish—a large group of fish that includes the flounder, halibut, and sole—are hatched, their eyes are located in the usual place, one on each side of the head. But after swimming around like other fish for a short time, a flatfish turns over on his side and begins swimming sideways. Shortly afterward, the eye on the underside of his head starts moving to the upper side, until the fish actually has both eyes on the same side of his head!

Amazingly, in cold waters the flatfish turns on its left side, and the left eye moves to the right side of the head; in warm waters, the fish turns on its right side, and the right eye does the moving! No one knows why temperature should have this effect.

Nurmi won two Olympic distance races in one day

On July 10, 1924, in the games held in Paris, Paavo Nurmi was entered in two Olympic finals. The Finn would run in the 1,500 meters, and also in the 5,000 meters; and the two events were scheduled but 50 minutes apart.

Not only did Paavo win both races, but he established two Olympic records in the process.

The 1,500 came first. At 100 meters, Nurmi took the lead. Shortly thereafter, he stretched his margin to 10 yards. Then with a lap to go, the Finnish speedster peered at his stopwatch, liked what he saw, and tossed his watch off to the sidelines. Nurmi fans knew what that meant: their blond hero was on schedule and was ready to step up the pace. As he crossed the finish line in 3:53.6—only a second off his world record—he kept on running, right into the locker room. There, he nibbled on dried fish, and then took a brief rest.

A half hour later, Paavo Nurmi was back on the track again for the 5,000. For the first 3,000 meters, Nurmi maintained his pace, often referring to his stopwatch. Ritola, another Finn, and an arch rival, stayed close at Willie's heels.

Then Ritola burst into the lead. Thirty thousand throats at Colombes Stadium broke into a roar as the two Finns battled step for step. Then Nurmi looked at his watch again, decided he had had enough of this parrying, discarded his timepiece, and broke into a sprint. About 20 yards from the finish, Nurmi turned his head and saw Ritola nearly abreast of him. Then Paavo put on a final burst, and won by a yard. His time was 14:31.2.

Nurmi's finish was so tremendous that Grantland Rice, dean of American sportswriters, ecstatically reported, "The superman has arrived at last!"

The aardvark lives on ants and termites

Imagine a creature the size of a large hog, co-vered with thick tan skin and thin, gray-brown hair, with a piglike snout, a tall pair of rabbit's ears, a long tail, and sharp dragon's claws—and you've got the picture of an aardvark. When you first see this strange creature, you may think you are looking at an animal from Mars, but the aardvark lives on the plains of Central and South Africa.

In the language of the Boers of South Africa, the name *aardvark* means *earth-pig*. The name fits him well, for the aardvark actually lives in the earth. Although the ground on the plains where he builds his home is often as hard as brick, this clumsy mammal can scratch through the surface as if it were sand at a beach. Within a few min-utes he can burrow his way completely under-ground, and once he is inside his underground home, no man can pull him out.

The aardvark spends the entire day sleeping in his tunnel-home. At dusk he awakens and goes out to hunt for his dinner. Guess as long as you like, you could probably never guess the aardvark's diet—for the great, six-foot-long creature eats nothing but little ants and termites!

The African termites live in large cone-shaped earthen nests. These nests become as hard as cement from baking all day in the strong African sun. Some of them are taller than a man. Yet to get his dinner, the aardvark can slash them apart with his powerful claws. Once the nest is open, he gobbles up the insects inside with his long, sticky tongue.

Dickinson bowled a 299 game while standing on two artificial legs

No matter how crippling a physical handicap seems to be, there are always people who manage to overcome it. Indeed, some of these courageous, determined individuals succeed in performing feats that would be considered outstanding even if their physical conditions were normal.

Take the inspiring case of Lyman Dickinson, of Watervliet, New York. A few years back, both his legs were amputated, and were replaced with artificial limbs. Dickinson had to learn to walk all over again. Thanks to plenty of guts and hard work, Dickinson trained himself to use his new legs so well that he was once again able to engage actively in fishing, hunting, golf, and bowling.

Though hunting and golf involve a considerable amount of walking, bowling presents an even more difficult obstacle; for to roll a bowling ball properly, one has to start by taking a series of quick steps, and then come to a complete stop just short of the foul line.

On July 2, 1970, at a bowling alley in Albany, New York, Lyman Dickinson rolled a 299 game. As all bowling fans know, this is just one pin short of a perfect score, a feat very, very few bowlers ever attain.

The butterfly flies south for the winter

The butterfly actually has three lives. This beautiful creature begins as a wormy caterpillar. After growing to full size, the insect attaches itself to a twig and uses its own secretions to weave a heavy silk covering around its body. The caterpillar remains in this silk covering—called a cocoon—for a matter of days or months, depending on its species. Then the insect emerges at the suitable season as a beautifully colored butterfly.

But when cold winds begin to blow, whole flocks of butterflies—just like flocks of birds—fly south to spend the winter in the sunshine. These delicate creatures possess a miraculous sense of direction. One species travels six hundred miles over water from America to Bermuda!

In the spring great flocks of butterflies are seen flying up from the South. But no one is sure whether these are the same butterflies returning, or their children who were born in the Southland.

The Tombs of Petra are cut out of the sides of cliffs

The ancient city of Petra—the site of some of the most unusually constructed tombs in the world—lies hidden in a small desert valley deep within the towering red sandstone cliffs of southern Jordan. So remote is this valley that the 2,000-year-old city of Petra remained unknown to the Western world until 1812. When the city was discovered, the whole world marveled at the tremendous pink tombs that were hewn out of the very side of a cliff!

Petra was occupied as early as the 4th century B.C. and was alternately the site of a Roman outpost, a caravan trading center, a Moslem religious enclave, and—during the Crusades—a Christian stronghold. The steep cliffs that surround the valley made Petra an impenetrable fortress, for the valley could be entered only by means of a narrow canyon that winds between the cliffs. This passageway is so narrow that in places a man can stretch his arms and touch both walls! Here, a handful of soldiers could defend the city against an army of any size.

Over the centuries, the rich caravan merchants who made their homes in Petra constructed massive tombs and temples to rival those of any ancient city. Since the narrow entranceway hindered the transport of building materials to the city, the merchants and Petran kings built their tombs by simply carving out the inner walls of the cliffs.

And what masterpieces these tombs are! Colored rose pink like the sandstone cliffs, adorned with columns and pediments in the classical style, these mammoth structures look as if they were built for giants rather than for men. The largest of the tombs is as tall as a 15-story building, hewn right from the solid rock in one piece! The tomb's main door is over 40 feet in height, and the bottom sill is so high that a man would have difficulty climbing it, much less stepping over it. In fact, the tombs are so massive, so incredible in design and construction, that the Arabs who in-

habited the surrounding areas believed these tombs could have been built only by jinns, the Moslem spirits.

Throughout the 1,000-foot canyon, these giant tombs and temples are carved from the cliff walls. Each is a marvel in itself, more a colossal work of sculpture than it is a building. Together, the tombs of Petra comprise one of the strangest and most impressive sights in the world.

Edison was the world's greatest inventor

Thomas Alva Edison was born in Milan, Ohio in 1837. Seven years later, his family moved to Port Huron, Michigan, and young Tom took a fling at formal schooling. That lasted but a scant three months; by then, Thomas Edison had seen the inside of a schoolhouse for the last time.

Edison went to work as a newsboy on the Grand Trunk Railroad. As he grew older, he graduated to the position of telegraph operator. It was this experience which prompted his first invention: a transmitter-receiver for the automatic telegraph, and the quadruplex method of sending out four telegraph messages simultaneously.

In his long life, Thomas Alva Edison invented:

1. An electric vote recorder.

2. Paraffin paper.

3. An improved stock ticker system.

4. An electric pen which was later developed into the mimeograph.

5. The carbon telephone transmitter which made Bell's telephone commercially successful; it also laid the groundwork for today's microphone.

6. The phonograph.

7. The first practical electric light.

8. Electric generators, motors, light sockets, and other components of a complete electrical power system.

9. An efficient electric storage battery.

10. Many components of an electric railway system, including the automatic signal.

11. The dictating machine.

He also developed:

1. The first practical typewriter.

2. The vacuum tube that makes modern radio and television possible.

3. A motion picture camera and sound system that prepared the way for talking pictures.

4. Synthetic rubber.

At his death in 1931, Edison held over 1,300 U.S. and foreign copyrights!

Hetty Green, a millionairess, lived liked a pauper

Hetty Green, born in New Bedford, Massachusetts, in 1835, inherited a substantial fortune upon her father's death. Managing her investments shrewdly, she eventually built up her father's estate to over 100 million dollars. Among financiers, she was known as the "Wizard of Wall Street."

Yet for all her riches, Hetty Green lived the life of a pauper. For example, while she and her two children resided in Bellows Falls, Vermont, her son Edward broke his leg. Hetty did not call for a doctor—the expense was too great, she felt—and instead took him to the charity hospital, where she passed herself off as a beggar. Unfortunately, the condition of young Edward's leg steadily worsened, and it became clear that amputation was necessary if the boy's life were to be saved. Hetty had the operation performed in her rooming house, to save the lying-in fee at the hospital.

In her later years, Hetty lived in an unheated tenement and subsisted on a diet of cold eggs and onions, to spare the cost of heating her food. She wore newspapers for underpants, and allowed only the lower half of her petticoats to be laundered.

All the while, her fortune grew. At her death in 1916, Hetty's estate was 125 million dollars!

The Human Pillar of Oslo contains 121 intertwined figures of men, women, and children

Rarely is the work of an artist so closely associated with a city as the work of Gustav Vigeland is with Oslo. Few cities can boast a more impressive outdoor art attraction than the Frogner Sculpture Park, which is devoted entirely to the work of Vigeland, Norway's most famous sculptor.

In 1921, the 51-year-old Vigeland—already a renowned artist—entered into a unique contract with the Oslo municipal authorities. He agreed to bequeath to the city almost all of his work, both past and future; in return, the city built Vigeland a spacious studio where the artist lived and worked until his death in 1943. Today the studio-residence forms the Vigeland Museum, which contains 1,650 sculptures and thousands of Vigeland's woodcuts and sketches.

But Vigeland's greatest gift to Oslo is the nearby Frogner Sculpture Park, which the artist designed to display his most monumental works. The verdant park, over one-half mile long, contains hundreds of figures carved in granite, iron, and bronze. The works include a bridge with 58 bronze figures adorning its parapets, and an ornate fountain.

The most spectacular of all Frogner Park's many sculptures is the obelisk known as the Human Pillar. Vigeland began designing the Pillar in 1924, but not until 1943 was the cutting of the stone completed. The Pillar is set in the middle of a circular mount of broad steps, on which 36 large granite groups of figures are set. Cut from a single piece of stone, the Pillar rises 55 feet, with a base diameter of eight feet, and contains 121 figures of men and women at all ages of life clambering in a spiral toward the summit. At the bottom, corpses are piled on top of one another; at the top, children are held aloft by their mothers. The complex intertwining of forms, symbolizing the development of man, displays a superb mastery of modeling and detail.

Frogner Park was opened to the public in 1947, and is visited by thousands each year. The Human Pillar stands as Vigeland's most memorable work, and one of the finest non-functional structures ever created.

The silkworm spins a thread twelve thousand times as long as its body

The silkworm is a moth larva that rarely measures more than three inches in length. Yet to build its cocoon this insect spins a continuous yellow or white silken thread more than a thousand yards long, wrapped tightly around its body. That's comparable to a six-foot man spinning a thread fifteen miles long!

Silkworm eggs are so small that 35,000 of them weigh just one ounce. Within a month of birth, however, the voracious, mulberry-eating creature has grown into a three-inch larva. The silkworm then attaches itself to a twig and spins its silken cocoon, A moist substance called fibroin, manufactured within the larva's body and mixed with small amounts of wax, is emitted through an orifice in the lip. The fibroin dries quickly in the air, and the larva is eventually surrounded by a half-mile-long silk thread!

Thomas Stevens rode around the world on a high-wheeled bicycle

In the 1880's, the bicycle consisted of an enormously high wheel in the front and a minuscule wheel in the rear. It was hard enough to handle on paved roads, and practically impossible to ride on the rough roads in the country. But Thomas Stevens vowed that he would pedal his way around the world.

Stevens was up against a few obstacles from the very start. For one thing, he didn't know how to ride a bike. But a little matter like that didn't seem to bother him. After just a few days of practice, Tom was off.

He left San Francisco in April, 1884. In August, pedaling over more than 3,000 miles of rough roads and trails, he reached Boston. There he ran into another obstacle: he was broke. After a few months' delay, Colonel A.A. Pope, a prominent manufacturer of bicycles, agreed to back the adventurer, and Stevens sailed for Europe.

The tour through Europe on a bike was quite enjoyable. The sights were interesting, the roads were good; and when his giant front wheel broke down, there was no lack of mechanics who could put the bike back in shape. By early 1885, thousands of Americans were following Stevens' adventure through newspaper accounts.

As Stevens traveled through Persia, India, and the Far East, the trip became more onerous. He was loaded down with gifts from Persian potentates and enthusiastic Chinese villagers.

Mile after mile the tireless Stevens pedaled on. Since he occasionally had to struggle against pranksters and animals who blocked his path on the roads, he refused to make time a factor. On some days he just didn't ride at all; on other days, he moved only by daylight.

But in January of 1887—less than three years after he had left home—Stevens returned, bicycle and all, to San Francisco. He was now famous, and his fame yielded him a considerable income through lectures and writings.

Gophers like to eat telephone cables

For centuries the gopher—a rabbit-size burrowing rodent—has been content to dig only about a foot deep in search of food. Blessed with sharp, strong claws, he has no trouble burrowing down as deep as the vegetable roots he likes to munch on. But recently the gopher has learned to supplement his diet with an occasional snack of underground telephone cables!

These thick, lead-sheathed cables crisscross the Western plains about thirty-six inches below ground. Gophers will frequently burrow for roots, then go right on digging until they can sink their powerful teeth into the metal cables.

No one knows why the gopher is so fond of lead, but this uninvited dinner guest creates quite a problem in transcontinental telephone service. For often the gophers' gnawing exposes the wires to moisture, thereby causing service interruptions. Having caught on to the gophers' taste for lead, telephone workers now wrap thin steel tape around the lead sheath to discourage the pesky nibblers.

The floating leaves of the Victorian water lily can support three men

At one time or another, you've no doubt seen a drawing or a photograph of a frog seated comfortably on a lily pad, floating on the surface of a fresh-water pond. Did you know that there is a water lily whose pads are large enough to support the weight of a man?

You'll find such an aquatic giant—it's called the Victorian water lily—in the Amazon region of South America. The round, padlike leaves of this jungle monster are sometimes over *six feet* in diameter. The English explorers who discovered and named the plant reported that it could safely support the weight of *three* men without being submerged!

The size of the Victorian water lily's leaves is in effect the plant's best defense against insect pests. Birds frequently alight on the pad to eat swimming insects which approach the plant —insects which would otherwise harm the floating giant.

Levitt made 499 straight free throws in a basketball contest

Four thousand basketball fans hied to the Madison Street Armory in Chicago on April 6, 1935, to witness various basketball contests held under the auspices of the Amateur Athletic Union. At 7:00 p.m. that night, Harold Levitt—"Bunny," as he was called—stood on the foul line and heaved foul shots into the basket. Before the clock struck midnight, Levitt had dunked 499 consecutive free throws with his underhanded, two-hands-on-the-ball pitch. He then missed on his 500th shot.

At this point the crowd was through but Levitt wasn't. He just stood at the same spot and threw in 371 more shots without a miss. It was now 2:30 in the morning, and since an impatient janitor wanted to close up, Levitt was obliged to stop.

Later, Bunny hooked up with the world-famous Harlem Globetrotters, who offered $1,000 to any man who could beat Levitt in a contest of 100 foul shots. The money was never claimed. The best any challenger ever scored was 86; the worst performance Levitt ever turned in was 96.

It becomes germane to ask why, if Levitt was such a matchless foul shooter, did he never achieve fame as either a college player or a basketball pro. The reason is simple: Bunny stood only five feet, four inches tall.

Telephone wires can grow "beards" of Spanish moss

One of the most striking spectacles afforded by the plant kingdom is that of a swamp or forest draped with wispy, dangling strands of Spanish moss. Although chiefly tropical, Spanish moss can be found in many areas of the southern United States. The Florida cypress swamps, for example, teeming with Spanish moss, create eerie, almost dreamlike landscapes a visitor is not soon to forget.

The grayish-green, threadlike leaves of Spanish moss form tangled strands that either hang from trees like long beards, or stretch from branch to branch like hairy festoons. Some of these strands may be over 25 feet long. In contrast, the plant's flowers are tiny and rarely seen.

Spanish moss is not a moss but an epiphyte, a plant that grows nonparasitically on another plant. An epiphyte, or air plant, obtains its moisture from the air rather than the soil. Unlike most parasites, epiphytes can carry on photosynthesis, and they depend upon the host plant for support only. In fact, the host need not always be a living plant. Spanish moss has been known to thrive on telephone wires!

The Eiffel Tower is the tallest structure in Europe

In the late 1880's, the city of Paris was swept by a storm of protest over a planned tower for the upcoming International Exposition. The proposed structure—intended to symbolize the glory of France—was decried by artists, writers, and officials alike as a useless monstrosity, an affront to the history of great monuments in its use of the then despised material, steel. Yet, despite these protests, the pressures of time, and a limited knowledge of the necessary structural techniques, Alexander Gustave Eiffel pressed on with his design. Almost 90 years later, this structure—the Eiffel Tower—is the highest (excluding TV towers), grandest, and most famous tower in the world, and the symbol of a nation.

The tallest structure in Europe (again, excluding TV towers, navigational masts, and chimneys), the Eiffel Tower rises 1,052 feet over a long landscaped promenade near the River Seine. At its base, four huge masonry pillars anchor four steel columns, which join at a height of 620 feet to form one slender spire. A football field could be placed between these pillars with room to spare.

Construction of the massive tower was completed in only 17 months, in time for the International Exposition of 1889. The design, a combination of the arch and the obelisk, called for the use of 12,000 component parts weighing a total of 7,500 tons. Despite the lack of sophisti-cated safety measures, there were no fatal accidents during the entire period of construction. Equally surprising, the total cost of over $1 million was recovered from sightseers within *one year!*

Today, the Eiffel Tower is one of the most popular tourist attractions in the world. Elevators rise aslant along the columns to observation decks at three levels, which provide a vista of Paris and the surrounding countryside up to 90 miles away!

Although the tower was decried as useless from its very inception, from 1925 to 1936 it supported the largest advertising sign ever erected. This electric "Citroen" sign, consisting of 250,000 lamps, was visible from as far as 24 miles away. Today, the Eiffel functions as a radio and TV broadcast tower, a meteorological station, and of course, as France's greatest tourist attraction.

Frenchwoman Renée Bordereau fought in 200 battles

During the French Revolution of 1789, many people in the provinces refused to side with the rebels. In the vanguard of those faithful to the King were the people of the Vendée, in western France. They rose against the Revolutionary regime in 1793, and for six years fought to restore the Bourbons to the throne.

The great heroine of this revolt was Renée Bordereau, sometimes called "The Second Joan of Arc." Renée's father was killed before her eyes by revolutionary soldiers, and at the age of 23 she enlisted in the Vendéean army.

Dressed as a man, she always led the attack and sought the most dangerous posts. Renée's comrades-in-arms, who did not for a moment suspect that she was a woman, greatly admired her courage.

Even after the Vendéean revolt had been put down by Napoleon, he feared to permit Renée to remain at liberty lest she lead a new rebellion. Instead, he put a price of 40 million francs on her head. She was captured, and Napoleon had her imprisoned for five years.

Two years after the final overthrow of Napoleon in 1815, Renée Bordereau was received with honors at the court of the French king, Louis XVIII.

Max Hoffman was revived and lived after burial

In 1865, in a small town in Wisconsin, five-year-old Max Hoffman came down with cholera. Three days later, the doctor pulled the sheets over the boy's head and pronounced him dead.

Little Max was laid to rest in the village cemetery. That night, his mother awoke screaming: she had dreamt that her son was turning over in his coffin, trying to escape. Trembling with fear, she begged her husband to go to the cemetery immediately and raise the coffin. Mr. Hoffman did his best to calm his wife, assuring her that while her nightmare was indeed hideous, it was still just a dream. Assuaged, Mrs. Hoffman returned to bed.

But the next night, Max's mother had the identical dream, and this time she would not be denied. Resignedly, Mr. Hoffman asked his eldest boy and a neighbor to help him exhume the corpse. They dug up the coffin, opened the lid, and incredibly, there was Max, *lying on his side!* Though he showed no signs of life, Mr. Hoffman brought the boy back to the house so the doctor could have one last look at him.

At the Hoffman home, the physician labored to revive him. After an hour, Max's eyelid fluttered. The doctor immediately placed heated salt bags under the boy's arms, rubbed his lips with brandy, and watched for signs of recovery.

Recover Max did. After a week, he was out playing with his comrades. And the boy who died at five lived well into his 80's in Clinton, Iowa. For his entire life, Max Hoffman's most treasured memento was the metal handles he had taken from his own coffin.

Daniel Dancer was the world's worst miser

In the annals of miserdom, no account is more pitiable than that of Daniel Dancer and his sister, who lived and died in 18th-century England. Daniel, however, was the stingier of the two, for in the worship of Mammon, he sacrificed his sister's life.

Lying on the heap of rags that was her bed, the dying Miss Dancer worsened from day to day, yet received no medical attention. When asked why he did not call a doctor for his sister, Daniel replied, "Why should I waste my money in wickedly endeavoring to counteract the will of Providence?"

All the while his sister lay ill, Daniel made no change in her customary diet of one cold dumpling and a strip of fatty meat. When she objected that so meager a supper would not suffice for one who was sick, Daniel told her, "If you don't like it, you may go without it."

The Dancer siblings were by no means poor: they had an annual income of 3,000 pounds a year from their farmlands in Harrow, just south of London. Yet they were so frugal that on one occasion, while walking on their grounds, they came upon the rotting carcass of a sheep that had obviously died of disease. They skinned this decaying hulk, and made meat pies with what little flesh remained.

Daniel Dancer would obtain fertilizer for his fields by walking along the common road, stuffing his pockets with the cow dung he found there. While he had his nose to the ground for manure, he also foraged for old bones; what meat was on the bones would go toward his dinner, while the bone would go to his dog.

From time to time, the Dancers received the charity of one Lady Tempest. On a frigid winter night, she sent Daniel a trout stewed in claret. During transport, the trout froze. Dancer was faced with a formidable challenge: he would not eat the trout cold, for fear of contracting a toothache; yet he would not warm the fish on a fire, not wanting to expend the wood. So in a miserly stroke of genius, he sat on his dinner like a hen until the delicacy thawed.

The king cobra can kill an elephant

The great king cobra of southeast Asia is one of the most dangerous creatures in the world. The largest of all poisonous snakes, an adult king cobra may be as long as eighteen feet! Its poison sacs are enormous, and the venom they secrete is one of the deadliest known.

Moreover, the king cobra is one of the few snakes that will attack with little or no provocation. These serpents are especially aggressive during mating and breeding time. During this period, the male keeps close to the nest where the female is guarding her eggs, and stands ready to attack anything appearing on the scene.

To be confronted by a king cobra with four or five feet of its length reared upward would be a most nerve-shattering experience!

In Siam, even a huge elephant may fall victim to the attack of a king cobra. The snake strikes either at the tender tip of the elephant's trunk, or at the thin-skinned spot where the elephant's toenail joins its foot. An elephant thus bitten usually dies within three hours!

Milo of Crotona carried an ox across the stadium at Olympia

The greatest wrestler and strongman of the ancient world was a Greek named Milon. He hailed from the southern Italian city of Croton, a Greek colony founded in the 8th century B.C. by settlers from Achaea. He is more commonly known by the Latin form of his name: Milo of Crotona.

Milo was a man of diversified interests and attainments. Skilled as a soldier and singer, he

was a favorite disciple of the famous philosopher-mathematician Pythagoras, and he was himself the author of the *Physica,* a book on science and natural history. But above all, Milo was renowned as an athlete. His specialties were wrestling and feats of strength.

Milo won the wrestling championship at each of the six meetings of Olympic Games between 540 and 516 B.C. He was the only man in the history of the ancient Olympics (776 B.C. to A.D. 393) to win so many victories in any sport. Milo's

achievement becomes even more impressive when one notes that his active career as a wrestler covered more than 24 years, an extremely long time for an athlete to maintain himself at championship peak.

Milo's amazing feats are recorded in the writings of such reliable ancient historians as Pausanias, Plutarch, and Strabo. According to their reports, Milo's fingers were so powerful that no one could bend them when he extended his hand horizontally. On one occasion, Milo enclosed a tender pomegranate in his mighty fist. Scores of other athletes tried to get it away from him but none succeeded. When Milo finally opened his hand, there was not the slightest bruise on the fruit.

Milo is best known, however, for a feat he performed on the opening day of one of the meetings of the Olympic Games. Carrying a full-grown ox on his shoulders—the ox must have weighed at least a ton—Milo strolled effortlessly into the stadium at Olympia. Before the amazed eyes of thousands, he carried the ox across the playing field. The story goes on to say that he slaughtered the ox, which he may have, but the legend that he ate all the meat on that same day seems apocryphal.

Tragically, it was Milo's incredible strength that proved to be his doom. Walking in the wilds one day, Milo chanced upon a tree whose trunk was partially split. Never one to turn away from a challenge, the giant tried to rip the two parts asunder. However, Milo's hand became caught in the tree trunk and, with no companion to free him, Milo was devoured that night by wolves.

The aspidistra is pollinated by snails

Many bees, beetles, flies, wasps, birds, and bats participate in the pollination of various plants. But the oddest pollinator of all must certainly be the snail. These crawling gastropods are responsible for the pollination of the aspidistra, a genus of ornamental plants found in parts of eastern Asia.

The aspidistra produces small, bell-shaped flowers at ground level. As the snail stops to nibble on the petals, it picks up grains of pollen, which are subsequently transferred to another aspidistra plant!

The ostrich can outrun a racehorse

The ostrich is the largest bird in the world, standing about eight feet tall and weighing up to three hundred pounds. A bird this size can't fly, of course, but the ostrich is certainly no slowpoke on land. A running ostrich can cover twenty-five feet in one stride, and at top speed can reach almost sixty miles an hour—faster than many racehorses!

According to popular belief, an endangered ostrich will bury his head in the sand. Actually, the bird is capable of outrunning almost any enemy. And even if he is cornered unexpectedly, this swift creature is far from defenseless—one kick of his powerful legs can kill a man!

In some parts of the world ostriches are raised for their feathers. Gauchos in the Argentine Pampas use bolas to bring down the big birds.

Menuhin was a great violinist at 11

When Yehudi Menuhin was 11 years old, he was hailed by many music experts as the most gifted natural violinist ever to have appeared on the concert stage. Wearing shorts and an open shirt, he performed Beethoven's "Violin Concerto," accompanied by the New York Philharmonic Orchestra. His technical virtuosity and musical insight was such that both critics and public could hardly believe their ears. Even members of the orchestra wept.

The son of a chicken farmer and a schoolteacher, Menuhin achieved world fame with a minimum of musical training. In fact, his violin instructors were so overwhelmed by the effortless purity of his playing that they hesitated to meddle with his style at all. Menuhin played classical compositions at the age of four, and made his stage debut with the San Francisco Symphony Orchestra at seven.

Nor was the young Yehudi's genius restricted to the stage. As a boy he could also read such classic writers as Dante in Italian and Descartes in French.

Now nearing 50, Menuhin remains one of the world's great violinists. Unlike many prodigies, he has grown up to be both a happy and successful adult. Still, there are critics who say that with maturity Menuhin has lost some of the natural beauty of style he exhibited as a child genius.

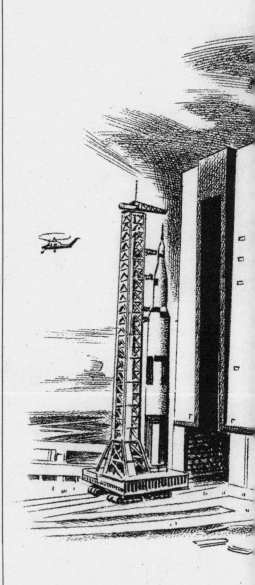

The Vertical Assembly Building is the most capacious structure ever built

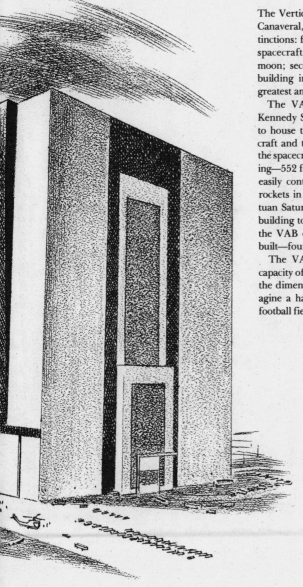

The Vertical Assembly Building (VAB) at Cape Canaveral, Florida, can boast two significant distinctions: first, within this structure was built the spacecraft that carried the first men to the moon; second, the VAB is the most capacious building in the world—that is, it encloses the greatest amount of space.

The VAB, at Complex 39 of the John F. Kennedy Space Center, was completed in 1965 to house the construction of the Apollo spacecraft and the Saturn V rocket that would carry the spacecraft into space. The steel-framed building—552 feet high and 710 feet in length—could easily contain a number of 363-foot Saturn V rockets in a vertical position. Since the gargantuan Saturn rockets had to be moved from the building to the launching pad upon completion, the VAB can also boast the largest doors ever built—four doors, each *460 feet high!*

The VAB sprawls over 10 acres and has a capacity of 129,000,000 cubic feet. To appreciate the dimensions of this mammoth structure, imagine a hangar the length of two-and-one-half football fields and as high as a 50-story building!

The Earl of Bridgewater used to dine
with a dozen dogs

The Rev. Francis Henry Egerton, Earl of Bridgewater, was a Prince of the Holy Roman Empire, a scholar, and a patron of the arts. In addition, he was enormously wealthy. During the last few years before his death in February, 1829, Lord Egerton took to heart the adage that

a man's best friend is his dog.

Lord Egerton was a permanent resident of the prestigious Hôtel de Noailles in Paris. Each night, he would sit down to a formal dinner with a dozen guests—all of them canine. In a Parisian journal of 1826, there is this account of a typical evening with the Earl:

"No less than a dozen favorite dogs...daily partake of milord's dinner, seated very gravely in armchairs, each with a napkin round his neck, and a servant behind to attend to his wants. These honorable quadrupeds, as if grateful for such delicate attentions, comport themselves during the time of repast with a decency and decorum which would do more than honor to a party of gentlemen; but if, by any chance, one of them should without due consideration obey the natural instinct of his appetite, and transgress any of the rules of good manners, his punishment is at hand. The day following the offense, the dog dines, and even dines well; but not at milord's table; banished to the antechamber, and dressed in livery, he eats in sorrow the bread of shame, and picks the bones of mortification, while his place at table remains vacant till his repentance has merited a generous pardon!"

After dinner, Lord Egerton liked to take a fast turn about town in his elegant carriage. For company, he would bring along a pack of his pampered pooches, each outfitted with four tiny boots to protect its paws from the mud of the Paris roadways.

The anteater has neither teeth nor jaws

Take a look at the giant anteater and your first reaction might well be: "How does he eat?" For this odd looking South American native seems to have no mouth! His snout is shaped like a long, crooked broomstick, and contains neither teeth nor jaws. But don't worry, this long-nosed fellow has no trouble swallowing his dinner. What nature has forgotten in the ways of jaws, she's more than made up for with one of the longest, most agile tongues in the animal kingdom.

The anteater's snout is actually a tube with a small opening at the end. Through this tube the anteater worms a thin, sticky tongue that looks like a piece of pink wire. And a long piece at that—it's often over a foot long!

Here's how the anteater uses his special gift: When he finds an anthill, the snake-tongued beast walks up and swipes it with his forepaws, spreading thousands of stunned ants on the

ground before him. Then he lashes his serpentine tongue at the scurrying hordes, catching a few hundred ants at a time on the flypaperlike surface of his tongue. When he's got a full load, he sucks his tongue back through his tubular snout and swallows the ants whole, in one gulp. Then out comes the tongue again for another quick meal. Before he's finished, this walking vacuum cleaner may devour almost the entire ant colony.

The anteater may seem to be a gentle, unvoracious creature, but don't be fooled—he's a strong, vicious character who inspires terror

among man and beast alike. First of all, the giant anteater is large, about the size of a brown bear. In fact, he's often called the ant bear. The three claws on each of his front feet are like razor-sharp daggers, and the anteater uses them as slashing weapons, backed by his tremendously powerful leg muscles. Behind the claws of each foot is a spiny heel, strong as a steel spur, that can easily punch a hole in a man's chest. Even savage jungle cats give this giant a wide berth!

Jean Theurel served as a soldier in three centuries

In 1699, a spirited lad of fifteen named Jean Theurel joined the Touraine Regiment to defend France's honor in the war against Holland. Theurel probably figured that he would see action in a few skirmishes, and then return to his native Dijon with boasting privileges for life.

But the boy proved to be a demon on the battlefield, and opted for a career in the military. He distinguished himself in hundreds of battles, and in later years hooked up with the First Company of Paris. Finally, in 1777, Louis XVI promoted him to captain. At the time, His Majesty suggested that since Theurel was now 92, he might contemplate retirement.

Nonetheless, Theurel continued to live in the First Company barracks and remained on the active rolls. Theurel's tenure was not challenged again until 1802, when Napoleon learned of his status. This time, Theurel was officially deactivated, and given a pension of 1,500 francs. Whether civilian life agreed with this soldier who served in three centuries no one can say. All we know is that Theurel died in 1807, at the age of 123.

Thirty people can stand in the observation deck at the crown of the Statue of Liberty

Towering above the harbor of New York, the gateway to America, the Statue of Liberty has stood as a welcoming beacon to millions of immigrants and visitors for close to 100 years.

What a thrill it is, after a long voyage, to slip through the Narrows Channel into the Upper Bay and suddenly view the vast panorama of New York City, with the great lady standing tall in the midst of the busy harbor, facing the open sea, her torch held high above her head in welcome.

The full name of this world-famous monument is The Statue of Liberty Enlightening the World. As befitting a monument to universal liberty, the Statue was erected not by any monarch or government, but by citizens of France and the United States, the twin vanguard of democracy.

An organization known as the Franco-American Union was founded in 1875, the year before America's centennial celebration. A proposal by the Frenchman Edouard Laboulayé was adopted whereby donations from American and French citizens would be used for the design and construction of a monument to commemorate the American and French Revolutions, and to symbolize the long-standing friendship between these two nations.

French citizens raised money for the statue, and a design was accepted from Frederic Auguste Bartholdi for an iron-and-steel frame statue covered with copper sheets. American citizens raised the money for the granite-and-concrete pedestal. Bartholdi, during a visit to the United States, suggested that the statue be placed on 12-acre Bedloe's Island, in the middle of New York Harbor.

American builders constructed the pedestal atop an 11-point star formed by the walls of old Fort Wood, which had previously occupied the island. Rising atop the pedestal was the iron-and-steel frame designed by Charles Eiffel—who was later to build the Eiffel Tower. When the 300 sculptured copper sheets were fixed to the frame, the copper-colored colossus was left

towering above the bay. (Copper oxidizes with age, and today the statue is entirely green.)

The Statue of Liberty was dedicated on October 28, 1886, and in 1924, it became a National Monument. In 1960, the name of Bedloe's Island was officially changed to Liberty Island.

The statue itself is a 152-foot figure of a woman in long robes, raising a lighted torch above her head. In her left hand she holds a tablet on which the date July 4, 1776—the date of the signing of the Declaration of Independence—is inscribed. Around her feet lie broken chains, symbolic of the breaking of the bonds of oppression that the statue commemorates. The pedestal adds nearly another 150 feet, giving the monument a total height of over 300 feet.

Visitors can take an elevator to the top of the pedestal, then climb a narrow, winding staircase that twists up into the Lady's crown. There, an observation room 260 feet above the water affords up to 30 people a spectacular view of New York harbor. In earlier days, visitors were permitted to climb to the arm of the statue and emerge on a platform surrounding the torch, but this passageway has been closed off in recent years, due to suspected structural weaknesses in the arm.

Whether one views the city from atop the statue or admires the statue from the city and harbor below, the Statue of Liberty remains an inspiring monument, a structural wonder, and the symbol of a nation.

Alvin York captured 130 German prisoners by himself at one time

It was on October 8, 1918 that a small group of American soldiers were surrounded by Germans in the Argonne Forest of France. On all sides were German machine-gun nests. The wounded sergeant of the troop, unable to continue, passed command to a young corporal named Alvin York. Capture seemed imminent. But the boy from Fentress County, Tennessee did not give up. Instead he stood up and, flattening his body against a tree, began to fire. Twelve Germans fell

in short order. In stark amazement and fury, eight Germans charged down a hill at the lone American soldier. York fired eight times and slew all eight. The other Germans, not knowing that they had surrounded a handful of American soldiers, thought that they *themselves* were outmanned. They abandoned their positions to surrender.

Soon York discovered that he had captured *92 prisoners*. The six Americans under York's command were really in a spot: they were in German territory, and they were vastly outnumbered by their prisoners. But again, young York was equal to the task. He marched the prisoners ahead of him, toward the American lines. Whenever they came to another German machine-gun nest, the gunners assumed that a large army battalion was behind the group of prisoners walking toward them. By the time York reached the American lines, he had collected 132 prisoners and had put out of action 35 machine-gun nests. He later received the highest governmental awards from the U.S. and France.

Gama, a 5-foot 7-inch Indian, was the greatest wrestler in history

Although much smaller than most wrestlers you see on TV, Gama of Patiala, India, made up for his size, and then some. Generally acknowledged to be the top wrestler of all time, this 5-foot 7-inch, 260-pound battler had a hard time finding competition. Most wrestlers feared Gama so much they would not enter the ring with him. Gama reigned as world champ well into his fifties.

In London in 1910, the Indian challenged any 20 wrestlers to meet him in combat, promising to throw them all in succession within an hour. But the Britons wouldn't take on the Indian terror. Indeed, throughout his career, Gama was able to lure only two Occidentals to do battle with him. One was an American named B.F. Roller; the other a Pole, the world-famous professional wrestler Stanislaus Zbysko, a gigantic hunk of a man, and generally regarded by sports writers as a very competent athlete. Neither lasted more than half a minute.

The trunk of the baobab is large enough to house a family

"The devil plucked up the baobab, thrust its branches into the earth, and left its roots in the air." To the Arabs who developed this legend, there seemed perhaps no other way to explain the preposterous shape of the baobab tree, an African and Indian relative of the cacao. With its broad, bulging trunk and dense network of root-like branches, the baobab does indeed appear to have been thrust upside down into the earth.

The trunks of these giants—second in bulk only to the sequoias—are extraordinarily fat in relation to their height. While the average baobab is only about 45 feet high, its diameter often approaches 35 feet, and some specimens are actually broader than they are tall!

The pulpy inside of this trunk is so soft that a bullet could pass right through it. African natives take advantage of the tree's softness and girth by hollowing out the trunk and using it as a dwelling. One famous South African specimen has been hollowed out and used as a bus shelter!

In addition to its unique shape, the baobab can boast one of the most extensive root systems in nature. The horizontal roots of some specimens spread out as much as 300 feet around the plant.

Baby Clark was born without a brain

On May 26, 1788, a 26-year-old woman named Mary Clark gave birth in the Carlisle Dispensary, England. The child was perfectly developed, except for a somewhat soft head. The doctor passed this off, since the child cried, kicked, ate, and otherwise behaved quite normally; moreover, a baby's head is normally rather soft.

After five days, inexplicably, the tot died. An autopsy revealed the startling fact that the child's skull contained neither a cerebrum, nor a cerebellum, nor a medulla—in short, *no brain*.

Incredible as this case may seem, it is not the only instance of a human being living without a brain. In 1935, another such child was born in St. Vincent's Hospital in New York City. Just like the Clark child, this babe acted normally for all the days of its life—27.

The cause of death was unknown until an autopsy revealed that the infant's head contained nothing but water.

Benjamin Franklin was the most versatile man who ever lived

Benjamin Franklin said, "I wish the good Lord had seen fit to make the day twice as long as it is. Perhaps then I could *really* accomplish something."

Thus spoke this many-sided man who did any number of things—and did them all amazingly well. He was a painter, writer, publisher, scientist, statesman, inventor, businessman, philosopher, and humanitarian.

Franklin's father, a poor Boston candlemaker, hoped to make Benjamin, one of 17 children, a minister. But lack of funds forced young Franklin to leave school at the age of 10. Apprenticed to an older brother, a printer, Benjamin managed to educate himself by giving up meat and using the money saved to buy books. Young Benjamin not only educated himself in such basic subjects as arithmetic and English grammar, but also navigation, algebra, geometry, and philosophy.

In 1723, at the age of 17, Ben left Boston to try his luck in Philadelphia. He arrived in that colonial town with little money and no friends. Yet within a very few years, Franklin became a famous author and publisher. His sharp wit and common-sense advice, published in his *Pennsylvania Gazette* and *Poor Richard's Almanack*, were known throughout the American colonies.

Marked up to his credit is a series of diverse achievements never equaled in American history. Here are just a few of his accomplishments:

As a scientist and inventor, Franklin:

1. Proved that lightning consisted of electricity.

2. Invented the lightning rod.

3. Invented the Franklin stove, an economical and useful heating device.

4. Invented bifocal glasses.

5. Invented the platform rocking chair.

6. Wrote a scientific essay which for the first time described the existence of the Gulf Stream.

7. Discovered that poorly aired rooms spread disease.

In the realm of literature, Franklin:

1. Was an original and highly talented writer, whose *Poor Richard's Almanack* and *Autobiography* have assumed a permanent place in the American literary heritage.

2. Founded a popular publication, the *Pennsylvania Gazette,* later to become *The Saturday Evening Post.*

As a humanitarian and tireless contributor to the public welfare, Franklin:

1. Organized the first fire department in Philadelphia.

2. Helped establish the first hospital in America.

3. Founded the first lending library in America.

4. Created the first efficient postal system in America.

5. Founded an academy which later became the University of Pennsylvania.

6. Headed the first society in America to oppose slavery.

7. Established the first American fire insurance company.

8. Founded a club that later became the American Philosophical Society.

Though his accomplishments in any of these fields would have assured Franklin a lasting imprint on American history, it was his role in founding a new nation that gave Franklin his special place in the hearts of his countrymen. Although he had already attained the advanced age of 70 when the Revolutionary War broke out in 1776, Franklin's guiding hand was felt every-

where during the struggle against the British. As Postmaster General of the colonies in rebellion, he contributed his entire salary to help the American wounded. Franklin also took a major part in reorganizing the Continental Army into an efficient fighting force. He helped draft the Declaration of Independence and, as America's envoy to France, did much to forge the alliance that in 1778 brought French aid to the hard-pressed American troops. And it was Franklin's wisdom and gift for compromise that, once the

Revolution was won, helped the colonies become a united nation under a federal constitution.

A year before Franklin's death, George Washington wrote the following words to this universally admired American. "If to be venerated for benevolence, if to be admired for talent, if to be esteemed for patriotism, if to be beloved for philanthropy, can gratify the human mind, you must have the pleasing consolation to know you have not lived in vain."

Salo Finkelstein was a mathematical machine

Some few years before World War II, the Polish Treasury Department began an economy drive by hiring Salo Finkelstein of Warsaw. Dr. Finkelstein merely replaced some 40-odd people, each of whom had operated a calculating machine. And the Polish Government vouched for the fact that during the five years in which Dr. Finkelstein tossed huge columns of figures around in his head, he did not make a mistake.

For Salo Finkelstein was a genius if ever there was one. You could give him a large number like 3,108, and in less than one minute he would reduce it accurately to the following squares: 52^2, 16^2, 12^2, and 2^2—a simple little maneuver that would take most of us half an hour or more to work out, if we could do it at all. The Doctor could look at an arithmetical problem like 6,894 x 2,763, and in just seven seconds, without paper and pencil, come up with the answer.

In his public performances, Finkelstein did use a blackboard. He drew a square containing five rows of five spaces, or 25 spaces in all. Then he turned his back to the board.

Folks in the audience came up and filled in the spaces with numbers. Finkelstein turned around and took one quick glance at the blackboard. Then, either blindfolded or with his back turned to the board, he recited the 25 numbers, going from left to right, then going from top to bottom, then moving diagonally, then spirally; or in fact, in any way that you might ask him to juggle his figures. And an hour later, after his mind had been filled with every conceivable sort of calculation, he would repeat those 25 numbers.

You see, the numbers were engraved on that photographic mind of his just as if they had been impressed on a gelatin plate. He remembered pi to 300 decimal places. He could recite logarithms from 1 to 100 to the seventh decimal and from 101 to 150 to the fifth decimal. He could conjure up, without a second's hesitation, thousands of square roots, cube roots, products, quotients, and number combinations. These numbers never failed him. They were there in his mind, and they stuck!

The Kaufmann house at Bear Run, Pennsylvania is built directly over a waterfall

"Fallingwater" is the popular name for one of the best-known private residences in the country, the Edgar J. Kaufmann house on Bear Run, Pennsylvania. The name is appropriate, for this home—designed by America's premier architect, Frank Lloyd Wright—was built directly over a waterfall!

When Mr. Kaufmann commissioned Wright to design a weekend retreat for his family on his Pennsylvania property, he wanted the architect to take full advantage of the picturesque site: a wooden glen with a slowly running stream, a clear pool, and a small waterfall. And Wright more than fulfilled his expectations, designing a striking three-story structure anchored on a small cliff overlooking the pool, with a portion of the house cantilevered directly over the running water.

Built almost entirely of masonry, the home features six reinforced-concrete terraces extending over the waterfall and pool. Most rooms offer access to a terrace and a breathtaking vista of the waters below. A stairway suspended from the lower story reaches to within a few feet of the waterfall itself. Viewed from the pool, Fallingwater seems to rise from the boulders around it, and the stream appears to run directly through the house, as if the structure were part of the natural site rather than an addition to it.

The unusual site and construction of Fallingwater earned the home much publicity when it was completed in 1936, and the home remains one of Wright's best-loved works. Fallingwater is open to visitors.

The 300-year-old secret of Stradivarius remains unsolved

Antonius Stradivarius was born in 1644. Initially a woodcarver, he learned to play the violin and consequently became interested in the making of violins. At eighteen he became an apprentice to Niccolo Amati, the famous violinmaker of Cremona.

In 1680, he left Amati's shop and began to work for himself. He experimented with his violins, giving them many different shapes. He was obsessed with the desire to make his violin sound as lovely as a beautiful human voice. He decorated his violins so exquisitely—inlaying them with mother of pearl and ivory and ebony—that not only are they the world's most wonderful violins because of their exquisite tone, but they are also the most beautiful violins ever created.

By the time he was 40 years old, he was a renowned and extremely wealthy man. He kept his notes safely locked up. Not even his two sons, who labored with him in his workshop, knew his secrets. During his long life of 94 years, he made at least 1,116 instruments.

The hunt for the secret of Stradivarius has been carried on ever since his death in 1737. His violins have been carefully measured and copied in every detail, and some very fine violins have been made; but they have never attained the perfection of the master's instruments. Vuillane, a famous French violinmaker of the early 1800's, spent all his life searching for the secrets of the great Stradivarius. At last, he finally got in touch with Giacomo Stradivarius, the great grandson of the master. Giacomo told Vuillane that he had discovered in an old family Bible a formula for varnish which he believed to have been Antonius Stradivarius' own special formula. Giacomo said he had told no one about it and, even though he was sorely tempted during financial straits to sell it, he had made the decision that he would give nobody the priceless prescription except a member of the family, should any one of them decide to pursue the trade of violinmaker.

Diverse suppositions have been made about what makes the violins of Stradivarius supreme. Some have attributed the characteristic sound of his violins to the physical properties of the wood, or to the shape of the instruments; others maintain that the secret lay in the interrelation of the various parts of the instruments. Still others regard the answer as the special pitch which Stradivarius derived from the sap of trees then growing in Italy which have since disappeared. But the most widely believed theory is that Stradivarius' secret lies in the special composition of the varnish with which he coated his violins. Chemists have attempted to analyze the composition, and indeed, some violinmakers have greatly improved the tone of their violins by imitating as closely as possible the composition of Stradivarius' varnish. Nevertheless, no one has been able to discover his secret. It is as much a mystery today as it was nearly 250 years ago.

Edgerton won a professional fight at age 63

When ex-boxer Walter Edgerton, age 63, challenged ex-boxer John Henry Johnson to a fight, Edgerton was at an age when most men would prefer to be puttering in their gardens. Johnson was no kid, either—he was 45.

Back in the 1880's Edgerton had been a well-known featherweight—"Kentucky Rosebud" by name. But this was February, 1913, and his fighting days should have been long behind him.

One fine day at a bar, Edgerton got into an argument with another ex-boxer. Herman

Taylor, a young promoter, heard about the quarrel and understood that the two wanted to settle their falling out with their fists. The age factor didn't faze them at all. So Taylor suggested they go into the ring at the Broadway AC. Not only would they end their altercation in the time-honored manner, but they would pick up some prize money as well.

And they did. The night Edgerton and Johnson squared off, the little AC was packed to its 800 capacity.

When he entered the ring at Philadelphia's Broadway Athletic Club, Edgerton didn't show an overabundance of push and go. At the start, it wasn't the fastest-moving bout on record. But Edgerton was conserving his strength. Before the fourth round was over, the young John Henry, Edgerton's junior by 18 years, was laid out like a plank, felled by the "Rosebud's" knockout punch.

The narwhal's tusk is often half as long as its body

The narwhal is a large aquatic mammal that makes its home in the coastal waters of the Arctic Ocean. This curious-looking creature has only two teeth in its upper jaw, and in the male of the species, one of these teeth develops into a long, straight tusk—giving him the appearance of a seal with a spearlike horn projecting straight ahead. Although the narwhal averages only thirteen or fourteen feet in length, occasionally growing to twenty feet, narwhal tusks are sometimes nine feet long—almost half as long as the creature's body!

The function of this oversized tusk is not known. The narwhal uses it neither as a digging tool nor as a weapon in combat. But during the Middle Ages this ivory spear was highly prized by man as the fabled horn of the unicorn.

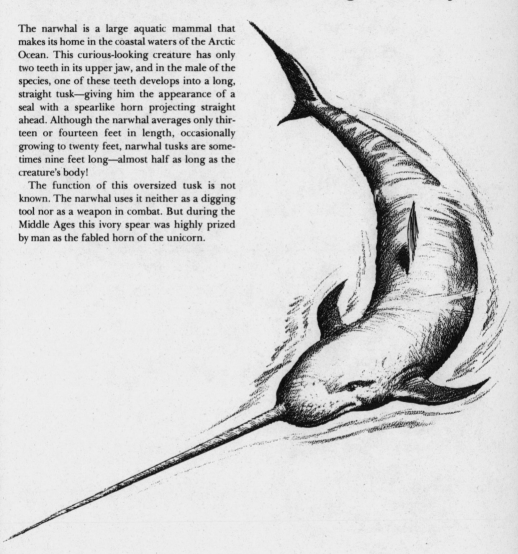

The opossum faints when frightened

When threatened by an enemy, some animals will stand their ground and fight, others will turn tail and run. The opossum, a small American marsupial, prefers another tack: When in danger, the opossum goes into a faint and plays dead!

Once this timid fellow has passed out, his body becomes as rigid as steel. A perplexed predator can poke him, pick him up, roll him over—and still the opossum will remain utterly motionless. Most predators will not eat an animal they have not killed themselves, and, after a few exploratory jabs, will move on to seek other prey. After perhaps twenty minutes of immobility, the opossum will open one eye, glance around to make sure all is well, then climb lazily to his feet and amble off.

Of course, the opossum's sham is not always successful, and many of these helpless creatures never live to awaken from their feigned slumber. But the possum population is certainly in no danger of extinction, for these cowardly creatures are the most prolific mammals in existence. An opossum may bear three litters in a single year—with as many as eighteen babies in each litter!

A seed of the Seychelles coconut can outweigh a bushel of apples

When you think of a seed, you're likely to call to mind an apple or melon seed, or an orange or cherry pit, all of which are roughly the same size. But just as plants themselves vary greatly in their dimensions, so do their seeds. Certain orchids produce seeds so small that 35 million would weigh just an ounce. At the other end of the scale, the seed of the Seychelles coconut can weigh more than a bushel of apples!

The Seychelles coconut is a palm tree found only in the Seychelles, a group of small islands off the east coast of Africa. It is often called the double coconut, because the shape of its seeds resemble two coconuts joined together. The seeds also bear a remarkable resemblance to the female pelvis, and as a result, magical properties have traditionally been attributed to the plant. The palm is sometimes known by yet another name, *coco de mer* (coconut of the sea), for its seeds have floated around the world and washed up on many distant shores.

Technically, the "seed" of this rare palm is a fruit, for it consists of a fleshy, fibrous jacket surrounding a hard, two-lobed seed. But since each fruit contains only one seed, many naturalists consider the Seychelles' fruit as a seed—indeed, as the largest seed in the world. (In fact, the largest true seed is that of the South American *Mora* tree, which can grow as long as six inches.)

The giant "seed" of the Seychelles coconut takes up to 10 years to ripen, sometimes attaining a length of 18 inches and a weight of 40 or 50 pounds!

Blake surf rode a wave for almost a mile

In popular fancy, good surfers are imagined capable of riding a wave for several miles. This is a misconception, for even at Honolulu's Waikiki Beach, generally considered to offer the finest surfing conditions in the world, the average ride is no more than 200 yards. Occasionally, though, when surf and tide conditions are right, longer rides become possible—at least for the best surfers, *if* they are lucky enough to be in the right place at the right time.

Commonplace 200-yard rides take place at Waikiki when the surf is running at "blow-hole-break," which is just about every day. (A break is a point where a wave slows, builds up, and then scatters.) At "first-break," which occurs somewhat less often, a good surfer can make 300 yards. When the surf breaks at Kalahuewehe, or "castle-break," he can make 500 yards, but this condition occurs only about three times a year. Even less frequent is "chuna-break," a condition when half-mile rides are possible. The longest rides of all occur when the surf comes in at "zero-break," something that very rarely happens.

It did happen, though, just before sundown one evening early in June 1936, and Tom Blake, probably the top surfer of all time, was on the spot and ready. In fact, Tom had been ready and waiting for a chance like this for six years.

The tide was running extremely high off Waikiki that day, so Blake knew something big was coming; though, of course, he had no way of predicting that it would be "zero-break." Along with several other skilled surfers, he took to the water and calmly edged his board into position far out at the mouth of Waikiki Bay.

Watching intently, Blake suddenly observed a set of monster waves rearing up about a half-mile off. Here, indeed, was the big one!

Catching the second wave of the set, Blake began riding in toward the beach atop a 25-foot-high solid wall of water stretching across the full width of Waikiki Bay. None of his companions made it, but Blake, progressing rapidly from "first-break-south-castle" through "public-baths break" and "chuna-break," soon reached the shore opposite Lalani Village. He had completed a surf ride of about a mile, the longest ever recorded.

Salmon will fight a current for one thousand miles

Of all the earth's sea creatures, the salmon is the finest and most determined navigator. This remarkable fish will swim great distances against a current to spawn in the precise stream in which it was born.

Salmon mature in the ocean, often growing to a length of four feet within one or two years. But at the appropriate season, depending on the species, they suddenly seek out freshwater and begin swimming upstream. During this frenzied upriver climb, salmon will buck a current and swim at thirty miles an hour, fighting rapids and leaping waterfalls as high as fifteen feet—no small feat for a fish that often weighs over seventy pounds. Their silvery scales turn a characteristic red as they hurry through rivers and streams, never pausing, not even to eat.

For most salmon, the journey does not end until the fish has found the stream in which it was born. Some of these extraordinary creatures have journeyed the length of the Yukon River to find their natal stream—a voyage of over one thousand miles. How do they find their way? Incredible as it may seem, experiments have shown that spawning salmon locate the right stream by means of a highly developed sense of smell! When the salmon arrive, they lay their eggs in gravel pits in the stream bed. Their duty done, many of the Pacific species then die, never to return to the sea again—although other species do survive a return trip.

Some of the young salmon that are born in these streams will descend immediately to the ocean; others—like the sockeye salmon—will live for as long as five years in freshwater before journeying downstream to the sea. And eventually each salmon will return once more to this parent stream.

Sohn glided to earth on canvas wings from almost four miles up

Man has always been intrigued by the thought of flying through his own physical power, without the aid of any heavy mechanism. The man who has come closest to that dream was Clem Sohn.

Sohn, an air-show performer in the 1930's, had perfected a way of gliding through the air with home-made wings. He had himself dropped from an airplane at a height of approximately 20,000 feet, and then he would float downward some three miles or so until he was but 800 or 1,000 feet from the ground, at which point he would open up his parachute for the final descent.

Clem, who hailed from Lansing, Michigan, made his wings out of zephyr cloth and mounted them on steel tubes to form a large web which was clasped to his hips. A loose cloth formed another web between his legs. His large goggles off, Clem had remarked, "I feel as safe as you would in your grandmother's kitchen." But during his descent on that day, his parachute didn't open. A terror-stricken crowd of 100,000 watched him frantically tug on the ripcord of his

gave him an appearance which justifiably led to his becoming known as *"The Batman."*

Sohn's amazing act came to an end on April 25, 1937, in Vincennes, France. Before taking emergency chute, but that failed, too; and Clem Sohn, only 26 years old, plunged to his death.

Marcgravia flowers are natural Christmas tree ornaments

For sheer visual peculiarity, nature has produced few plants more remarkable than the marcgravia. The flower clusters of this South American forest dweller dangle from their stalks like delicate Christmas tree ornaments. The flowers suspended from the clusters resemble tiny mobiles. But this fanciful structure is far from accidental, for the marcgravia—like almost all flowers—is expressly designed to facilitate its pollination.

Each flower cluster consists of five nectar pouches and a number of much smaller flowers. The pipe-shaped pouches hang vertically, with the acorn-shaped flowers suspended above in a horizontal whorl. Hummingbirds which visit the pouches to extract nectar cannot avoid bumping the flowers as they leave. Pollen is thus left on the birds' heads, and deposited on the flowers they subsequently visit, thereby pollinating those plants.

The marcgravia is notable also for the unusual formation of its leaves. The lower portion of each stem produces two rows of stalkless leaves. But higher up, near the flower, the leaves are stalked and arranged spirally around the stem. The change from one arrangement to the other is abrupt—and its cause unknown.

Bats fly by radar

As the expression "blind as a bat" indicates, bats have extremely poor vision. Yet these creatures—the only flying mammals in existence—can navigate easily in the blackest night, gobbling up insects that would be invisible to the sharpest human eye. How do they do it? Surprisingly enough, bats fly by radar!

When a ship is negotiating a difficult strait in fog or darkness, it sends out radio signals that strike nearby objects and bounce back to the ship. The time it takes for these signals to reach the object and return to the ship indicates how far away that object is.

The bat's "radar" system works on the same

principle. As he flies through the air, the bat opens his mouth and sends out a steady series of rapid little cries, from thirty to sixty per second. These cries are much too high-pitched to be detected by human ears, but the bat can hear sounds pitched as high as 100,000 vibrations per second. If the sounds strike an object, they bounce back, like an echo. The bat's remarkable ears pick them up and tell him where the object is located.

The radar system of this airborne creature is so precise that a totally blind bat can fly about in a crowded room without touching an obstacle with so much as a wing tip. But tape his mouth shut and he'll crash into everything—including the wall!

Mathias won the Olympic decathlon at age 17

No title is held in greater esteem than the Olympic decathlon. The champion in this event is generally regarded as the greatest athlete in the world. There is no doubt that the performances in the 1968 decathlon in Mexico City were watched on television by more viewers than any other Olympic event. The decathlon performer must be able to run, to jump, and to throw. He must be able to sprint, and to have sufficient endurance to last a long distance. He must blend agility with strength.

Just a few months before he was tapped to carry the hopes of the United States in the 1948 Olympics in London, 17-year-old Bob Mathias had never touched a javelin. Nor had he ever pole-vaulted. And to top off his inexperience, the 400-meter distance and the 1,500-meter dis-

won the U.S. championship. In a short six weeks, the boy found himself in the international arena in London.

Here Mathias took on the world's best as if he were a veteran. The schoolboy ran the 100 meters in 11.2 seconds; the 400 meters in 51.7 seconds; the rugged 1,500 meters in 5 minutes and 11 seconds; the 110-meter hurdles in 15.7 seconds. He broad-jumped 21 feet 8 inches; high-jumped 6 feet 1¼ inches, and pole-vaulted 11 feet 5½ inches. In the weight events, he threw the javelin 165 feet 1 inch; the shot put, 42 feet 9 inches; and he hurled the discus 144 feet 4 inches. His 7,139 points easily led the field.

When the two-day ordeal ended on August 6, an onlooker asked Bob what he would do to celebrate his victory. "Start shaving, I guess," said Bob.

tance were quite unfamiliar. His enthusiastic high school coach suggested to his young charge that he try out for the Olympic team anyhow. The lad weighed 190 pounds, was strong, willing, and was an exceptionally good competitor. Bob Mathias was the cool type. The coach believed that he wouldn't make the team, but that he would gain valuable experience for the next competition, four years later.

However, Mathias exceeded everyone's hopes, including his own. He won the very first decathlon meet he entered, defeating several well-known college stars. Less than a month later, he

The toucan's bill is larger than its body

Toucans, a family of tropical American fruit-eating birds, have extremely large bills. Indeed, among some members of the family, the bill is actually bigger than the bird's body! This over-sized beak gives the toucan an ungainly, somewhat comical appearance, but the thin-walled bill is light and not hard for the bird to carry.

Rastelli juggled 10 balls

Enrico Rastelli was one of the greatest jugglers and acrobats of all time. A magnificently coordinated athlete, he had the highest paid novelty act of any kind when he worked the Keith-Albee-Orpheum vaudeville circuit in the United States in the 1920s.

The son and grandson of performers, Rastelli was born in 1896 in Samara, Russia, where his parents were on tour with the famous Circus Truzzi. He learned juggling from his father, and at the age of 12, he displayed his budding talent by doing a handstand on his father's head while juggling four lit torches.

The wiry 5-foot 6-inch Rastelli soon gained fame for many incredible feats. He would do a handstand on a lamp which stood on a table, while he was also holding an 8-foot flagpole (which flew the Italian flag) with one foot, and juggling two balls with his other foot. Rastelli could also juggle six 24-inch sticks while keeping a seventh stick balanced on his head, and he could juggle eight plates at one time.

However, his most famous stunt was the one in which he flashed ten balls at one time— that is, simultaneously kept five balls constantly moving with each hand. No juggler since has been able to duplicate this feat.

Poon Lim survived for 133 days on a life raft

On November 23, 1942, the S.S. Lomond, an English merchant manned by a crew of 55, was torpedoed in the South Atlantic. Only one of the seamen survived—a 25-year-old Chinese by the name of Poon Lim. He had been catapulted off the deck by an explosion of such force that the very clothes were blown from his back.

Lim swam in the neighborhood of the wreck for two hours, and then grabbed a drifting life raft on which he survived for 133 days, naked and exposed to the elements. The raft carried enough food and water for him to live through 60 days. After that, his very life depended on the fish he could catch.

Poon fashioned a hook from a spring which he extracted from the raft's flashlight, and he trolled for small fish. He used these small ones as bait for larger game. Occasionally, he would grab at and catch a sea gull for a meatier meal.

But hunger was not his only trial. Verily, Poon Lim was like Coleridge's "ancient mariner," who bemoaned:

> Alone, alone, oh! all alone,
>   Alone on a wide, wide sea;
> And never a saint took pity on
>   My soul in agony.

For more than four months, Lim drifted through calm and squall, and at long last neared the coast of Brazil. On April 5, 1943, he was spotted by some fishermen who took him aboard. He was palpably ill, and his legs were wobbly, but yet his rescuers found it hard to believe that this 5-foot, 5-inch little mite of a man could have possibly endured through better than a third of a year on an exposed raft, bobbing at random in the middle of the ocean.

When the story reached Britain the tale met with a different reception. The British knew about the torpedoing of the S.S. Lomond. King George VI, deeply impressed with Poon's fortitude, presented him in 1943 with England's highest civilian award, the British Empire medal. Speaking of his incredible record, Poon Lim said "I hope no one will ever have to break it."

There is a crab that can kill a man

The giant spider crab—or *Macrocheira kampferi*—is undoubtedly the king of crustaceans. This nightmarish creature, who lives in the waters off the Ryukyu Islands southwest of Japan, stands three feet high and often weighs as much as thirty pounds. His powerful legs can spread as wide as twelve feet, and his savage claws have torn the flesh from men who have challenged him.

During the day, the spider crab lurks deep in his ocean home, but when the sun sets, he clambers ashore and ambles along the beach, looking like a grotesque creature from another planet. Japanese fishermen capture him with huge nets, and it often takes several men to hold the net once this monster has been snagged!

Bangkok contains 400 Buddhist temples

Bangkok, Thailand, is the home of some of the most stunning Buddhist temples in the East. In all, there are some 400 Buddhist monasteries within the limits of this canal-crossed city, often called the "Venice of the East."

248

In addition to the Emerald Buddha, the Wat Phra Kaeo includes a depository of ancient Buddhist scriptures, memorials to white elephants, statues of venerated holy men, and a great stupa or reliquary. The Royal Pantheon—which is open to visitors only one day each year—contains life-sized bronze figures of former Thai kings. Throughout the grounds,

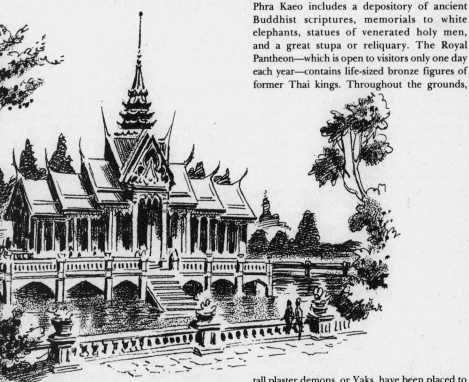

Perhaps the most well-known of Bangkok's many religious structures is the Temple of the Emerald Buddha. Since the 15th century, when King Tiloka adopted the structure as the spiritual safeguard of Thailand, the Temple of the Emerald Buddha has been the center of all Thai religious life. The Temple is the home of the most sacred objects in Thailand, chief among these an immense statue of a meditating Buddha mounted on a pedestal under the Temple's high roof.

The Emerald Buddha forms only a part of a larger religious complex, called the Wat Phra Kaeo, situated on the banks of the Chaophraya River in the Thai capital. The complex is surrounded by a wall four and one-half miles long, 13 feet high, and 10 feet thick. Sixty-three ornamented gates permit entry to the sacred grounds.

tall plaster demons, or Yaks, have been placed to ward off evil spirits.

In every building of the temple complex, each door, window, statue, tower, and pillar tapers upwards. The most striking features of these buildings are the "sky licks," curving, pointed pieces of ornamental metal that resembles licks of flame.

Directly across the Chaophraya River from Wat Phra Kaeo lies the small Wat Arun, or Temple of the Dawn. Here, as in the Wat Phra Kaeo, the brick walls are intricately inlaid with bits of shell, pottery, and porcelain. The various levels of the Wat Arun are supported by rows of columns sculpted in the form of demons.

The two temple complexes, bordering the river with their needlepoint towers glittering in the sun, form one of the most memorable panoramas in the East—or for that matter, in the world.

William Beckford was England's mad builder of towers

William Beckford was but a child when he inherited his father's West Indies plantation, a million pounds, and a sumptuous estate in Wiltshire, England. His guardian saw to it that he obtained the finest education possible. On the Continent, he learned piano from Mozart, and Arabic and Persian from private tutors.

In 1786, at the age of 26, Beckford wrote an Arabian romance called *Vathek* which was greatly admired by Byron, and is still studied in universities today. For some unknown reason, the Englishman Beckford wrote his book in French, *and then hired someone to translate it into English,* the language in which it was first published.

In Beckford's novel, an Arabian sultan named Vathek builds an enormous tower, hoping to fathom the secrets of the universe through a study of astrology. In the 1790's, the sultan's preoccupation in the novel became Beckford's preoccupation in reality. Beckford hired England's greatest architect of the time, James Wyatt, to build him a tower as magnificent as Vathek's.

Beckford was terribly impatient for Fonthill Abbey, as he named the structure, to be completed. He had 500 men working on the job night and day, in two shifts. He pressed the workers so hard that they were compelled to take many structural shortcuts.

In 1800, the 300-foot tower was completed. Beckford prepared to move in. But not one week after the tower was completed, the first mild zephyr broke it in half, and reduced the structure to rubble.

Beckford went to work again, this time determined that his tower would *not* fall. He invested seven years and 273,000 pounds to erect it. For 15 years, Beckford lived in this 300-foot tower, until financial reverses forced him to sell it to a man named John Farquhar. Not long after Farquhar moved in, the tower collapsed in a gale.

Beckford's next and last construction was the maddest of his career. On a hill outside the resort town of Bath, Beckford built a modest tower of 130 feet, and stocked it with dwarfs. By now, the middle-aged Beckford had acquired a considerable aversion to women, which he formalized in stone. He had special niches constructed in the hallways, so that his maids could hide themselves when they heard his approach.

The axolotl resembles a fish with legs

Few creatures, land or sea, are more improbably shaped than a Mexican amphibian known as the axolotl. This exotic lake dweller is unusual in that it permanently retains its larval features—as if it were a tadpole, which, instead of developing into a frog, simply grew into a larger tadpole. As a result, while other amphibians have lost their gills by the time they reach adulthood, most axolotls retain external gills throughout their lives. And a full-grown eight-inch axolotl looks much like a fish with stubby legs!

Cote covered ten miles on snowshoes in a little over an hour

Gerard Cote was an athlete for all seasons. In warm weather, he was a distance runner who had won the famous 26-mile Boston Marathon three times. In winter, he was a snowshoer.

One fine day in 1938, the French Canadian ventured down to Montreal from his home in St. Hyacinthe for the national championships. Wearing standard 10" by 33" snowshoes, the 24-year-old newsboy, who stood only five feet, six inches tall and weighed a mere 130 pounds, clomped over the 10-mile course in 63 minutes and 45 seconds—a record performance.

The piranha is the world's most ferocious fish

In the streams and lakes of the South American tropics lurks a small, harmless-looking fish with a silver- and brown-speckled body—the piranha. But don't let the size of this creature fool you, for the piranha is the most ferocious fish to be found anywhere in the world. A school of these flesh-eaters can strip a man's skeleton clean in a matter of minutes!

The piranha's powerful jaws are lined with teeth as sharp as razor blades. Each tooth is shaped like a small triangle, and a row of them resembles the points of a king's crown. The natives of South America use these knifelike teeth as tips for their arrows.

Armed with these deadly razors, the piranha will not hesitate to attack any creature, no matter how large. One piranha would be troublesome enough, but these treacherous fish always attack their prey in schools of a hundred or more. And no animal of any size can withstand their vicious onslaught.

Strangely enough, piranhas will not bite the feet of cows crossing a stream in which they are swimming. But let a cow scrape its foot on a sharp rock and lose a drop of blood, and the piranhas will descend, ripping into the cow's feet until the poor animal keels over. And once the wounded cow has fallen, it will be only a matter of minutes before the blood-crazed piranhas have torn every bit of flesh from its bones!

The piranha's voracious appetite makes him an easy fish to catch, as he'll go for almost any bait. But if the other piranhas in a school see that one of their brothers has been hooked, they'll strip his bones clean too! A fisherman has to be quick indeed if he wants to find a piranha in one piece on the end of his line.

Lillian Leitzel chinned the bar 27 times with one hand

By profession, Lillian Leitzel was an aerialist. She had performed in a number of circuses, including the famous Ringling Brothers and Barnum & Bailey production. This pint-sized acrobat —only 4 feet, 9 inches tall and weighing 95 pounds—was gifted with a strength that was almost unbelievable.

The record for one-handed chin-ups by a male athlete at the time was held by an Englishman named Cutler, who in 1878 completed 12 one-handed chin-ups. The difficulty of chinning with one hand is well recognized.

So when Lillian came to Hermann's Gym in Philadelphia in 1918 to work out with some acrobats, the gymnasts who were present scoffed at her claim that she could best the world's record for one-handed chin-ups. Lillian was 36 years old at the time.

Responding to the offer of a small, friendly wager to test her boast, Miss Leitzel took to the bar and clicked off 27 right-armed chin-ups in a row. After the pay-off and a short rest, Lillian had one more shock left for the bystanders. She leaped to the bar—this time with her LEFT hand!—and did 19 more one-handed chin-ups—a performance that again broke the male right-hand record.

Some snakes have two heads

Although many kinds of animals are known to have been born with two heads, such freaks are rare. But for some reason, an unusually large number of snakes are born with two complete heads growing out of one body. Many of these snakes also have two tails!

As a rule, both heads are fully developed. In such cases, two heads are definitely no better than one, for they certainly do not make the snake any smarter.

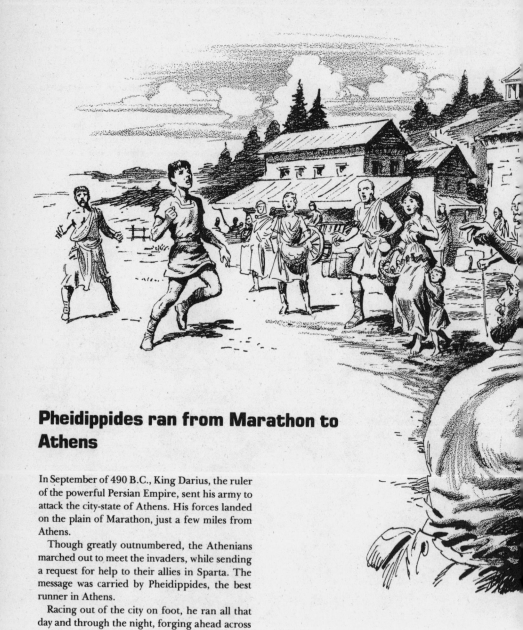

Pheidippides ran from Marathon to Athens

In September of 490 B.C., King Darius, the ruler of the powerful Persian Empire, sent his army to attack the city-state of Athens. His forces landed on the plain of Marathon, just a few miles from Athens.

Though greatly outnumbered, the Athenians marched out to meet the invaders, while sending a request for help to their allies in Sparta. The message was carried by Pheidippides, the best runner in Athens.

Racing out of the city on foot, he ran all that day and through the night, forging ahead across rough, rocky terrain in which the road was often barely suitable for mules and mountain goats. The next morning, having covered a distance of 140 miles, he arrived in Sparta. After delivering his message and getting the answer, he set out to rejoin the Athenian troops, once again covering the distance in a day and a night.

rest up from his magnificent two-way run, Pheidippides participated in the battle as an infantryman.

Contrary to expectations, the Athenians decisively defeated the Persians. Like his fellow soldiers, who had fought so hard against the numerically superior enemy, Pheidippides was exhausted when the fighting came to an end. Nonetheless, he gamely accepted the Athenian commander's request to carry the news of the victory to the anxious inhabitants of the city. Casting off his heavy armor, the exhausted Pheidippides set out on his last and greatest run.

The distance from Marathon to Athens is 22 miles 1,470 yards. Pheidippides covered it in just a few hours, but the ordeal was too much for his already overtaxed system. Shouting, "Victory, victory" with his last breaths, he staggered into the central marketplace of Athens, then dropped to the pavement—dead.

The Athenians never forgot this noble patriotic sacrifice; and in the years that followed, they established a series of memorial games, including running events of various kinds, in memory of Pheidippides. When the Olympic Games were revived in 1896, a road-race called the marathon was made a regular event. In 1924, its distance was standardized at 26 miles 385 yards.

Just a few days later, the Athenian and Persian armies clashed in the now famous battle of Marathon. Though he'd had only a short time to

The Kremlin is the largest fortress in Europe

Today, Moscow's Kremlin is synonymous with the government of the Soviet Union. But the Kremlin is also a construction of extraordinary beauty and size. In fact, this age-old complex is the largest fortress in all Europe.

In medieval Russia, a kremlin was a walled bastion within a city which provided protection for the rulers who resided there, and served as the administrative and religious center of the surrounding district. A kremlin customarily included palaces, churches, barracks, storehouses, and markets, and hence, was a small city in itself.

The kremlin at Moscow, now known simply as the Kremlin, was the seat of the Czarist government until 1712, when the Russian capital was moved to St. Petersburg (now Leningrad). In 1918, after the Bolshevik revolution, the capital was relocated in Moscow, and the Kremlin became the center of administration for the Soviet Union.

This massive city-within-a-city was built in stages over a period of six centuries. The first stone structures were erected in 1365, and the

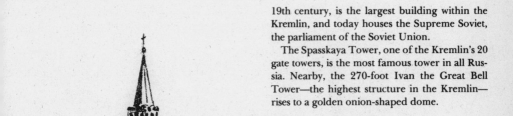

19th century, is the largest building within the Kremlin, and today houses the Supreme Soviet, the parliament of the Soviet Union.

The Spasskaya Tower, one of the Kremlin's 20 gate towers, is the most famous tower in all Russia. Nearby, the 270-foot Ivan the Great Bell Tower—the highest structure in the Kremlin—rises to a golden onion-shaped dome.

Czar Ivan III rebuilt the entire complex a century later. Over the years, the Kremlin has many times survived the destruction of Moscow itself. In 1812, during Napoleon's occupation, the Kremlin alone withstood the inferno that burned almost the entire city to the ground.

The Kremlin is situated on a small hill overlooking the Moscow River. The fortress consists of a complex of varied buildings surrounded by a triangular wall one-and-one-quarter miles around. In all, the Kremlin extends over an area of 90 acres.

Many of the structures that comprise the Kremlin are world-famous in themselves. The Palace of Facets, built by Italian architects in the late 15th century, is a charming milk-white palace noted for the diamond-shaped facets that adorn its facades. The Grand Palace, built in the

The renowned King of Bells, the largest bell in the world, is on display near the Bell Tower. This gigantic instrument, cast in 1733, weighs 216 tons and is over 20 feet high. Twenty-four men were required to swing its clapper. Unfortunately, the bell fell to the ground after only three years of use, and has not been tolled since.

The Kremlin also contains the largest cannon in the world, a gun so huge it has never been fired.

On the eastern side of the Kremlin lies the famed Red Square, the site of the incredibly beautiful cathedral of St. Basil. This ornate church, built in the later 16th century, is remarkable for its multi-colored onion-shaped domes. Another feature of Red Square is the black marble tomb of Lenin.

The "sensitive plant" droops immediately if stimulated

One of the most remarkable examples of a plant's ability to react to external stimuli is the movement exhibited by a plant known as *Mimosa pudica*. So strong are the reactive properties of this species of mimosa that it is commonly termed "the sensitive plant." If you were to perform some simple experiments, you might believe that this plant is capable of experiencing both fright and fatigue!

When flourishing, the long, thin leaves of the sensitive plant extend straight outward from their stem in symmetrical pairs, with the stem itself erect. But when one of the leaves is touched, all the leaves immediately raise themselves vertically and fold over until each pair has joined together near the stem. The stem then bends downward limply. These drooping movements, which take just seconds, give the impression that the entire plant is wilting from fright before your very eyes!

The mimosa will react to strong wind, warmth, vibration, sudden darkness, and other stimuli as well as touch. After a short time in the wilted, closed-up condition, the leaves will begin spreading slowly until they have returned to their normal position. But another touch can send them drooping again.

Curiously, a sensitive plant can be overstimulated. If the plant is touched repeatedly within a short period of time, it will cease to react after a few openings and closings—as if it had become exhausted by its movements! Moreover, in certain temperature ranges the mimosa will not react at all.

These unusual movements are due to small cushion-like bodies, called pulvini, found at the base of the leaf stalks. When the leaves are extended, the pulvini are firm and filled with water. When the plant is stimulated, an electrical impulse is transmitted throughout the plant, and the water quickly passes out of the pulvini and into the stem. The deflated pulvini can no longer buoy up the leaves, and the plant wilts with "fright."

A 20-pound porcupine can kill a 200-pound lion

If you've ever stumbled into a cactus plant, you know what it would be like to trip over a porcupine in the dark. This odd creature has hundreds of treacherous quills protruding from his back, sides, and tail, providing him with one of nature's most unusual—and most successful —defense mechanisms.

Many people erroneously believe that the porcupine shoots his quills like darts. Actually, the quills are very loose and come off at the slightest touch, so that in a fight it may appear that the porcupine is shooting them. Nevertheless, this thorny fellow—who is no bigger than a large tomcat—is capable of killing a beast as huge as a mountain lion!

Ordinarily lions—as well as bears, wolves, and other woodland predators—wisely keep their distance from this walking pincushion. But occasionally a hungry cat will leap on a porcupine.

When attacked, the slow-footed rodent merely turns his back. After one bite the foolhardy cat's mouth is bristling with sharp quills.

The tip of each quill is barbed like a fish hook, and the more the lion struggles to spit out the unwelcome lunch, the deeper the quills sink into the tender lining of his mouth. Swallowing only breaks off the ends of the quills and pierces the membrane of his throat. In a few day the lion, unable to eat, will die of starvation.

There's only one animal clever enough to overcome the porcupine—the fisher, a member of the weasel family. The fisher walks quietly up to the porcupine and, instead of scratching or biting, merely turns the spiny beast over on his back and slits his soft belly with his claws.

The porcupine's own diet consists mostly of the juicy underbark of trees. Occasionally, though, a porcupine will lumber into a campsite

Rollings did 17,000 consecutive sit-ups

Sit-ups are a standard form of exercise used in many calisthenics classes. To do a sit-up, one lies on one's back with hands folded behind the head. The idea is to keep the legs stretched flat on the floor and then to raise the rest of the body up, bending the trunk at the waist until the elbows touch the knees. Generally speaking, 20 or at the most 30 of such sit-ups are all the average man or woman can perform. An individual who has been honed to especially good condition may do 100 sit-ups.

On September 13, 1971, Wayne E. Rollings, a 30-year-old Marine captain stationed at Kaneohe, Hawaii, summoned official witnesses and medical aides to the gymnasium of his military post to authenticate his feat.

Wayne began doing sit-ups, and didn't stop until he had done a total of 17,000, achieving this number in 7 hours 27 minutes.

in search of his favorite dish—salt.

The porcupine's love of salt is nothing short of phenomenal. He will even lick the wood on porch steps if people have walked barefoot on the boards, for there is enough salt in human sweat to send the porcupine into gustatory ecstasy. And if you've wondered why deer antlers are so hard to find in the woods, blame it on the porcupine's passion for salt. The thorny rodents chew the horns up and swallow them for their salty flavor!

The sloth's belly is almost constantly filled

The title of "the laziest animal in the world" must go to a small, tropical American mammal known as the sloth—his very name means "slow"! This sluggish creature spends almost his entire life clinging erect to the trunk of a tree or hanging upside down from a branch. He doesn't make a single move unless it's absolutely necessary!

The sloth is a queer-looking fellow with a rounded head and a grotesque, flattened face. One species of sloth has two toes on his forelegs; another species—also known as the ai—has three toes. Both species have sharp, curved claws for clinging to trees, and both species are equally lazy—but with good reason. For the sloth cannot walk—if he ever moves along the ground he does so by pulling his body along with his claws.

And his belly is almost constantly filled! It may take a sloth more than a week to digest a meal, and in the meantime, he does nothing but hang motionless from a branch.

Despite his sluggishness, the sloth has little to fear from other creatures of the jungle. Suspended from a branch, this little loafer resembles a clump of dead leaves, and during the rainy season he derives additional camouflage from a green alga that grows in his hair. And should some rude creature on the ground below disturb a slumbering sloth, the lazy fellow can investigate the noise-maker with a minimum of effort—due to an unusual arrangement of neck vertabrae, a sloth can turn his head through a 270-degree angle!

Woods disc-jockeyed for more than 11 days nonstop

Tommy Woods was an undergraduate at William Paterson College in Wayne, New Jersey, and also was active as a disc jockey on WPSC, his college's AM station. In December 1972, he came up with a wild idea: to go on the air and stay on longer than anyone ever had.

Woods began his broadcasting marathon at 8 a.m. on Monday, December 11, 1972, alternating hard-rock music with a steady flow of mellifluous DJ patter. Periodically, a registered nurse stopped in at the studio to check out Woods' physical condition. However, despite fatigue, eyestrain, and increasing hoarseness, Woods remained awake and on the job for more than 11 consecutive days.

Before very long, Tomy became a hero on campus and in the surrounding community. An audience of millions who lived outside WPSC's small listening area vividly followed his progress as reported by TV newsmen in nearby New York City.

Finally, at 4 p.m. on December 22, 1972, Tommy Woods played his last record, said a few final, elated words, and signed off. He had been on the air continuously for a total of 272 hours—a world's record.

Theogenes fought and killed 1,425 opponents

In ancient days, the rulers of Greece and Rome would amuse themselves and their subjects through gladiatorial combats in which men fought to the death for the amusement of the spectators. History records that the greatest of these gladiators was a Greek called Theogenes, a native of Thasos.

Theogenes served a cruel prince named Thesus, who reigned about 900 B.C. Thesus delighted in sadistic spectacles and ordained a combat that was especially vicious. The two contestants—if they can be called such—were placed facing each other, almost nose to nose, each on a flat stone. Both men were strapped into place. Their fists were encased in leather thongs which were studded with small, sharp metal spikes. At a given signal, they would strike at each other, and the combat would continue, without rest, until one of the contestants had been beaten to death.

During a long career, Theogenes—strong, skillful and savage—faced 1,425 men and killed every one of them.

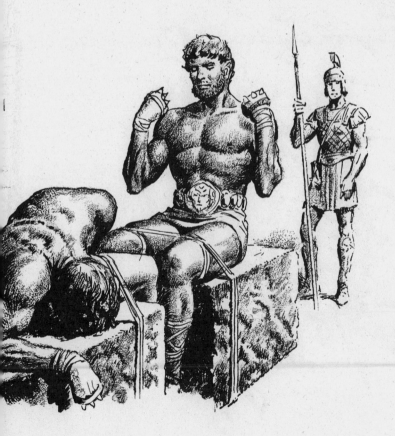

The walking leaf is actually an insect

The Ceylonese insect known as the walking leaf can claim the world's most unusual camouflage. This odd creature so resembles a leaf that its presence in a tree cannot be detected. The insect's body is shaped and colored exactly like a leaf, and streaked with the vein-like markings of a leaf. The legs resemble smaller leaves, and their slightly yellowed edges suggest that bits of leaf have been nibbled away by insects.

When the wind blows the tree in which the walking leaf makes its home, the insect wiggles gently, imitating perfectly the movements of wind-shaken leaves.

LeBel jumped over 17 barrels on skates

The rules of jumping on skates are quite specific: the barrels must measure 16 inches in diameter and be 30 inches wide; the skater must clear the barrels cleanly without touching any one of them. Since the hazard of crashing is great, the barrels are made of a fibrous composition that has some give to it. Nevertheless, failing to jump over a barrel at great speed involves danger to limb and neck. Only those of great courage and confidence essay this sport.

On December 18, 1965, Kenneth LeBel, a native of Lake Placid, New York, and Jacques Favero, a Canadian, met at the Grossinger Hotel in Liberty, New York, to compete in a match which would determine the world's champion barrel jumper. After Favero had catapulted himself over 16 barrels, the 180-pound LeBel circled the rink a couple of times to get up speed. Then he roared down the 200-foot straightway, leaped, and sailed through the air at a speed of 40 miles an hour. LeBel had jumped over 17 barrels, darting through the air for a distance of 28 feet and 8 inches!

The Alhambra is the fairy-tale fortress of Spain

An invitation to choose the most beautifully ornamented building in the world will naturally result in some difference of opinion, but a structure that is sure to top many lists is the exquisite citadel of the Alhambra, in Granada, Spain. This massive, sumptuously adorned complex of halls,

tured Granada. In 1812, the towers of the fortress were blown up by Napoleon's troops, and in 1821, an earthquake heavily damaged the complex. Extensive restoration was undertaken after 1828, and today the 700-year-old Alhambra has regained much of its age-old charm.

The hilltop citadel is so extensive that it would take a visitor more than an hour to walk around the surrounding walls. (It is to these red-brick walls that the citadel owes its name, for "Alhambra" means "the Red" in Arabic.) But it is not size that earns the Alhambra its fame.

The older Moorish section of the complex—the Alcazaba—is a magnificent work of interior design and sculpture. Here, intricate carvings in marble, alabaster, plaster, and glazed tile adorn the walls and ceilings. Palm-like marble pillars and stalactite vaultings form shady arcades; rich mosaics decorate the halls; delicate fountains embellish the many sun-bathed courtyards.

The Palace of the Kings is perhaps the most elegant of the many buildings in the Alhambra. In the center of this palace is the famed Court of Lions, with its alabaster basin supported by white marble beasts. Nearby, in the Hall of Ambassadors—which boasts a 75-foot high dome—water spouts through the mouths of yawning lions. In the Court of Myrtles, a 10,000 square-foot pond glistens with the reflection of nearby Myrtle trees, while underneath glimmering goldfish swim in the clear, still waters.

Through the years, the Alhambra has given birth to many legends, and ghosts are said to roam its quiet halls and courts. These spirits, according to legend, are the souls of the Alhambra's Moorish and Spanish residents, who would not forsake an earthly habitation of such heavenly beauty.

towers, palaces, and courts is perhaps the finest example of the Moorish architecture that once dominated much of North Africa and Spain.

Resting atop a 35-acre plateau overlooking the historic city of Granada, the Alhambra was for many years the home of the Moorish kings, serving as palace, fortress, and administrative headquarters for their Spanish empire. Built chiefly between 1230 and 1354, the Alhambra remained the last bulwark of Islam in Europe until Granada fell to the Spaniards in 1492.

During its tempestuous history the Alhambra has survived many calamities. The Spaniards destroyed much of the citadel when they recap-

Bamboo is the world's largest grass plant

Can you imagine grass growing to the height of a 10-story building? Well, bamboo, whose woody, pole-like blades are sometimes used as crude fishing poles, belongs to the same plant family as the grass on your front lawn. And some species of bamboo grow in tufts to a height of 100 feet!

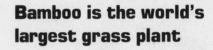

The growth rate of most bamboo plants is unbelievably rapid. The Molocca bamboo, for instance, can grow two feet in just 24 hours! But while the blades of the bamboo grow prodigiously, the growth of its flower is extremely slow—some bamboo plants do not flower until they are about 20 years old.

Of course, bamboo has many uses throughout the world in addition to fishing poles. The blades provide paper, fuel, and construction material for homes, furniture, utensils, plumbing pipes, and ship masts. And anyone who has ever dined in a Chinese restaurant is familiar with that Oriental delicacy, the pickled bamboo shoot.

Houdini stayed underwater in a sealed coffin an hour and a half

No locks, no chains, no manacles could hold Harry Houdini, the greatest escape artist of all time. Born as Erich Weiss in 1874, this boy from Appleton, Wisconsin, did not take long to make headlines.

His handcuff act became so famous that he was invited to "escape" from London's Scotland Yard. Superintendent Melville, chief of this, the most famous police force in the world, placed Houdini's arms around a pillar and then hand-cuffed him. Before Melville was out of the building, Houdini had freed himself and caught up to the chief!

Houdini could open any lock in the world in a few minutes. Once, on a tour through Europe, the continent's most famous locksmiths pre-sented him with what they considered foolproof locks, the result of countless years of work. Houdini opened the locks so astonishingly fast that the master mechanics hardly knew what was happening.

During his European tour, Houdini escaped from jails in the cities of Liverpool, Amsterdam, Moscow, and The Hague. He duplicated these feats in almost every large city in the United States. The plain fact was that Houdini could enter or leave virtually any room, building, or cell at will.

His repertoire of escape acts fascinated mil-lions all over the world. So uncanny were his performances that many believed Houdini pos-sessed supernatural powers. Though Houdini vociferously denied being gifted with anything more than human attributes, his performances were so baffling that even his stout denials failed to squelch the talk. No one could fathom just how his stunts were accomplished; and it was not until after his death that his notebooks revealed how he contrived to do things which seemed beyond the powers of mortals.

One of his favorite stunts was to have himself bound by the police in a straitjacket used for the violently insane. No one, the police averred, could break out of this. But, in addition to the straitjacket, Harry had the police load him with iron shackles and ropes. Houdini was turned up-side down, and hauled aloft in mid-air by means of a block and pulley. Then, in full sight of an astounded audience and an absolutely dumb-founded police detail, the incredible man would wriggle free.

How did he do it?

Houdini was one of the greatest athletes that ever lived. From his early youth on, he had prac-ticed body control. He could flex virtually every muscle in his body. His fingers had the strength of pliers; and his teeth were so strong that they could be used like a can opener. His strength was so great that he could bend iron bars, and his tactile sensibility so fantastic that while blind-folded he could tell the exact number of tooth-picks he was kneeling on.

Still, how did Houdini get out of that strait-jacket? Answer: He contracted his muscles in such a way that he could slip one hand out of its bonds. By similar contractions and maneuver-ings, he would set his limbs free. Then the great locksmith would free himself from his iron fet-ters.

Houdini left explicit directions as to just how the stunt could be accomplished, but so far no athlete has come along with enough physical dexterity to perform the feat.

Unsurpassed as a magician, Houdini displayed courage and daring equally unmatched. In the days when the airplane was still a new and un-proved machine, Houdini jumped from one air-plane to another—3,000 feet above the earth—*while handcuffed!*

On August 26, 1907, Houdini leaped off a bridge in San Francisco Bay with his hands tied behind his back and 75 pounds of ball and chain attached to his body. He came up out of the water unharmed.

On another occasion, Houdini was thrown into the East River in New York City, handcuf-fed inside a box to which 200 pounds of iron had been attached. But what were handcuffs, irons, and a river to Harry? He emerged within two minutes.

And then, on August 5, 1926, as if to cap all his former feats, he allowed himself to be sealed in a coffin which was then lowered into the waters of a swimming pool. Before a whole deputation of doctors and newsmen, he remained in the coffin under water *a full hour and a half!*

Immediately upon emerging, he was examined by physicians who all agreed that he had suffered no ill effects. Houdini contended that it was panic, not lack of air, which usually caused suffocation. His own muscle control was so phenomenal that he may have accomplished this stunt by means of suspended animation.

Yet despite the fact that the physicians gave Houdini a clean bill of health on August 5, 1926, the great magician and athlete did not live to see 1927.

277

The Astrodome was the first enclosed arena in which outdoor sports can be played

Upon its completion in 1965, the Harris County Sports Stadium in Houston, Texas—better known as the Astrodome—could lay claim to a number of impressive superlatives: the largest indoor arena in the world, roofed by the largest dome ever constructed, and the only sports stadium in the world that did not contain a single blade of grass.

The Astrodome is truly a landmark of modern engineering and a harbinger of things to come. The stadium sprawls over nine-and-one-half acres and can seat 66,000 spectators. The surface of the field is covered with "Astroturf," a synthetic grass specially designed for the stadium. A scoreboard 474 feet long and four stories high features a 10,000-light screen that can show messages, shorts, cartoons, and anything else that can be put on film. But without doubt, the most revolutionary feature of the $20 million structure is the massive dome.

Constructed of transparent plastic panels supported by a steel lattice, the dome measures 710 feet in diameter and rises to the height of 208 feet over the playing field. The dome of the Pantheon in Rome—the largest dome of the ancient world—had only *4 percent* of the surface area of the Houston dome.

The dome also provides for year-round fair weather inside the stadium. An air-conditioning system circulates 6,600 tons of air *each minute*, and keeps the temperature inside the stadium at a constant 74 degrees. If on a humid day the air conditioning were turned off, an entrance of warmer air could cause it to rain in the stadium!

The mammoth dome has resulted in some unexpected problems for players in the stadium. During the first few baseball games played on the new field, players complained that balls hit high into the air could not be seen against the backdrop of the dome. After a number of embarrassing muffs of fly balls by hometown players, the plastic panels of the dome were painted over to provide for better vision.

And, during a baseball game in the 1974 season, Philadelphia's Mike Schmidt did what had been considered impossible—he hit a ball against a public-address speaker affixed to the roof, 329 feet from the plate and 117 feet above the field. The would-be tape-measure however dropped in center field and Schmidt was held to a single.

In 1971, a domed stadium with a retractable panel overhead was completed in Irving, Texas, and the massive "Superdome" in New Orleans was ready a few years later. Undoubtedly, most of the sports stadiums built in the future will be domed—following the footsteps of the original, the Houston Astrodome.

The squid throws up a smokescreen

The cuttlefish, or squid, has a singular way of
escaping from its enemies. When closely pressed,
the squid shoots out a cloud of black sepia. Leaving its enemy in the dark, the clever cuttlefish
then makes its getaway.

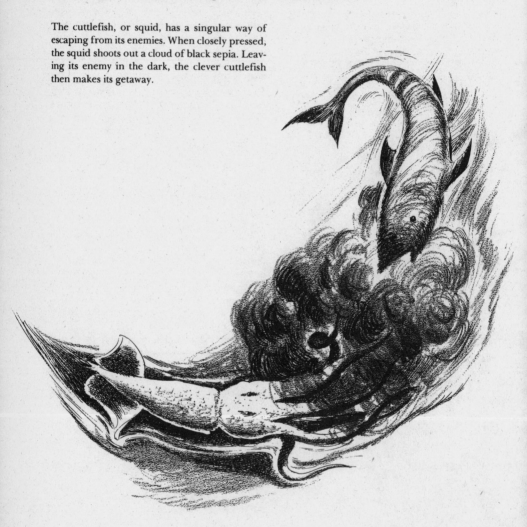

The Shayad Tower symbolizes modern Iran

In 1971, Iran—which describes itself as the world's oldest monarchy—celebrated the 2,500th anniversary of the first Persian Empire. Heads of state from around the world came to view the gala celebration staged near Persepolis by Shah Mohammed Reza Pahlavi, the reigning monarch since 1941. And in Teheran, the capital city, construction began on a striking new monumental tower, the Shayad, to commemorate the anniversary.

The Shayad Tower was completed in 1972, and stands today as the gateway to bustling Teheran. The bold design of the tower combines both modern and traditional forms, symbolizing the illustrious past and the promising future of this oil-rich nation.

Yielding walked on stilts 22 feet high

He grew up in Great Yarmouth, England, among a family of circus performers, and he grew up dabbling in all sorts of circus stunts. After years of practice, Harry Yielding became expert on those awkward high-rise contraptions called stilts.

During the early 1900's, Yielding performed dressed as a clown, and how the crowd did roar when they saw him walking along on stilts 22 feet high—just about two stories above the ground.

The cheetah is the fastest animal on earth

The swiftest man cannot run much faster than twenty-five miles an hour. The greyhound, fleetest of dogs, dashes at forty miles an hour. Racehorses can run from forty-five to fifty an hour, and the graceful antelope can leap along the ground at close to sixty. But no animal can keep pace with the most astonishing of all the world's runners—the magnificent jungle cat known as the cheetah.

Of all the great cats, the cheetah is the sleekest and most graceful. The golden coat of this Asian and African speed demon is covered with black spots smaller than those of the leopard, and his legs are longer and thinner than the legs of the lion or tiger. When hunting an antelope, this fleet fellow can sprint at the phenomenal speed of *seventy miles an hour!* Once the cheetah decides to give chase, there is no animal that can escape him.

Morris skipped rope 22,806 times in two hours

Thomas Morris had a strange mode of locomotion. He got a great kick out of skipping rope, and once he traveled from Melbourne to Adelaide and back, a distance of 1,000 miles, skipping rope all the way.

On November 21, 1937, Morris began skipping before a timer in Sydney, Australia. Morris wanted to make some sort of an official test as to his prowess and speed. He set off at a rate of 200 beats a minute, better than three skips every single second. The pace was so grueling that his audience was stunned into silence. After one hour had passed, it was recorded that Morris had completed 12,000 skips. Since he was still fresh, he decided to go on for another hour, and without missing a beat, he continued. At the finish, his timers were as worn out as he was. For they had tallied an astonishing 22,806 skips. If each skip were accounted as the step of an average man, Thomas Morris, in those two hours, would have walked about 12 miles!

The Colossi of Memnon were statues that sang

In the 15th century B.C., the Egyptian king Amenhotep III erected a funeral temple near the city of Thebes, with two colossal stone statues guarding the entrance. In the following centuries, Egyptians were startled to hear, at each dawning, mysterious musical sounds emanating from one of the colossi!

The Greeks, equally baffled by the harp-like noises, named the 60-foot statues after the demigod Memnon. The daily song, they believed, was the voice of Memnon greeting his mother Eos, the goddess of dawn.

After an earthquake damaged the two colossi, the Roman Emperor Septimius Severus had the statues repaired. But when the restoration was completed, the strange cries of Memnon ceased forever, as mysteriously as they had begun (although visitors today sometimes claim to hear eerie sounds emanating from the statues). Today the funeral temple is gone and the colossi stand on the desert alone—and silent.

The explanation for the strange cries? The rapid change in temperature as the desert sun rises at dawn produces strong air currents. These currents probably resounded through the loose joints of the colossus before Severus repaired it. The acoustic principles responsible for the curious sounds are similar to those of an organ pipe—making the statues the most oddly shaped organ pipes in history!

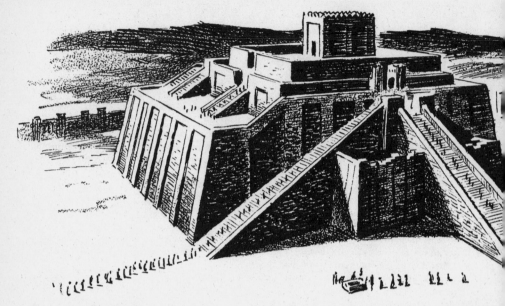

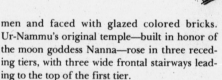

The Ziggurat was the emblem of a great ancient culture

The ziggurat form was in common use for pyramidal temples in the ancient kingdoms of Sumer, Babylonia, and Assyria. At one time, hundreds of these huge structures—often called step pyramids—stood in the various kingdoms of Mesopotamia (now Iraq). The Biblical story of the Tower of Babel relates one attempt to build such a temple, although ziggurats were never as high as the tale suggests.

In ancient times, the most widely known of these structures was the Great Ziggurat at Ur. The city of Ur was the capital of the Sumerian culture and was, the Bible says, the home of Abraham. Under the reign of King Ur-Nammu (c. 2060 B.C.), Ur became the most important city in Mesopotamia, populous and wealthy, an important trading center on the Euphrates River. In the middle of the city, Ur-Nammu built a high terraced ziggurat as the city's chief temple.

This imposing structure, towering above the low mud-brick houses of Ur, was built of sun-baked bricks set in a kind of mortar called bitu-

men and faced with glazed colored bricks. Ur-Nammu's original temple—built in honor of the moon goddess Nanna—rose in three receding tiers, with three wide frontal stairways leading to the top of the first tier.

Despite the angular appearance of the Ziggurat, there was not one straight line in the entire structure. The ancient Sumerians understood the technique of entasis, whereby supposedly straight lines were curved slightly so that a wall or pillar would appear straight when viewed from the ground.

It was the Babylonian king Nebuchadnezzar who made the Ziggurat at Ur the greatest ziggurat of the ancient world. After the Babylonians had captured the city, Nebuchadnezzar ordered that the Ziggurat be rebuilt. Where Ur-Nammu had built a pyramid of three tiers, Nebuchadnezzar built a seven-tiered tower. Each

Nebuchadnezzar and a subsequent king, Nabonidus, more than doubled the height of Ur-Nammu's Ziggurat. At 160 feet, it became one of the highest structures in all Mesopotamia. The base itself—210 feet by 150 feet—was 40 feet high. At the top of the last tier, a couch and table were left for the moon goddess to use on her visits to earth.

The city of Ur was destroyed many times by conquerors and eventually abandoned. For thousands of years, the Great Ziggurat lay crumbling and covered with sand in the midst of a barren desert. During this century, however, the ruins of Ur were unearthed. The sandy rubble that the archaeologists found can hardly suggest the size and majesty of the ziggurat, the greatest structure of a great civilization.

of the steps in the three frontal stairways was relaid bearing the name of this great king. A series of stairs and passages rising from the first tier gave the impression that a staircase wound around the tower in spiral fashion. Indeed, one could ascend to the apex via a spiral route, but a multitude of other paths were possible.

Tamerlane built pyramids from the skulls of his victims

In 1336, an obscure tribal chieftain, living near the Central Asian city of Samarkand, celebrated the birth of a son. The Mongol chieftain named his baby Timur. Later, when Timur was crippled by an arrow, he received his nickname, Timur-i-Leng, or Timur the Lame. To the Western world, he is more familiar as Tamerlane.

Making Samarkand his capital, Tamerlane set out on a decades-long campaign to subjugate the world to his rule. He created an empire that stretched from the Ganges River in India to the very gates of Europe. Much of present-day Russia, including Moscow, was incorporated into his domains.

Merciless to his enemies, Tamerlane ravaged huge areas, reduced great cities to rubble, and slaughtered hundreds of thousands. Indeed, he left cruel testimonials to his victories by building great pyramids from the skulls of his victims—70,000 at Isfahan, 90,000 in Baghdad, and 100,000 at Delhi. At Sebsewar in Persia, the merciless monarch enclosed 2,000 live people inside a brick and mortar tomb.

The mongoose can kill the dreaded cobra

The deadly poisonous cobra strikes fear into the hearts of men and animals alike. And no wonder, for this snake's venom can kill a grown man within minutes. But there is one creature who'll never shrink from the cobra—the mongoose, an animal so plucky that he does not hesitate to attack this killer snake, four times larger than himself.

The mongoose, a native of India, is only about thirty inches long, with a sharp, pointed snout, short legs, tiny ears, and a tail as long as his body.

A bright, friendly creature, the mongoose makes an excellent pet, and has been used throughout the world to combat rats. But it is in battle with the cobra that the mongoose earns his medal for bravery.

When a mongoose encounters a cobra, both become so tense that the air seems electrified. The huge cobra coils into a tense spring, and two flaps under its head puff out like a hood. Slowly the killer sways from side to side, its thin black tongue darting nervously in and out of its mouth.

In front of the cobra stands the mongoose, his short legs tense and his back arched like a spitting cat's. Every hair in his rough coat stands erect. Inching forward, he follows every movement of the cobra. One bite from those sharp fangs means instant death. Both animals seem to move together, their noses only a few inches apart.

Suddenly the snake strikes! The mongoose leaps backward at lightning speed, untouched. The cobra strikes again, and again the mongoose is quick enough to dodge him. The cobra lunges angrily, but time after time the clever little mongoose escapes his thrust, holding his ground and waiting for the cobra to tire.

When the snake begins to slow, the mongoose gets ready for his own attack. He waits for the moment when the cobra does not withdraw its head quickly enough from one of its thrusts, then leaps forward and sinks his teeth into the back of the cobra's head.

Now the cobra's fangs are useless, for the mongoose has its head in an unshakable grip. The snake thrashes about madly, trying to coil its long body around the mongoose, but the furry creature keeps his jaws tightly clamped and hangs on. Not until the last breath has left the body of the cobra does the mongoose open his jaws for a well-earned rest. After the kill the mongoose will eat the entire snake, including the poison glands.

Some mongooses were considered sacred in ancient Egypt, and were often mummified. Before the introduction of domesticated cats, the mongoose was used to control rodents. One species, the Indian mongoose, was introduced into Jamaica and Martinique to combat viper infestation. The mongooses succeeded in controlling the snakes, but soon began preying on poultry. Eventually they became subject to vigorous control measures themselves.

Calverley's 55-foot basketball shot tied a major tournament game

In basketball, it's size that counts. That's why oddsmakers made the five giants from Bowling Green a 12-point favorite over little Rhode Island State on March 14, 1946, in the opening game of the National Invitation Tournament in New York City. A record 18,548 fans crowded the old 49th Street Madison Square Garden. Standing five-foot-ten, Ernie Calverley of underdog Rhode Island jumped against the six-foot-eleven Don Otten of the Ohioans at the tipoff.

Rhode Island State surprised, and the game was close all the way. On 13 occasions, the score was tied. Then, with 3:20 minutes left on the clock, the Ohioans lost Otten on fouls. But Bowling Green still had the height to control the game. With only ten seconds remaining, Bowling Green held onto a 74-72 lead. As the tension mounted, Rhode Island moved the ball down the court. In order to stop the advance, a Bowling Green player barged in and risked a one-shot foul—a pretty smart maneuver, for under the rules in effect at the time, if Rhode Island chose to shoot the foul, they would lose the game even if their player had sunk his foul shot. Time would just run out.

parabola and descended cleanly through the mesh, not even touching the rim. Calverley had tied the game, and the Garden broke loose in pandemonium!

After that, in the overtime, Bowling Green, still in the throes of shock, was no match for the little Rams, who won by a final score of 82 to 79.

Opinions differ as to the exact point from which Calverley let fly. The ball zoomed at least 50 feet—no one disputes that. However, some observers estimated the distance at 65 feet. A Garden official close to the scene claimed that he recalled the exact point from which the ball took off, and the officials measured it at 55 feet. But wherever it was, Ernie had certainly made the most famous basketball shot in history.

So Rhode Island elected to waive the foul shot, and took possession of the ball. Only three seconds were left now to move the ball the full length of the court, and make a basket. It was a practical impossibility. The Bowling Green players tightened their web around the Rhode Islanders. Somehow, Calverley broke loose. He was well behind the mid-court line when a teammate threw the ball to him. Almost without pause, Calverley let fly for the basket—a target which seemed miles away. Here was a desperation shot if there ever was one. But Ernie's long-distance two-hander executed a perfect

The stonefish has poisonous fins

The stonefish gets its name from the hideous wartlike texture of its skin, which looks as if it were studded with small pebbles. In fact, the stonefish can easily be mistaken for a pile of stones, for it spends most of its time almost motionless on the bottom of the tropical ocean, or lounging amid the coral and rocks. But pity the creature that disturbs this ugly sluggard! The stonefish's dorsal fin contains a venom gland, and through a groove in this fin the stonefish can shoot a deadly poison—sometimes powerful enough to kill a man!

Johnny Eck walked on his hands

Johnny Eck did not walk on his hands as a stunt; that was the only way he could get around, for he was born without a body below the waist. Johnny's arms were longer than his body, and so powerful that he could stand on one hand easily. He did have two feet, but they were malformed and useless.

Eck made his living in the circus, where he was bluntly called The Half Man. But Johnny lived a whole life; he was an excellent pianist and saxophonist who for a time had his own orchestra. He was also a first-rate actor, as he revealed in the films *Freaks* and *Tarzan*.

A fungus looks like an egg-filled nest

Botanists in the seventeenth century were fascinated by a strange fungal growth that strongly resembles a small bird's nest with a clutch of tiny eggs. This fungus, *Cyathus striatus,* was thought by some to actually contain eggs. Others believed the egglike lumps inside the cup of the plant were seeds. Still others claimed to have seen these lumps give birth to live birds!

Of course, none of these claims were true. The spongy lumps within the acorn-sized cups are actually spore sacs, filled with thousands of tiny spores. The plant's resemblance to a bird's nest appears to be completely incidental. The fungus derives no benefit from its inadvertent mimicry.

Annie Taylor rode over Niagara Falls in a barrel

She was a childless, widowed, 43-year-old schoolteacher from Bay City, Michigan, and for the task at hand, her credentials were rather bland. For a first-time adventurer, her stakes were high.

On October 24, 1901, she would go over the 160-foot-high Horseshoe Falls in a barrel. Where others had failed, Annie Edson Taylor was willing to gamble. As it was, her life was going nowhere; if she succeeded, fame and fortune would follow.

On that big day, she made her entrance in a long black dress and fluttering hat. Only just before getting into her barrel would she change into a short skirt. For one thing she was prudish; for another, she weighed 160 pounds.

At Grass Island, Annie was lowered into the oak cask. From there, a rowboat took her out to where the currents would carry her to the Falls. Of course, it was no ordinary barrel. Bound by seven iron hoops, it was four and one-half feet high, four feet in diameter, and it weighed 160 pounds. A hundred pound anvil was tied to its bottom as an anchor, to keep the barrel upright when it floated.

The cheering throngs that gathered along the Niagara gave Annie the attention she craved. "Au revoir," she told them majestically, as she was turned loose. "I'll not say goodbye because I'm coming back."

As the barrel was picked up by the strong current, the throng fell silent and wondered.

The barrel bobbed and flipped, and then it splashed over the break. For Annie, strapped inside, there could be no strategy other than to use her strong muscles to brace herself. Luckily, when the barrel hit bottom, it bounced away from the Falls, and her aides fished her out. It wasn't until later that they learned she couldn't swim!

For Annie, there was immediate fame; but sadly, no fortune. Brokenhearted, she again became an unknown, but never again an adventurer.

Stonehenge is an age-old enigma

One of the world's simplest, yet most astounding structures—Stonehenge—lies in eerie solitude on the marshy Salisbury Plain of Southwestern England. This remarkable construction of massive stones, built by an unknown people thousands of years ago, has been a puzzle to archaeologists and historians for centuries.

Although many of the stones have now fallen to earth, we know that the original arrangement of ditches, holes, and rock constructions was basically a series of concentric rings. A circular ditch 300 feet in diameter forms the outermost ring. Moving in toward the center, the next ring consists of 56 circular holes filled in with earth. These "Aubrey holes," so-called after the British antiquarian who studied Stonehenge—are each six feet wide and four feet deep. Within this ring are two circles comprised of smaller filled-in-holes, known as the Y and the Z holes.

The third ring is a circle of large Sarsen stones, each about 13½ feet high, arranged in post-and-lintel (upright-and-crossbeam) forma-tions. The innermost ring is a circle of upright Bluestones, without lintels.

Within this Bluestone ring, we find a horseshoe of five hugh trilithons: massive stones as much as 24 feet high, with lintels across the top of the upright post stones. Each trilithon weighs over 30 tons! The horseshoe surrounds an ovoid formation of Bluestones, which is in turn wrapped around the center "altar" stone.

The amount of work required of a prehistoric people just to place the huge lintels atop the stone posts is staggering. But these hard rocks were not only hoisted; they were first smoothed with hammers. Incredibly, some of the rocks in Stonehenge came from quarries which were as far away as 30 miles! But the actual distance that the stones were carried was nearly twice that fig-

ure. Archaeologists have shown that the Blue-stones must have been transported from the Prescelly Mountains in Wales, and that the simplest route must have covered at least 240 miles over land and water. Even with the use of rafts and rollers, this is a mind-boggling feat.

The heavier Sarsen stones were apparently brought from Marlborough Downs, about 20 miles distant from Stonehenge. This job would have required the work of 800 men.

The construction of the inner rings of Stonehenge is thought to have taken about seven years. The entire structure required an estimated total of 1.5 million man-hours of labor!

Why these prehistoric men worked so hard to construct this curious monolith remains a mystery. For centuries, it was thought that the structure was used as a pagan temple, for cremated bones were found in the Aubrey holes. But early in this century, the proposition was advanced that Stonehenge was constructed as a sort of seasonal clock, its main axis pointing directly toward the rising sun on midsummer day (June 24).

Each of the five post-and-lintel trilithons in the horseshoe frames the position of the sunset or sunrise on a key day. The Stonehenge structure could have been used by the ancient builders as a primitive alarm clock, advising when to plant and when to harvest. Calculations have shown that the risings and settings of the sun, as seen through the openings in the trilithons, are remarkably precise.

The electric ray shocks its prey

The queer-looking, circular-shaped fish called the electric ray has a most unusual method of catching its dinner. This soft-skinned creature is equipped with two muscular organs, one on each side of its head, which are capable of giving off strong electrical impulses. The ray captures its prey by "butting" the victim with these organs and thereby stunning or killing it with an electrical shock.

The ray also uses its electric organs to fight off enemies. Any creature that tangles with one of these deepwater fish is in for a rude shock, for the current produced by a large electric ray is powerful enough to kill a man!

Philippe Petit walked a tightrope 110 stories high in the air

Early one morning in August, 1974, the skyline of lower Manhattan was altered in a small but stunning way: the twin towers of the World Trade Center, second tallest buildings in the world, were linked by a one-inch steel cable—and perched on that cable was a fellow named Philippe Petit. For 45 minutes, this 25-year-old French acrobat and juggler thrilled thousands of Manhattanites as he danced in mid-air at the dizzying height of 1,350 feet.

When Philippe grew bored with life at the top, he put his feet down on firmer terra and was promptly arrested for disorderly conduct. To police and newsmen, Petit made it clear that his conduct was, for him, the very model of order. In fact, his high-wire antics 110 stories up were the culmination of 10 years' study and practice.

At the age of 15, Philippe quit school and joined the Omankowsky acrobatic troupe in the Loire Valley. In 1971, he became a celebrity in France by walking a high wire strung between the towers of Notre Dame cathedral. Shortly thereafter, he traveled to Sydney, Australia, and traversed a cable from one pylon of the giant Harbour Bridge to the other.

Petit's boldest venture required six months' study of the World Trade Center. He rented an apartment in New York and, with the help of friends, "cased the joint." Often, he and his friends had to don hard hats or pose as French architectural reporters to mask their real purpose. At last, in August 1974, they hid in one tower overnight and, with a crossbow, shot their cable across to the other tower. The next morning, Petit took his stratospheric stroll.

A reporter asked Petit the inevitable question: why did he do it? "I see three oranges," Petit responded, "I have to juggle. I see two towers, I have to walk."

Madame Regnier, though able to, did not talk for 30 years

Here is a cautionary tale for henpecked husbands. After reading about Madame Regnier, you may have second thoughts about telling your wife to button her lip.

Madame Regnier lived comfortably in Versailles as the wife of a French Royal Procurator, or crown attorney. One fine day in 1842, she was prattling about something or other when her husband admonished her, "Be silent, woman, you talk nonsense."

Madame Regnier stormed out of the room in a huff. For days afterward, she would not speak to her husband—nor to anyone else. At last, Monsieur Regnier went to his wife's chamber and abjectly apologized. His wife looked at him impassively, and said not a word.

Days stretched into weeks, and weeks into years, while Madame Regnier continued to hold her tongue. Even when her daughter came to ask for permission to marry, Madame Regnier only nodded her assent.

From that day in 1842 to her death 30 years later, Madame Regnier never uttered a sound.

The Pentagon is the world's largest office building

Not long before America's entry into World War II, General B.B. Sommervell proposed the construction of a building to house all the agencies of the U.S. War Department. While many people viewed his proposal as an unnecessary extrava-gance for a nation that might soon become embroiled in a world war, others felt that this contingency was precisely the reason why the erection of centralized offices was imperative.

The latter view prevailed, and construction of

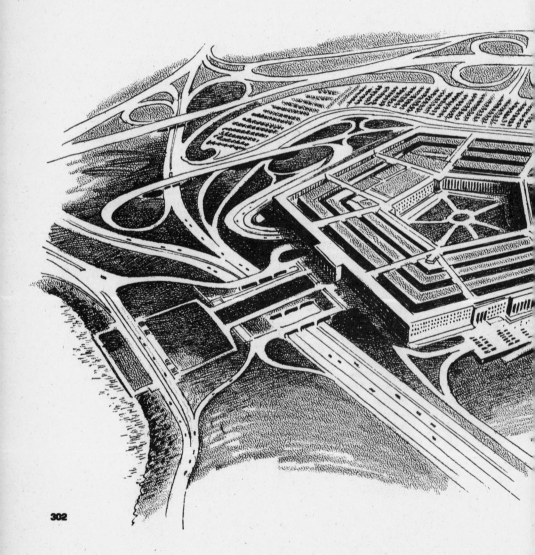

the building began in September 1941, on a 34-acre site across the Potomac River from Washington, D.C. More than 13,000 workers were employed on the giant project; 6 million cubic yards of earth were moved; 41,492 pillars were sunk into the marshy earth; 410,000 cubic yards of concrete were poured; and 680,000 tons of sand and gravel were dredged from the bot-

tom of the Potomac. War Department workers began moving into the building even before it was completed in January 1943.

Today, this building—known familiarly as the Pentagon—is synonymous with American military might, and stands as the largest office building in the world. Its total floor area could fill a square whose sides were *one-half mile*. The building consists of five concentric pentagons connected by ten "spokes." The outermost pentagon extends 921 feet on each of its five sides. The innermost pentagon encloses a large open courtyard. Paved courts and roads for delivery vehicles separate the other rings. The ingenious design of the building assures that, despite its size, no two offices are more than 1,800 feet—or six minutes walking time—apart from each other.

The Pentagon is truly a city in itself. Five stories plus a mezzanine and basement comprise a total area of 6½ million square feet, *three times* the floor area of the Empire State Building. Thirty miles of roads and interchanges girdle the site, while 17½ miles of corridors thread through the gigantic complex. Each day, the Pentagon houses more than 30,000 Defense Department workers.

Like any small city, the Pentagon has its Main Street. The long corridor known as the Concourse is lined with shops and showrooms of every kind, from shoeshine parlors and barber shops to airline agencies, a bus depot, and a post office. The two restaurants, six cafeterias, and ten snack bars alone employ a staff of 700.

The Pentagon's total cost of $83 million was considered astronomical at the time of its construction. Yet today, the rental of office space of an equal size would cost the government more than $20 million per day!

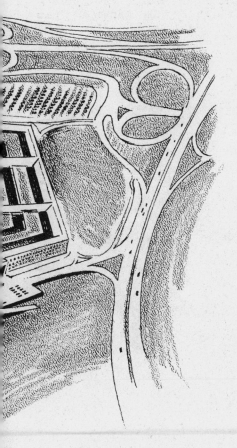

Mildred Didrikson Zaharias was a champion in track, golf, and baseball

In 1950, the Associated Press polled its sports writers and sportscasters to choose the greatest female athlete of the first half of the 20th century. The Associated Press people selected "Babe" Didrikson Zaharias (nee Mildred Didrikson). It was an easy choice, for the Babe from Beaumont, Texas, was generally considered to be the greatest woman athlete who ever lived.

The Babe first came into national prominence as a basketball player. During her teens, she was nominated on All-America teams for three straight years, though she stood merely a shade over five feet tall. In one of her games, she scored over 100 points.

In 1932, Mildred entered the Amateur Athletic Union national track championships as a one-woman track team representing the Employers Casualty Company of Dallas. Other competing teams consisted of 10 to 22 members. Yet on that weekend in Chicago, the 18-year-old Babe entered eight events and scored points in seven. She won five outright, setting three world records in the process. Before the close of 1932, the 105-pound girl added two Olympic titles to her collection of medals, winning the javelin throw and the hurdles.

In baseball, Mildred toured the country with a professional barnstorming team—a team composed only of men; and she played only against men. But the Babe could throw a ball almost 300 feet on a straight line.

As the Babe grew older, she found her favorite sport in golf. During her career, she won more than 50 major tournaments. She once ran up a streak of 17 tournament victories. With the help of a wind, she once drove a ball 346 yards!

In 1954, after undergoing an operation for cancer, Mildred Zaharias won her third National Open. Had her brilliant career not been cut short by the dread killer, Mrs. Zaharias, who passed away in 1956 at the age of 43, would have undoubtedly added still more laurels.

A 35-pound peccary will take on a lynx—or even a locomotive

The peccary, an odd-looking, piglike mammal whose habitat ranges from the southwestern United States to Brazil, looks like a curious cross among half a dozen animals. The peccary's head and body resemble a boar's; his flat nose looks like the end of an elephant's trunk. He has a scent gland like the skunk, runs on legs as delicate as a deer's, and has sharp, two-inch tusks in

both his upper and lower jaws. But don't sidle up for a closer look—this queer fellow is one of the most dangerous fighters in the animal kingdom!

The peccary seldom measures more than forty inches in length and averages about thirty-five pounds, although in the tropics he may weigh as much as seventy pounds. Don't let this porcine character's size fool you, though. Those tusks can rip through flesh as if it were tissue paper.

And where there's one peccary, there are usually a few dozen more. Against a combined peccary assault few animals have a fighting chance.

What makes the peccary even more dangerous is his unparalleled courage. This animal apparently never shows fear! Without batting an eye he will attack anything from a German shepherd to a jaguar. Peccaries have even been known to attack a railroad train!

The leaves of the compass plant point north and south

If you're ever lost in the country, a compass plant could come in handy. This North American herb, also known as rosinweed, orients its leaves to the points of the compass. The leaf surfaces almost always point towards the rising or setting sun—that is, east or west—with the surfaces exactly parellel to the sun's rays at midday. Thus, the ends of the leaves usually point due north or south as dependably as the needle of a compass!

Hall scored three goals in three and one half minutes of soccer

Soccer is a low-scoring game—especially in international matches. Generally, a score will run two goals or three goals a game, rarely as many as six. So the nonpareil outburst by a British stalwart, G.W. Hall, must rank among the greatest soccer feats of all time.

On November 16, 1938, England stunned its arch-rival Ireland in a one-sided contest that ended 7-0. What was remarkable was that three of those goals were scored by one player in the space of three and a half minutes. Never in major competition has any soccer player tallied in such a rat-a-tat fashion.

With England leading 1-0 in the first half, 40,000 witnesses at the Old Trafford stadium in Manchester saw London's inside-right turn the trick. Hall scored his initial tally set up in front of the goal-mouth by his brilliant team-mate, Stanley Matthews. Moments after the ensuing kick-

his back turned to the goalie.

And Willie scored still once more when the redoubtable Matthews, dribbling past two men, flicked a pass which Hall converted. That made five for Willie for the afternoon.

off, Hall scored again—this time on a low corner shot from inside left. When the ball was put back in play, the Irish goalie was determined to stop the barrage. Charged with more enthusiasm than wisdom, he ventured out too far after Hall, and the net was an easy target. Hall tallied again, and the crowd went wild!

But Hall wasn't through. Ten minutes after the intermission, the Britisher connected again with a fine spinning shot that he hooked in with

The chimpanzee can be taught sign language

Chimpanzees are undoubtedly the most intelligent non-human creatures in the world. It has long been known that any normally bright chimp can be taught to use simple tools such as the brush, cup, spoon, and hammer, and to mimic many human gestures. But recent experiments have shown that this remarkable ape has a learning potential far greater than had been previously supposed. Some chimps have even been taught to use forms of language!

In one experiment, a young chimp was taught a sign language with which he communicated with his trainer. This chimp was able not only to learn the correct signs for forty different subjects, but to grasp and use language concepts such as the adjective, verb, and adverb as well!

Another experiment showed that a chimpanzee can construct "sentences" once he learns a number of words. A chimp taught the correlation between certain words and a set of marked tokens was able to place these tokens in such an order as to make a statement expressing what the chimp felt, even though these "sentences" were usually as simple as: "me want banana now please."

And still another experiment demonstrated that these smartest of all nonhumans could be taught to use money. Chimps learned that by placing a certain chip in a slot machine they could obtain grapes from the machine. It didn't take these clever creatures long before they began working for their chips, hoarding them—even fighting over them!

Spitz won seven Olympic gold medals in swimming

When Mark Spitz arrived in Munich, West Germany for the 1972 Olympic Games, the whole world was watching him. The dark, handsome, powerfully built Spitz had already established himself as the most outstanding swimmer of modern times. He had been swimming since early childhood, and set his first U.S. record in 1960—which still stands—in a 50-yard butterfly competition for nine- and ten-year olds.

Spitz, who lives in Carmichael, California, had won two gold medals at the 1968 Olympic Games in Mexico City, and at various times had broken 28 world freestyle and butterfly records. In 1971 alone, he had won four national and two collegiate championships in the United States, and had set seven world and two U.S. records.

For the 1972 Olympics, Spitz was entered in four individual competitions and three relay events. He had a chance to win seven gold medals, two more than anyone had ever won at a single session of the Olympic Games.

All the spectators at Munich's 9,000-seat Schwimhalle were aware of this record-shattering possibility as Spitz leapt into the pool for his first test, the 200-meter butterfly, on the afternoon of August 28, 1972. Spitz reached the finish line first, beating the world record which he himself had set several weeks before at the U.S. Olympic Trials in Chicago.

A few hours later, as a member of the winning U.S. team in the 400-meter freestyle relay, Spitz won his second gold medal. The next evening, finishing first in the 200-meter freestyle, he won his third.

Spitz won two more medals on September 1: the 100-meter butterfly, in which he set a new world record, and the 800-meter freestyle relay, in which he anchored the winning U.S. team. On September 3, by winning the 100-meter freestyle, Spitz became the first Olympic athlete ever to garner so many gold medals at one Olympiad.

Finally, on September 4, swimming the butterfly leg for the U.S. team in the 400-meter medley relay, the 22-year-old Spitz won his seventh medal.

At Chichen Itza, thousands of victims were hurled to their death

In the centuries preceding Columbus's voyage to the New World, the Maya Indians developed a highly advanced civilization centering in the Yucatan Peninsula of Mexico. One of their greatest cities was Chichen Itza, "the city of the Itzas at the mouth of the wells." First settled by the Mayas in 514, this city was once the home of close to 100,000 people, and the mecca of Mayan pilgrims throughout Central America.

Chichen Itza was abandoned in the 15th century and subsequently overgrown with jungle. But from these ruins modern man has been able to learn much about not only Mayan architecture, but the customs of these ancient people as well.

While all wooden and earthen structures in Chichen Itza had disintegrated long before this century, the stone buildings remain almost intact. These massive white-stone constructions are

ornamented with heavy decorative sculpture —with the feathered serpent as the most prominent motif—and enclose dark, cramped interiors.

Among the most striking structures of the ancient city is the Caracol, a round stone tower 41 feet high which probably served as an astronomical observatory, for the Mayas were skilled astronomers. A large stadium and game courts are located near the center of the city. Nearby is the Temple of a Thousand Columns, which gets its name from the rows of stone columns that surround the building.

Yet the most interesting by far of all Chichen Itza's monumental structures is the sacrificial complex leading to the deep well from which the city gets its name. The Mayas built their city beside two such wells: one was used to draw water for irrigation and drinking; the second—called the Cenote—was considered sacred, the home of the rain god Yum-Chac. Into the depth of this sacred well the Mayas hurled precious artifacts and, often, human sacrifices.

Near the Temple of a Thousand Columns, a tall step pyramid rises 100 feet in nine tiers, topped with a small stone shrine. In this shrine

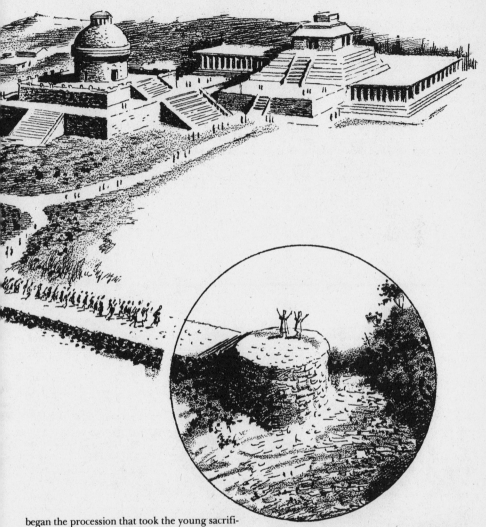

began the procession that took the young sacrificial victims to the well of the rain god. Ninety steps lead down one side of the pyramid to a quarter-mile stone causeway.

The solemn procession followed this causeway to a small altar at the edge of the 60-foot well. There, the victims were plunged down into a 60-foot ravine to appease the bloodthirsty Yum-Chac. At the bottom of the ravine lay the well, whose murky waters were sixty feet deep and over 150 feet wide.

The walls of the ravine are too steep to have allowed the victims, had they survived the plummet into the well, to escape the clutches of the rain god. However, these victims were usually so laden with jade and metal that it is unlikely any of them survived the 60-foot plunge or the waters below. When the sacred well was dredged earlier in this century, many precious objects were discovered among the bones in the thick silt below the waters.

Knievel, on a motorcycle, jumped over 20 automobiles

From the mountains of Butte, Montana, came Robert Craig Knievel, daredevil stunt rider, who, to dramatize his billing, chose the nickname of "Evel." And Knievel certainly had an eye for the dramatic.

On May 30, 1967, at the Ascot Speedway in Gardena, California, Evel Knievel gunned his Triumph motorcycle and jumped off a ramp at a speed of 80 miles an hour. That allowed him to clear 16 automobiles standing in a row.

To prove the stunt was no fluke, Knievel attempted 16 cars again—four more times, to be exact. Twice he made it. The other two times proved how dangerous the feat is: once he broke his lower spine, the other time he suffered a brain concussion.

This type of daredeviltry earned the 29-year-old Montanan about $100,000 in 1967. Now Knievel planned a bigger spectacular. The ornamental fountains at *Caesar's Palace,* one of the largest hostelries and casinos of Las Vegas, had been advertised as the largest privately owned fountains in the world. On New Year's Day, 1968, Knievel set forth to scale these waterspouts.

A ramp was especially built for him. He took off at 100 miles an hour and catapulted his 198-pound body to a height of 30 feet. He was definitely over the fountains with a leap of 150 feet. But evil pursued Knievel, and as his Triumph motorcycle hit the descending ramp at

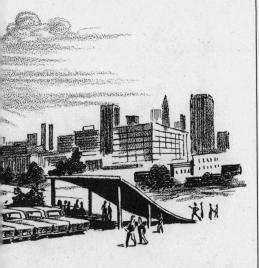

a speed of 70 miles an hour, the front wheel went askew, and Knievel lost control. He sped along over the neighboring asphalt parking lot for 165 feet, and then wound up in the hospital.

Was Evel daunted? Not so that anybody could make out. Four years later, he cleared 20 cars!

A pigeon can find its home from fifteen hundred miles away

The homing instinct of the carrier pigeon is so strongly developed that these birds can fly more than a thousand miles over unfamiliar territory and never fail to find their way home.

A pigeon's training begins at the age of three months. Released by its keeper a short distance from home, the young bird quickly flies back to its dovecote. The distance is gradually increased until the pigeon is able to return from more than 1,500 miles away to the spot where it was bred.

Messages placed in a metal container can be attached to the foot of the bird. Unless the homing pigeon, a small target indeed, is shot as it wings its way through the air, there is little chance of intercepting the message it carries.

Priscilla Lauther was known as the Monkey Girl

On a rainy, windswept night in 1929, Carl Lauther was about to close up his tent show for lack of customers. Just as he went to turn out the lights, a drenched, shabbily dressed couple walked up to him. The woman carried a bundle in her arms. She threw back the folds of the blanket to reveal an incredible sight—a baby girl covered from head to foot with silky black hair.

The couple knew that their child was "different," and thought that since Lauther was a circus showman, he might be interested in taking her. Lauther immediately recognized the gold mine that this infant represented, and gladly took the girl from her relieved parents. Lauther and his wife named the child Priscilla, and legally adopted her.

Priscilla grew to be a healthy, well-developed teenager and the star attraction of the Lauther's show. She played with her pet chimpanzees before the crowds, and was billed as "The Monkey Girl Who Lives with Apes." Apart from the hair which covered her body, Priscilla's only physical problem was that she had two sets of teeth, one row behind the other.

In 1946, when Priscilla was 17, a wealthy woman offered to pay for all of Priscilla's dental needs. In exchange, the woman asked only one thing: she wanted to crossbreed one of her pet apes with Priscilla!

At this point, an unusual "knight in shining armor" arrived on the scene—a young circus performer whose skin affliction caused him to be labeled "The Alligator Boy." He and Priscilla married, and performed together as "The World's Strangest Couple," which they surely were.

This incredible marriage brought crowds streaming to the carnival. With the new-found profits, Priscilla's parents could easily afford the dental operations she required. These were successful, and The Monkey Woman and The Alligator Boy lived, as far as anybody knows, happily thereafter.

The kangaroo rat never drinks water

The kangaroo rat, a tiny desert rodent, is in no way related to its much larger namesake, the kangaroo. In fact, in nature the two creatures have never laid eyes on each other—the three-inch kangaroo rat makes his home in the arid southwestern United States, while his seven-foot marsupial mammal can be found only in Australia. The only connection between the two is

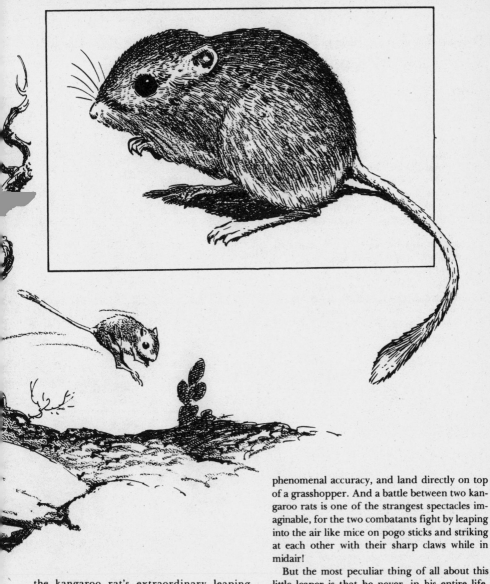

the kangaroo rat's extraordinary leaping abilities.

This remarkable rodent has proportionately the same long, powerful legs as the kangaroo, and the same strong tail that the animal can use to sit on. Catapulting up from the ground like a popping watch spring, the kangaroo rat can jump right over a man's outstretched hand, with

phenomenal accuracy, and land directly on top of a grasshopper. And a battle between two kangaroo rats is one of the strangest spectacles imaginable, for the two combatants fight by leaping into the air like mice on pogo sticks and striking at each other with their sharp claws while in midair!

But the most peculiar thing of all about this little leaper is that he never, in his entire life, takes a drink of water—or any other liquid, for that matter. Living in the dry, hot deserts of the Southwest, where water is scarce, the frisky little fellow gets moisture from prairie roots and herbs. These plants, no juicier than the vegetables you eat at dinner, provide all the liquid the kangaroo rat needs.

One termite queen can produce half a billion children

Termites, like ants and bees, live together in large colonies. Some species of this wood-eating insect build their homes belowground, while others construct massive nests aboveground, using wood, leaves, and a sticky substance from their mouths. Such steeple-shaped nests can rise as high as twenty feet! But there is one thing that all termite colonies have in common—there is only one queen.

Termite queens are easily the longest-lived insect specimens in the world—some survive for more than fifty years. And a healthy queen can produce over thirty thousand eggs in one day. That means that over the course of her lifetime, a queen termite could conceivably give birth to about a *half a billion* children!

The Temple at Madura is ornamented with 30 million idols

According to legend, the Hindu temple of Siva at Madura, India, is adorned with *30 million* intricately molded idols. This figure may indeed

In the 16th and 17th centuries, the city of Madura was the capital of a large Hindu kingdom. In this city, King Tirumula began the construction of a massive walled temple complex. But Tirumula's temple was not to be one of delicate grace and beauty to honor a glorious and benign Hindu deity. Instead, the temple at Madura was a shrine to Siva, the Destroyer, and depicted the god in all his grotesque forms.

The walls of this nightmarish temple are over 1,000 feet long on each side and surround a maze of courts, halls, and colonnades. Ten pyramid-like gate towers rise to the height of a 20-story building, and each is completely covered with tier upon tier of densely jumbled idols. These images—molded of plaster, painted in garish hues of red and green, and coated with rancid butter—depict gods and goddesses and demons and monsters of all shapes and forms.

Simply to count all the idols on the towers and walls at Madura would take years. The task of molding and painting them must surely have required decades of work by countless sculptors.

be an exaggeration, but even if there are "only" 1 million idols, Madura would still be one of the most elaborately ornamented temples in the world.

Georges Clemenceau slept fully dressed

Georges Clemenceau (1841-1929) was known as "The Tiger" for his passionate concern with the welfare of France. He was twice his nation's premier, the second time rallying the dispirited French to victory in World War I.

Clemenceau had the peculiar habit of going to bed each night in a full dress suit: trousers, waistcoat, coat, and even gloves! The only concessions to comfort he allowed were the exchange of his starched shirt for an unstarched one, and the wearing of slippers instead of street shoes.

Clemenceau slept in this manner his whole life; but in his final days, he was thwarted in his intention of meeting his Maker fully prepared. In a half-conscious state, he could offer no resistance to the doctors who removed his formal clothes.

One ferret can rid a farm of rats

You probably know that the expression *ferret out* means *search out* or *dig out*. But did you realize that the words originally had a more limited meaning: to use a ferret to flush another animal from hiding? For until the use of modern rodent poisons became widespread, farmers depended on the ferret—a white, cat-sized relative of the weasel—to rid their fields of destructive pests. And this furry creature is so well suited to the task you'd think nature placed him on earth to do nothing but help the harried farmer!

The ferret has a slender, silky body just perfect for crawling down into narrow ratholes, and a pair of pink eyes that can see in almost total darkness. Ferrets are trained and kept in cages on the farm, and when a field begins to get a bit overcrowded with vermin, the walking rat trap is brought to the rescue.

The farmer stuffs a ferret into his pocket and goes in search of ratholes. When he finds one, he places the ferret before it and gives the little fellow a shove. Like a tiger stalking its prey in the

underbrush, the ferret crawls through the dark underground passages until he finds the rat, and then snarls savagely.

The animals swipe at each other with their claws, but the rat soon learns that he is no match for his ferocious adversary. The rodent flees towards daylight, but the relentless ferret is right on his tail. No sooner does the terror-stricken rat emerge from the hole than his attacker leaps and sinks his teeth into the rodent's throat.

By systematically attending to all the holes and rock crevices in his field with these white wonders, a farmer can, well, ferret out all his rat enemies—and all he has to do himself is sit on the ground and wait!

Knox bowled a perfect game without seeing the pins

Bowling a perfect game, though admittedly rare, is not an unheard-of feat. Most every top professional has bowled a perfect game at one time or other during his career. But nobody has ever equaled the feat of Bill Knox, who in 1933 knocked down the tenpins 12 times in a row without ever seeing them.

Knox had a special screen built at the Olney Alleys of Philadelphia and instructed two pin boys to hold the screen about one foot above the foul line. The screen would hide the pins from the sight of the bowler and would even block off the sight of the lane itself. But the fans sitting in the stands could see over the top of the screen. Knox's purpose was to show bowlers the effectiveness of "spot" bowling—choosing a point on which to lay down the ball.

His control was so unbelievable that the sphere was in the perfect groove 12 times out of 12. Bill Knox had bowled a perfect game without ever seeing his target.

Cardinal Mezzofanti learned 114 languages

Joseph Caspar of Bologna, Italy, had very little schooling. At an early age, he was apprenticed to a carpenter. While working in the shop one day in the mid-1780's, he heard a priest next door giving lessons in Greek and Latin to some students. Though he was not even in the class, and had never seen a book in either language, the young carpenter proved to be the best pupil. In a short while, he was able to speak both languages fluently.

The would-be carpenter later became priest and eventually earned the title of Cardinal Mezzofanti. He spent most of his life studying languages, learning to speak at least 53 languages with considerable fluency. He spoke 61 additional tongues not quite so well, and understood 72 more dialects, although he could not speak them.

The only language to provide Cardinal Mezzofanti any difficulty at all was Chinese, which took the master linguist all of four months to learn!

How much does one have to travel to learn languages? Cardinal Mezzofanti never once left Italy in his whole life!

King Otto of Bavaria shot a peasant a day

Here's the life of another King Otto (see page 184), this time a real one from Bavaria. Otto gained the crown in 1886, but he was hardly fit to rule his subjects. For the previous 14 years, his raving lunacy had forced his family to keep him in a locked room. This constraint did not seem to bother Otto too much, because it did allow him the privacy necessary for his conferences with the spirits who lived in his dresser drawers.

One of Otto's more peculiar notions was that if he shot a peasant a day, he could keep the doctor away. The Mad King was enabled to gratify this whim by the compliance of two loyal guards. One guard would daily load Otto's gun with blanks, while the other would don peasant garb and hide in the bushes outside the King's window. When Otto would appear at the window with pistol poised, the "peasant" would emerge from his hiding place and amiably drop dead at the sound of the shot.

The mystery of the stone faces on Easter Island is still unsolved

On Easter Day, 1722, the Dutch explorer Jakob Roggeven chanced upon a small, remote island in the South Pacific, almost 2,500 miles from the coast of South America. There he found—amid the craters of extinct volcanoes and a small tribe of stone-age people—a collection of mysterious faces gazing stoically towards the ocean. Even today archaeologists have not solved all the puzzles posed by the immense monoliths of Easter Island.

The massive heads are set against the gentle slopes of the island's volcanic ridges. Imbedded deep in the soil, the almost identical heads rise from 10 to 40 feet above the ground, and many are estimated to weigh close to 50 tons! In all, over 600 statues dot the island, forming a strange gallery of somber faces on many of the island's slopes.

The figures were carved of tufa, a soft volcanic stone that was quarried in the center of one of the island's volcanoes—Rano Raraku. When explorers discovered the deserted quarry, they

found close to 150 additional statues that had never been moved to their intended places on the hillside. These figures, in various stages of completion, and the tools that still lay scattered about the quarry, gave evidence that the work on the monoliths had been interrupted quite suddenly and had never been resumed.

The more archaeologists investigated the island, the more they were startled by their discoveries. Bones and ash were found buried in the earth at the foot of the statues. Flat red rocks that lay beside many of the monoliths were shown to be "hats" or "topknots" that at one time rested on top of the heads. And when archaeologists began digging deeper in the soil around the faces, they discovered that the unknown sculptors had carved not merely faces but also full-bodied figures, many of which were now imbedded 30 feet in the ground!

How were the massive stones carried distances of up to 10 miles from the Rano Raraku quarry without losing their smoothly polished finish? How were the gigantic "topknots" hoisted atop the heads without pulleys? How did the bodies come to be so deeply imbedded in the earth? How long ago were the statues carved, and by whom, and for what reason? Why was the work halted so abruptly? All these are questions that decades of research and debate have not answered definitively.

Bees mistake the bee orchid flower for other bees

Most flowers produce nectar to lure insects to the reproductive parts of the plant, and thereby enlist the insect's aid in pollination. But some plants lack nectar. Nature has devised rather ingenious ways of attracting bees and other insects to these flowers. One of the most striking is that of the bee orchid, *Orchis apifera*.

The *Orchis* genus contains about 750 species of American and Caribbean orchid, most of which grow on or among other flowering plants. Since these other plants are most likely to be nectar producers, bees will be constantly flitting about in the vicinity of the orchid. How does the bee orchid lure bees from the nectar-secreting flowers to its own? Remarkable as it may seem, the bee orchid produces flowers that look just like bees!

Each bee orchid flower has three brightly colored petals, from the center of which protrudes a fuzzy, multi-colored growth that greatly resembles a particular large bee. This imitated insect is, in fact, an enemy of the pollinating bees found in the bee orchid's habitat. A male bee flying near the orchid mistakes the fuzzy growth for the enemy bee. It strikes at the plant in an effort to drive the invader from its territory. While striking at the flower the bee picks up and deposits pollen, thereby pollinating the orchid!

Fanny Blankers-Koen won four Olympic gold medals

When Fanny Blankers-Koen stepped up to the starting line at Wembley Stadium in London during the 1948 Olympics, few in the stands would guess that this attractive blonde was a housewife and the mother of two young children. When the gun blasted off, the trim Hollander dashed to the forefront, and stayed there until she reached the tape—the winner in the 100-meter dash in 11.9 seconds.

Mrs. Blankers-Koen then proceeded to carry off the honors in the 200-meter dash, covering the distance in 24.4 seconds.

In negotiating the 80-meter hurdles, she established an Olympic record of 11.2 seconds.

And to top off her performance, Fanny led the 400-meter relay team from the Netherlands to a first-place victory. The Dutch housewife had carted off four gold medals within a week's time—an Olympic record.

But there is more to be said. Unfortunately, the Olympic rules limited the blonde streak to entering three individual events. At a time when Fanny Blankers-Koen held the world's record in both the broad jump and the high jump, had she been allowed to compete in these events, it is safe to say that she would have done fairly well.

Flying fish use their fins as wings

There are at least sixty-five kinds of "flying fish" found in the oceans of the world—and none are capable of true flight. But these versatile creatures can glide for a considerable distance above the surface of the water, putting on one of nature's most unusual aerial shows.

The flying fish's tail furnishes the driving force required for takeoff. The one-foot long creature skims along the surface of the water, whipping its tail back and forth to generate speed. When the fish has developed sufficient takeoff speed, it suddenly spreads its pectoral

Daisy Ashford wrote a best-selling novel as a child

In 1909, Daisy Ashford won renown throughout the English-speaking world with her novel *The Young Visiters*. An uproariously funny book, *The Young Visiters* scored an immediate success and topped the 200,000 mark in sales.

Miss Ashford's characters were favorably compared with those of Charles Dickens. Her deft portrait of late Victorian society provides incisive social comment on the foibles of the period. But what really makes Miss Ashford so incredible is that she wrote this novel when she was only nine years old. Despite this early literary triumph, Daisy Ashford never wrote another book!

fins as if they were wings and soars into the air. Once in flight, the fish can bank and maneuver just like an airplane!

The flying fish's average flight lasts only a few seconds, but flights as long as twelve to fourteen seconds have been reported. These graceful creatures shoot out of the water at speeds of up to forty miles an hour, and can glide through the air for distances of up to six hundred feet and more!

Their performances take place at night as well as during the daytime. After dark, many are attracted by lights on ships and—like some birds and insects—fly toward the illumination. Flying

fish have been known to crash into a ship's side, land on deck, or even soar through an open porthole!

A foot-long sea hedgehog can kill a 20-foot shark

The sea hedgehog owes its name to the unusual composition of its skin. Like its landlubber cousin's, the sea hedgehog's fur is studded with sharp quills. Thanks to these quills, this sea creature, which measures less than a foot in length, is capable of killing a relatively huge enemy, the shark!

The sea hedgehog is often attacked and swallowed by sharks. Once it is in the belly of the shark, though, the sea hedgehog inflates its prickly body as if it were a balloon. The spearlike points penetrate the stomach of the shark and rip a hole through the monster's body. The sea hedgehog then calmly swims through the gap, leaving a fatally-wounded shark behind.

The Gateway Arch is the world's tallest monument

In the early 1960's, a massive construction project was undertaken in St. Louis, Missouri, to reconstruct much of the city's downtown area —particularly the Mississippi riverfront. The new structures in the restored area included a 51,000-seat sports stadium and the imposing Gateway Arch. Upon its completion in 1965, the Arch became the tallest monument in the world.

The Arch was built to commemorate the westward expansion of the United States after the Louisiana Purchase of 1803, and especially the important role St. Louis played in that expansion as the gateway to the West. The towering, graceful structure—designed by the noted architect Eero Saarinen—spans 630 feet along the Mississippi riverfront. The height of the arch is also 630 feet, which makes the monument as tall as a *60-story building!*

The vivid sight of the sun's rays glistening on the shining steel is visible from miles away. And each year thousands of visitors ride in 40-passenger cars that take them to the top of the colossal arch for a breathtaking view of surrounding Missouri and Illinois.

Though initially the arch met with some opposition from the citizenry at large, it has now come to be regarded as one of the finest achievements in modern architecture.

Beatty entered an arena that contained 50 lions and tigers

The greatest animal trainer who ever lived was just 5 feet, 5 inches tall. Until his death in 1965, Clyde Beatty was considered to be without peer results. Time and again, Beatty was clawed and he bore the scars from over 100 maulings by wild cats, some of which weighed over 500 pounds.

in the handling of wild beasts. He would enter a cage armed only with a .38-caliber pistol that could hardly kill a flea. His weapon was loaded only with blanks which he used at times simply to scare his charges.

During a long career, the curly-headed Midwesterner faced thousands and thousands of lions, tigers, leopards, bears, ocelots and jaguars. Of course, this exposure yielded its untoward

Beatty's routine called for him to spend about a quarter of an hour locked up in a cage with anywhere from 12 to 24 lions and tigers. But on one occasion, he undertook to handle 50 of the big cats. Nobody, either before or since, has ever essayed such a feat. But Beatty was really a master.

Holding a whip in one hand and a chair in the other, he kept all the animals in their places.

Using the crack of his whip, low whispers, blank shots from his pistol, and even screams, he kept this full menagerie of roaring, snarling beasts under control.

The feat is all the more remarkable when it is realized that it is virtually impossible for a man to keep 50 caged lions and tigers within the range of his peripheral vision. Clyde solved this problem by keeping his chair tilted toward the direction where he wasn't looking, while the animals

in the range of his glare felt the constant threat of being whipped. Whenever a lion threatened to lunge at Beatty, he froze stark still, stared the animal down, and held up his chair for protection. With his other hand, he threatened with his whip.

However, before the day was over, even the unusually game Clyde Beatty admitted that 50 animals on a rampage at one time would have been even too much for him to manage.

He never tried it again.

Seeds of an arctic shrub bloomed after 10,000 years

For how long can a seed retain its generative capability? No one knows for sure, but it seems that under the right conditions a seed's potentiality for producing a new plant is almost eternal. For example, seeds of a sacred lotus plant, found in a peat deposit in Manchuria, where estimated by carbon dating to be about 1,400 years old. Nevertheless, when punctured and watered, the seeds rapidly germinated and produced plants!

If that seems incredible, consider this: in 1967, seeds of an arctic tundra shrub, *Lupinus arcticus*, were found in a frozen lemming burrow with animal remains established to be at least *10,000 years old!* When placed in conditions favorable to growth, the seeds germinated within 48 hours. There is no reason to believe that this remarkable generative power is the sole property of the arctic shrub.

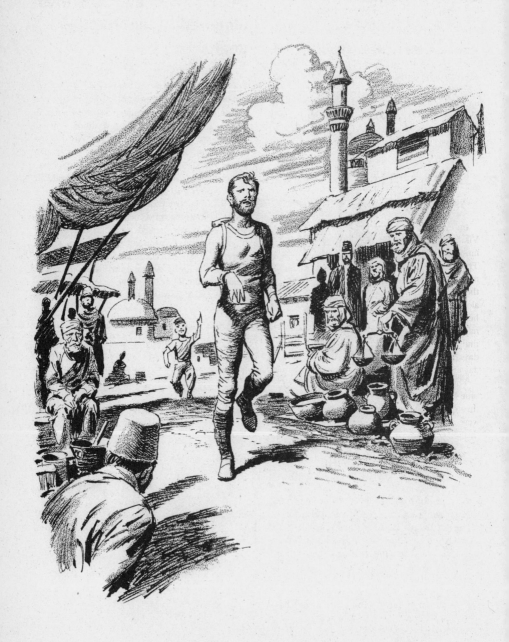

332

Ernst walked from Constantinople to Calcutta and back in 59 days

Mensen Ernst grew up in the heart of Norway's fjord country. Though he earned his living as a sailor, he made his fame as a landlubber. He traversed Europe, Asia, and Africa on foot in unbelievable record time.

Little jaunts like a march from Paris to Moscow, or a hike from Germany to Greece, were nothing for this Norwegian. He took those kinds of walks in stride, so to speak.

In 1836, when he was 37 years old, the sturdy Viking took off from Constantinople (now Istanbul) and headed for Calcutta in eastern India. The two cities were 2,800 miles apart. The trip meant crossing mountains, rivers, badlands, and the deserts of the Middle East. Ernst trekked along for almost 100 miles each day; and when he reached Calcutta he hardly took time off for a nap, but did an about-face to return to Constantinople. He completed his two-way trip in 59 days, and over-all average of four miles an hour day and night, counting sleeping hours, too.

This was a 5,589-mile hike accomplished at a time when many roads were not paved, and through areas where in some localities there were no roads at all. No man has ever equaled this walking achievement.

Grass of Parnassus fools flies with fake nectar

All that glistens is not gold, and in the plant world all glistening, sweet-smelling liquid is not nectar—as flies soon discover during their visits to a grass of Parnassus plant. This floral faker, known also as Parnassia, has "decoy" nectaries which dupe flies into fertilizing its flower.

In most plants of the Parnassia genus, approximately five sterile stamens alternate with an equal number of fertile stamens. The sterile decoys each bear a button-like gland which secretes a fluid resembling nectar. Flies are attracted to the glistening, scented droplets of this liquid only to discover they've been fooled in their search for nectar.

But there is a reward for the insect visitors after all. Real nectar collects in depressions on the upper surface of the petals, near the center of the flower. Once attracted to the plant by the glistening buttons, the flies continue into the flower for their reward. On their way they brush against the sex organs, and fertilize the plant.

The tern migrates halfway around the globe

The Arctic tern leads a strange life indeed, spending three months of each year in the Arctic regions, three months in the Antarctic—and almost six months in the air! For this small gull-like bird flies one of the longest migratory journeys made by any creature.

The tern summers in the Arctic, then heads south in the fall. Traveling at a leisurely thirty to thirty-five miles an hour, stopping to rest and eat on the ocean and on land, the tern meanders southward for three months. After a trip that may total eleven thousand miles, the well-traveled fellow at last reaches the neighborhood of the South Pole.

But when spring arrives, the tern is off again on another eleven thousand-mile journey back to his Arctic home. This remarkable bird thus flies a round trip covering as much as 22,000 miles—and he repeats his feat each year!

The Strasbourg Cathedral contains the most elaborate clock ever built

Visitors to Strasbourg, France will marvel at the gothic splendor of the city's main cathedral, whose 466-foot tower is the tallest medieval tower still standing in Europe. But the modern visitor is likely to be most intrigued by a more recent addition to the age-old cathedral: an astronomic clock that may well be the most elaborate timepiece ever constructed.

The Strasbourg Cathedral, completed in 1439, has displayed an astronomic clock since 1352. But the ingenious device that now stands in the cathedral is the work of Jean-Baptiste Schwilgué, who completed his clock in 1842. This intricate structural masterpiece is run by hundreds of hidden gears, and the various dials and figurines on the outside of the clock form a small mechanical circus, with performances every fifteen minutes.

Near the top of the timepiece, the four ages of man are represented by figures of an infant, adolescent, warrior, and old man. Every quarter hour, each figure in turn takes two steps forward. rings a bell, and then disappears. About the quartet, figures of the 12 apostles appear through a small doorway. A mechanical cock greets the arrival of the apostles by raising its head, bristling its plumage, opening its beak, and crowing three times. Two angels swing their hammers against bells, adding to the confusion of chimes and moving figures.

Below the angles, seven figures—representing the seven days of the week and the seven inner planets—revolve in a ring, with one figure visible each day. The clock also boasts an angel with a working hourglass, a figure of Christ, a revolving celestial globe, a figure of death who rings a bell with a bone, and sculptured panels depicting Copernicus, Uranis (the goddess of astronomy), the Resurrection, the Creation, and Schwilgué himself.

The clock faces illustrate three distinct methods of time-keeping: standard time, in

hours and minutes; apparent time, indicated by the sunrise and sunset, the phases of the moon, the coming of eclipses, and other movements of the sun and moon; and sidereal time, governed by the movement of the stars through the signs of the zodiac. Together, the various time-telling devices comprise not only one of the most intricate and amusing clocks in the world, but also one of the most accurate.

The squirting cucumber can propel its seeds up to 40 feet

The squirting lapel flower is an old practical joke, but there are many specimens of the plant kingdom that do indeed squirt liquid—some with great force. Among these is the squirting cucumber, a Mediterranean plant that depends upon the propulsion of fruit juice for the dispersal of its seeds.

The seeds of the squirting cucumber are contained in an oval fruit about one and a half inches long. When the fruit is ripe the inner tissue forms a liquid, in which the seeds float. The "cucumber" swells with liquid to the bursting point, then explodes and propels the juice and seed mixture through a small hole punched in the end of the fruit. The explosion is powerful enough to propel the seeds as far as 40 feet from the plant!

Brown beat six professional fighters on the same night

Most boxers prefer their fights just one at a time, with weeks of rest and training periods in between.

But consider the case of Preston Brown of Philadelphia's Broadway Athletic Club. One night in 1913, he announced that he would take on all comers, and no fewer than six ring-wise professionals arose from the ranks.

Every one of the challengers was bigger than Brown. Nonetheless the plucky 125-pounder took them on—one by one—and he walloped them all. He knocked out five of the six—in early rounds, no less. The sixth challenger lost on a decision.

Ewry won ten Olympic gold medals

When he was a child growing up in Lafayette, Indiana, Ray Ewry's legs were as wobbly as spaghetti: a case of polio had weakened his limbs. Ray's physician suggested that the lad strengthen his legs through constant jumping exercises.

Ewry followed this advice—and he did so, so perseveringly and so unstintingly, that he actually developed what were perhaps the strongest set of legs in history. In the 1890's, Ewry went to Purdue University where he captained the track team. After he graduated, Ewry earned a place on the United States Olympic team. He was then 26 years old.

On July 16, 1900, in Paris, Ewry won three

Olympic gold medals: the standing long jump, the standing high jump, and the standing hop, step and jump—all of which required a stationary start. In the standing high jump Ewry cleared 5 feet, 5 inches, nearly six inches better than his closest competitor.

In the 1904 Olympics, the lanky 6-foot, 3-inch athlete repeated his masterful performance. In 1906 (when a special Olympics was held), and in 1908, Ewry collected medals again for the standing long and high jumps. During a nine-year span, Ray collected 10 Olympic gold medals—no mean accomplishment when it is considered that no athlete, before or since, has won more than seven firsts in Olympic track and field events.

All European and North American eels are born—and die—in the same place

There are hundreds of species of eel to be found in the streams and rivers of Europe and North America, but all of these snakelike fish have one remarkable thing in common: They were all spawned in the same part of the ocean!

The Sargasso Sea is a large, relatively calm area of the North Atlantic noted for the dense seaweed that covers its waters. Once a year millions of eels leave their freshwater homes and swim to the Sargasso Sea, where they lay their eggs—and die. Ocean currents carry the newborn, tadpole-like eels to the continental shelves off Europe and North America to mature. The following spring, millions of eels form a dense mass, miles long, in many rivers and streams as they swim inland.

Some of these elongated fish will live as long as fifteen years in fresh water before returning to the Sargasso Sea to spawn and die. Thus, aside from those eels that are killed by man or other creatures while living in their streams, eels are not only born in the same place, but die there as well!

Oddly enough, drought will not prevent these fish from migrating back to the Sargasso Sea. Although classified as a fish, the eel can breathe through its skin when out of water, and therefore can migrate great distances over land!

Al Herpin never slept in his 94 years of life

Most of us get a full eight hours' sleep each night to perform at peak the following day. Others get along quite nicely with as little as three to four hours' shuteye. But it is universally agreed that a human being must eventually sleep, just as he must eat and drink. In fact, doctors are fond of saying that sleep is the brain's food; starve the brain and you die.

So what are we to make of the strange case of Al Herpin? A 90-year-old handyman of average intelligence and excellent health, Herpin lived in a tarpaper shanty outside Trenton, New Jersey, in the 1940's. When word spread of this ancient who claimed he had never slept, legions of doctors marched to his door, determined to expose the fraud and thus buttress their own medical theories.

Inside Al Herpin's house, the doctors found a rocking chair and a table—but no bed, no hammock, no cot, nothing on which a man might lie down. For weeks on end, medics attended Herpin in relays, waiting for the man to sneak a few winks. He never did. Naturally, after a hard day's work at odd jobs, he would be tired. But his way of resting was to sit in his rocker and read seven newspapers thoroughly until he felt refreshed.

Herpin himself contended that the cause of his lifelong insomnia was an injury his mother had suffered just a few days before delivering the infant Al.

Herpin finally closed his eyes for eternal sleep on January 3, 1947, at the age of 94.

The marmot has an air-raid warning system

High on the slopes of the Rocky Mountains lives a remarkable breed of small, burrowing rodents known as hoary marmots. These furry creatures, each about the size of a rabbit, make their homes in large colonies in the mountains. Each marmot family digs and maintains its own burrow, and a

colony can turn a barren, rocky slope into a bustling community. Peer down from the top of one of these slopes and you'll see hundreds of tiny brown heads popping out of holes all across the mountainside.

Hoary marmots play happily in the summer sun, nibbling moss and plant rocks, seemingly unconcerned about the danger of predators. But the marmots can afford to be lax in their vigilance. In each colony, one member of the group perches on a high rock and acts as sentinel. At the first glimpse of a dreaded enemy, like the golden eagle, the wary watchguard will fill the air with a thunderous whistle.

Instantly, each marmot scurries for cover in his own burrow. In seconds, a field teeming with busy animals becomes a barren, lifeless mountainside. But then, after the eagle has flown on, another loud whistle breaks the silence—the all-clear signal given by the marmot air-raid warden. And suddenly the slope is alive again.

The whistle of the hoary marmot is an extraordinary sound. Echoing over the rocks and through the valleys, the long, loud shriek sounds like the whistle of a freight train passing in the night. That such a loud sound could come from so small an animal seems unbelievable, for the marmot's voice box is no larger than a peanut. But the cry of this furry little fellow can be heard for a distance of *two miles* in any direction. It is the farthest-reaching sound made by any land animal on earth!

The "Scottish Brothers" had one body and two heads

In the late 15th century, the court of James III of Scotland featured one of the oddities of the age—the "Scottish Brothers." When young King James learned of a set of twins joined at the abdomen, with two legs, four arms, and two heads, he had the children sent to the royal court. James wanted not only to satisfy his curiosity, but also to save the freaks from possible harm in the rural backwater from which they came.

King James arranged for the "Scottish Brothers" to be educated, including special training in art, music, and foreign languages. As the brothers matured, they each developed passionate and sometimes contrary tastes in music, art, and letters. These antagonisms often reached the point of physical mayhem. The sight of the brothers' four fists raining blows upon their two heads must have looked like a helicopter.

The brothers lived under royal protection for the rest of their lives, until they were 28. One brother died five days before the other, who moaned piteously as he crept about the castle gardens, half dead and half alive.

Swahn competed in the Olympic games at age 73

As an accountant employed in the Stockholm office of the Swedish Telegram Bureau, Oscar G. Swahn must have seemed an ordinary enough person, but he was one of the finest riflemen who ever lived. During his 65-year career, he won more than 500 awards and prizes and he was a member of the Swedish shooting team at four meetings of the Olympic Games. His specialty was the running-deer event.

At the Paris Games in 1900, Swahn won a gold medal in the single-shot running-deer event. In 1908, at the London Games—where at age 61 he was the oldest participant in any event—Swahn again won a gold medal in the single-shot running-deer, a bronze medal in the double-shot, and helped win a gold medal for Sweden in the team single-shot event.

The 1912 Games were held in Stockholm, Swahn's home town. Competing before the admiring eyes of thousands of his countrymen, Swahn, again the oldest competitor, was a member of the gold-medal team in the single-shot running-deer event, and the bronze-medal team in the double-shot.

Because of World War I, the Olympic Games were not held in 1916. But at the first peacetime session of the Games, held in Antwerp in 1920, Swahn competed at the amazing age of 73. He helped win a team bronze medal for Sweden in the single-shot, and a team silver medal in the double-shot.

Four years later, Swahn once more qualified for the Swedish shooting team. At the last minute, though, he was prevented by illness from participating in the Games. He died in 1927 at the age of 80.

The genius of Sidis, a child prodigy, fizzled out as he grew older

William J. Sidis, Jr., son of an American psychiatrist, became his father's star pupil a short time after his birth in 1898. At the age of six months, William knew the alphabet. By the time he was two, the boy could read and write. By his eighth year, young Bill had completed 11 years of grammar school and high school. At nine, the boy entered Harvard University.

As an 11-year-old student at Harvard, Sidis delivered a lecture displaying his knowledge of the highly complicated fourth dimension, thoroughly amazing the members of the mathematics department. At the age of 16, he was graduated with honors, and at 19 he was made a full professor of mathematics.

Yet despite his virtually unprecedented scholastic achievements, Sidis failed to live up to the promise of his early years. At 26, the student who had been so brilliant in higher mathematics was discovered operating an adding machine in a New York store. In 1943, a lonely ex-genius, he died in a New York rooming house.

The hippopotamus's sweat is red

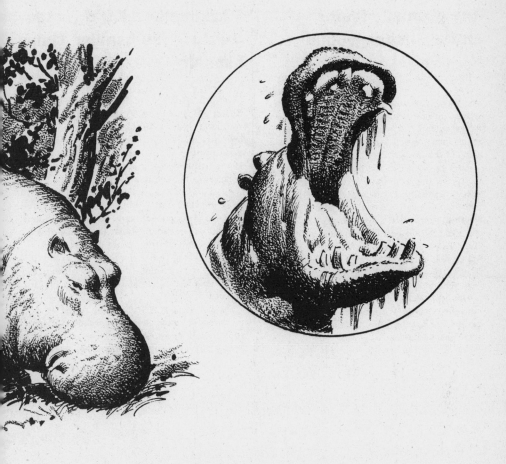

The hippopotamus is the second largest land animal in existence, giving precedence only to the elephant. This hefty relative of the hog grows to a length of thirteen feet, and a full-grown hippo can weigh more than six thousand pounds. Yet this African giant is a harmless, playful creature who spends most of his time frisking about in rivers, and never eats anything more than a leaf, root or blade of grass!

Understandably, the hippopotamus rarely gets excited. His great size makes rapid movement impossible, and in any event he is virtually without an enemy in the jungle. But when one of these three-ton titans does become excited, his thick, hairless hide exudes an odd carmine red perspiration that often inspires circus men to promise a "blood-sweating hippo" in their advertisements.

The peanut's fruits mature underground

When we think of a bizarre plant, we're likely to call to mind some exotic giant from the tropical rain forests. But often the plants that surround us have intriguing properties, too. The peanut is a good example. It is one of the few plants with the property of geocarpy, the underground ripening of fruit.

After pollinization, the peanut stalks holding the fertilized ovaries elongate and bend downward. Eventually this growth pushes the seed pods into the soil, where they mature. But the length to which these stalks can grow is limited, and the peanut plant has a mysterious way of "knowing" before pollination if the seed pods will be able to reach the ground. Thus, if the plant has grown too high, the upper parts of the plant will simply not produce any seeds!

Another "talent" exhibited by the peanut is versatility; George Washington Carver discovered several hundred uses for the various parts of the peanut plant.

Fitzsimmons KO'd a man 140 pounds heavier than himself

On April 30, 1900, in Brooklyn, New York, Robert Fitzsimmons, a 37-year-old Englishman, fought Edward Dunkhorst, an American heavyweight. "Ruby Robert," as he was known, stood five feet 11¾ inches in height, and didn't look particularly robust at 165 pounds. Dunkhorst tipped the scales at a hearty 305.

Fitzsimmons' strategy was clear. He would move in with a flurry of punches and then back off from his opponent, move in again and then back off. He intended to wear Dunkhorst down.

In the second round, Ruby Robert dropped the big, hulking Dunkhorst to the floor, and Ed never got up to continue the battle. Fitzsimmons had beaten a man who outweighed him by 140 pounds!

During his career, Ruby Robert, one of the great fistic names of all time, held the championship in the middle-weight class, the light-heavyweight class, and the heavyweight class.

The Winchester Mansion is the most bizarre house ever built

Mrs. Sara Winchester's mansion near San José, California, is without doubt the most bizarre residence ever constructed. This house—which began as a modest-sized dwelling in 1884—grew year by year into a nonsensical maze of rooms, corridors, and stairways, many of which served no function whatsoever. The most imaginative amusement-park funhouse could hardly compete with Mrs. Winchester's mansion in its freakishness of design.

This mansion owes its outlandish construction to Mrs. Winchester's odd fear—she was convinced she would die if she stopped adding rooms to her house! The wealthy woman was so certain of her conviction that she kept scores of carpenters, masons, and plumbers busy every day for nearly 38 years.

Some rooms in the mansion were built and furnished with the elegance of a royal palace, with gold and silver chandeliers, stained-glass windows, inlaid wood floors, and satin-covered walls. Other parts of the house were constructed only so that the eccentric resident could hear the reassuring bang of hammers. Some rooms measured only a few inches wide, and some stairways led nowhere. The mad mansion con-

Some cicadas live underground for seventeen years

Cicadas are the loudest singers in the insect world. These large, winged insects snap thin membranes on their thorax to produce a loud chirping that resembles the sound of locusts. In fact, some cicadas are often called "seven-year locusts" or "seventeen-year locusts," though they are not locusts at all.

The latter variety spends seventeen years eating and growing in underground passageways, then emerges for only a few weeks of sunshine before dying. Seventeen years later, a new generation of cicadas will emerge from the ground. These creatures thus constitute the longest-lived species in the insect kingdom!

tained 2,000 doors and 10,000 windows, many of which opened onto blank walls! The eight-story house also boasted three elevators, 48 fireplaces, nine kitchens, and miles of secret passages and hallways.

When Mrs. Winchester died in 1922 at the age of 85, her mansion contained 160 rooms and sprawled over six acres. The total cost of this insane structure was over $5,000,000!

Finn ran 100 yards in a sack in 14.4 seconds

Nowadays, sack races are usually held as entertainments during church outings or family picnics. But there was a time earlier in this century when the sack race was a regular event on many track and field schedules. The winner of such a contest scored just as many points for his team as did a pole vaulter or a miler.

The best sack racer ever was an Irish-American from Brooklyn, New York, by the name of Johnny Finn. On May 1, 1929, in New York's 106th Regiment Armory, Finn competed in the 100-yard race—the popular distance in sack events. Each of the contestants lined up at the starting line, each one standing up to his neck in a cumbersome burlap bag. The oddness of grown-up men enmeshed in a such a get-up brought the usual laughter from the crowd. However, with the crack of the starter's gun, everyone settled down to business. The athletes waddled, hopped, stumbled, and shuffled down the straightway.

At the finish, it was Finn as usual who was home first, breaking the tape at 14.4 seconds for a world's record. Just how fast that was may be gathered from the fact that on that same night—in the same meet—the 100-yard dash was won by a sprinter who covered the distance in 10.4 seconds.

The flying squirrel does not have wings

The name "flying squirrel" is a misnomer, for no mammal except the bat is capable of true flight. In fact, the flying squirrel does not even have wings. But these popeyed rodents could aptly be called "gliding squirrels," for that's just what they do—glide like paper airplanes from tree to tree.

Stretched between the squirrel's front and hind legs are thin, parachutelike flaps of skin, one on each side. By spreading these flaps wide as he pushes off from a branch, the flying squirrel can coast gracefully on air currents to another tree. Although some of these creatures are over two feet long, they can often soar between branches more than one hundred feet apart!

The birthwort "kidnaps" insects and then sets them free

The flowers of most insect-pollinated plants provide a convenient resting place and nourishing nectar for their welcome insect visitors. Some plants, however, can be rude hosts to the creatures they depend upon for pollination. Among the latter is the birthwort, which lures and then imprisons its insect benefactors, holding the creatures hostage until they've performed their unwitting duty.

Birthwort is the common name for a 600-member family of shrubs and vines most often found in the tropics. Some species are cultivated as medicinals, with their extract used in the treatment of snakebite. Other species, common to the steppes of Western Asia where goats frequently graze, produce flowers that both look and smell like goat droppings!

But the "kidnapper" among the birthwort is a European species. The flower of these plants forms a curving tube similar in shape to a saxophone, which exudes a foul odor attractive to some insects. When a visitor blunders in through the open end of the tube, it quickly becomes a hostage.

Still drawn on by the odor, the insect travels toward the swollen base of the flower tube. Stiff, downward-pointing hairs prevent escape. A transparent area in the wall of the tube, near the base, lures the captive further in search of an exit. Here the insect is likely to brush against the nearby stigma and pollinate the flower.

If the insect doesn't pollinate the flower, it cannot escape. But once the flower has been pollinated, the stigma grows erect and exposes the anthers, which "reward" the insect with a shower of pollen. Then the stiff hairs wither, and the captive is allowed to escape. In some cases, the thankless flower bends downward after pollination and rudely pitches the abused insect out!

The mouse deer can stand in the palm of a hand

If you were to come upon a mouse deer in the Malayan jungle, you might think you'd stumbled into the land of the Lilliputians. For this creature is the image of the full-sized deer that roams the forests of America, identical in almost every detail with its much larger counterpart—except that the fully grown mouse deer stands less than one foot high!

This miniature deer is incredibly dainty and beautiful. His legs are so slender they seem like sticks of fragile glass. His delicate head is even smaller than the head of a rat, and if the two animals meet, the rat would look the huskier of the pair.

For his size, the mouse deer is one of the fastest creatures in the jungle. He runs with a peculiar motion, something like the bouncing of a rubber ball, ending each few steps in a sprightly little leap.

The anableps has bifocal eyes

A tiny fish called the anableps, which makes its home in the American tropics, has eyes that function just like a pair of bifocal lenses. Each of its eyes is divided into two parts, the upper portion focused for vision above the surface of the water, the lower half for underwater sight. As the anableps swims at the water's surface, it can search for insects on the surface and at the same time watch out below for larger, deeper-swimming fish that would like to munch on the anableps. However, the little fish does have to duck its upper eyes under the water frequently to keep them moist.

St. Peter's is the largest Christian church in the world

For sheer size, the church of St. Peter's in Rome is an extraordinary structure, easily outstripping such great cathedrals as Rheims, Chartres, and Notre Dame de Paris. Yet St. Peter's is also one of the world's most renowned works of architecture, and boasts painting and sculpture by the greatest artists of the Renaissance. The crowning glory of an age, St. Peter's remains today the center of the Roman Catholic Church.

Even the site upon which St. Peter's rests is historically significant. It was here, on the left bank of the Tiber, that the Roman Emperor Nero built a large amphitheater to house his gory spectacles, in which thousands of Christians died for the viewing pleasure of the Roman masses. Among these victims was St. Peter, the Church's first pope, who was crucified and buried in a mass grave outside the amphitheater.

In the 4th century, the Roman Emperor Constantine the Great—the first Christian emperor—built a small church in place of the old amphitheater. The altar of this church was placed directly over the supposed site of Peter's grave. Here many popes and emperors—among them Charlemagne—were crowned.

By the 15th century, Constantine's church was crumbling, and portions were rebuilt by Pope Nicholas V. Then, in 1506, at the height of the Renaissance, Pope Julian II decided to construct a new church on the site, a grand church worthy of the most powerful institution in the world.

Julian's plan called for a church large enough to hold 80,000 people—at that time, the entire population of Rome! A monumental design by the architect Bramante was accepted, and the greatest construction project in the Church's history was underway.

Bramante's church was so large and elaborate that 12 architects spent most of their lives working on the project. Raphael was in charge of construction for a time. Michelangelo supervised the building of the immense dome, but he—like most of the artists who worked on the project —never lived to see the church completed.

The main section of St. Peter's is 700 feet long and 450 feet wide, enclosing an area of over seven acres. Most of the world's cathedrals could fit inside without difficulty. Imagine a church this large topped by a roof as high as a 15-story building!

Within the church are 44 altars, the largest being a huge work of bronze upon which only the Pope himself may conduct mass. Three-hundred-ninety statues—most of them quite large—adorn the interior and exterior. But the most extraordinary feature of the church is the massive dome designed by Michelangelo. For hundreds of years, the dome of St. Peter's stood as the world's largest. It is high enough to enclose the Capitol Building in Washington, D.C.—with 65 feet to spare!

Today, St. Peter's is only a part of the Vatican complex, with its numerous chapels, palaces, and gardens. But St. Peter's remains the greatest structure of the Vatican and the greatest church in the world.

It wasn't until 1626, 120 years after construction began, that St. Peter's was dedicated. And it was another 40 years before the vast piazza and colonnades in front of the church were finished. In memory of the thousands of Christians who had died in Nero's arena, an Egyptian obelisk that had stood in the center of the amphitheater was placed in the center of this piazza.

Robert Earl Hughes was the fattest man who ever lived

In 1926, a bouncing 11½-pound boy was born into the Hughes family of Fish Hook, Illinois. Christened Robert Earl, this Hughes boy was obviously bound for big things. At the age of six, he tipped the scales at 203 pounds; four years later, he weighed 378. He didn't stop adding avoirdupois until he had nearly tripled that weight.

In the last year of his life, spent with a touring carnival, Hughes had his dimensions reliably measured. His weight was 1,069 pounds; his waist was 124 inches around, exceeding the measure of his chest by two inches.

In July of 1958, Hughes came down with a case of measles. Though Hughes was gravely ill, he could not enter the hospital in Bremen, Indiana, where the carnival had stopped, for he could not pass through its door. Hughes' specially built house trailer was kept in the hospital parking lot, where oxygen could be administered and doctors and nurses could check on him.

All this attention proved to no avail. The measles cleared up, but were immediately followed by uremia—a failure of the kidneys. Robert Earl Hughes passed away on July 10, 1958. His coffin was made from a piano case, transported to a cemetery in Mount Sterling, Illinois, via a moving van. The weight of the coffin plus its occupant was over a ton; Hughes had to be lowered into the earth by a crane.

There is another American who is reputed to have weighed more than Hughes. Johnny Alee of Carbon, North Carolina (1853-1887), allegedly tipped the scales at 1,132 pounds, However, no reliable verification of this figure exists.

A camel can go without water for almost a week

The dromedary, or one-humped camel, is so well designed for desert travel that he has been called the "Ship of the Desert." While other animals would probably collapse from heat and thirst after a few hours in the desert sun, a fully laden dromedary can walk well over two hundred miles in the most parched desert—without so much as one drink of water!

It is the unusual arrangement of the camel's stomachs that suits him so well for desert travel. The dromedary's stomachs—he has several, like the cow—are lined with millions of tiny storage cells, which can retain enough water to sustain the hardy beast for close to a week.

The camel can also go without food for long periods of time. The hump on a dromedary's back holds layers of fat, and serves as a sort of food storehouse. Thus, a well-fed camel has a larger hump than an overworked, poorly fed one.

This walking reservoir has another talent that makes him particularly useful in the desert—a marvelous sense of smell. Camels can sniff out water holes from miles away. Many caravans would have perished if their "Ships of the Desert" hadn't found water for them.

Mistletoe is known as the "vampire plant"

The custom of kissing underneath a sprig of mistletoe has earned the plant a charming reputation. But there is another—hardly charming —side to this evergreen which is suggested by its gruesome nickname: "vampire plant." For as a vampire was thought to suck blood from its victims, so the parasitic mistletoe sucks the life's blood from its host plant.

Herbs and shrubs of the mistletoe family —there are 35 species in all—send modified roots, called haustoria, into the tissue of the host plant to obtain nourishment. Although mistletoe prefers trees, it can live on many different plants. Occasionally a mistletoe will even attach itself to another mistletoe! But the parasite can sap the strength from its host, and thus bring about the death of both plants.

Birds often assist in carrying mistletoe seeds to suitable host plants. As birds feed on the plant's waxy white berries, the seeds contained inside stick to their bills and feet. The birds scrape off the seeds on the bark of trees, and when the seeds germinate, the roots bore into the tissue of the newfound host.

One dwarf species of mistletoe has another way of spreading its progeny: its berries explode when ripe, sending seeds as far as 50 feet from the parent plant!

A wealth of folklore and superstition has surrounded mistletoe. Though often fatal to fellow plants, mistletoe was thought of as a panacea for many human ills. The plant was sacred to several early sects, among them the Druids, who apparently originated the custom of kissing underneath a sprig of the "vampire plant."

The armadillo rolls itself into an armor-plated ball

Various species of a bizzare-looking mammal known as the armadillo abound in the Western Hemisphere from the southwest United States to Argentina, and range in size from the fifteen-inch, twelve-ounce "pink fairy" armadillo to the five-foot, one 125-pound "giant." All species

have one thing in common: a body encased in a hard shell of small bony plates. When threatened by another creature, an armadillo will often roll itself up into a tightly compressed ball, pulling in its head and limbs and leaving little to attack but a mass of armor plates. One species, known as

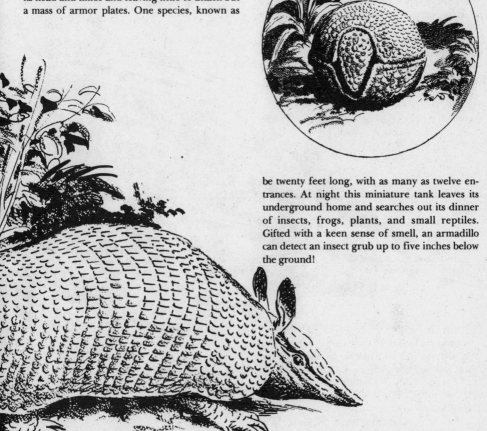

be twenty feet long, with as many as twelve entrances. At night this miniature tank leaves its underground home and searches out its dinner of insects, frogs, plants, and small reptiles. Gifted with a keen sense of smell, an armadillo can detect an insect grub up to five inches below the ground!

the three-banded armadillo, can curl up in a perfect ball, *completely* protected by its bony shell!

The armadillo is a nocturnal animal, and spends most of the day inside its burrow, a complex of underground passageways that it builds by scratching through the earth with its sharp, heavy claws. An armadillo's burrow complex can

Plaisted won a professional rowing race at age 74

When he was 17, Frederick Plaisted won his first professional rowing race, and with it $500 in cash. But it was his very last stake race—a race that occurred 57 years later—that earned Plaisted immortality.

Fred was 74 years old when he and two old professional rivals, Jim Ten Eyck and Jim Riley, set up a match in Saratoga to determine who was the best of the three. Plaisted, then of Philadel-

phia, found a backer who put up $1,000 for him. (Plaisted was finicky about his backers, and for good reason. He once went to China to race for $10,000 cash, only to find after his victory that $10,000 cash in Chinese money was worth $10 in American specie.)

At 5 a.m. on that morning in 1924, the three lined up before a crowd of 1,000 onlookers. The course was marked off at three miles—a good-sized race for rowers of any age bracket. The betting was fairly heavy.

For the first half-mile all three rowers seemed surprisingly strong. Then Ten Eyck, the rowing coach at Syracuse, faded. Riley, who had the advantage of being on his own course, pressed on, staying within striking distance of Plaisted.

But Plaisted, once a 240-pounder who now weighed in at 185, had power to burn. By the halfway mark, Fred was away by himself. As Riley grew weaker at the finish, Plaisted came in with considerable margin to spare, in the impressive time of 21 minutes, 4 seconds.

Fred Plaisted never raced again for money, but he did race again. He celebrated his 89th birthday by defeating John B. Kelly, an ex-Olympic champion and a much younger man, in a race on the Schuylkill in Philadelphia.

Crickets chirp more quickly in warm weather

The male cricket produces his characteristic chirping noises by rubbing his forewings together. The higher the air temperature, the greater the number of chirps he generates per minute. Thus, you can tell the temperature by counting a cricket's chirps! Provided that the thermometer reads between forty-five and eighty degrees, count the number of chirps you hear in fifteen seconds. Then add thirty-seven to this number. The result will tell you the exact air temperature at the time!

On his 91st birthday, Fred admitted to rowing three miles every other day, just to keep in shape. When interviewed, he said, "Technically, I am a better rower now than I ever was." He died when he was 95.

There is a fungus that can capture an animal

A carnivorous fungus known as *Zoophagus insidians* engages in a sort of microscopic fishing expedition to catch its dinner. Along the main stem of the fungus are short branches, called hyphae, which are appetizing to minute aquatic animals known as rotifers. When a rotifer bites into a hyphae, the tip of the branch begins to swell inside the animal. Like a fish snared on a hook, the rotifer is helplessly trapped on the swollen end of the branch!

As the victim struggles to escape, the fungus shoots out a glob of mucilage that helps to hold the prey. The fungus later ingests nutrients from the dead animal.

The llama spits when angry

Of all man's beasts of burden, only the llama is capable of carrying loads at very high altitudes. In the thin, freezing air of South America's Andes Mountains, this woolly camel is indis-

pensable to the Indians who reside there. He carries their burdens along the treacherous slopes, provides wool for clothing, and blankets and milk for Indian children. The llama's manure, when dried in the sun, provides the Indians with their only fuel. And when the beast dies, he is used to make leather.

But the llama, unlike the horse, simply refuses to be overworked. Knowing to the ounce just how much he can carry comfortably, the shaggy-haired carrier will drop to the ground and refuse to budge if so much as an extra pound is placed on his back. Furthermore, the llama will carry a burden only so far. After about twenty miles the arrogant fellow will begin a determined sit-down strike. Once the llama has decided to stop working, he can't be coaxed.

And what if an inexperienced master tries to make his llama work after the animal has decided to call it quits? Well, that man is in for an unpleasant surprise. An angry llama puckers his lips and spits in his tormentor's face—shooting a vile green juice from his mouth with surefire accuracy!

Chichester sailed around the world alone

During the 1920's and 1930's, a spare, simple-looking English real-estate magnate turned to flying. Combining skill with daring, Francis Chichester established a number of aerial records. However, one of his attempts led to his being invalided for five years. As soon as he was able to get around again, Chichester attempted a solo flight around the world, crashed into some telephone poles in Japan, and broke 13 bones, Finally, he decided to look elsewhere for his thrills.

When he was 52, Chichester set forth on the greatest adventure of his life: to sail around the world alone in his boat, the Gipsy Moth IV, a sea-going ketch 53 feet in length—a boat that was normally manned by a crew of six.

On August 27, 1966, Francis Chichester departed from Plymouth, England. It was to be a harrowing trip. When he reached the treacherous waters of Cape Horn, squalls as strong as 100 knots an hour rocked his ketch and frigid waves spilled over the deck. Five times the cockpit was flooded, and Chichester was constantly in mortal peril.

Yet against all odds, the man succeeded. Francis covered 28,500 miles in a voyage that took him 226 days. Queen Elizabeth was so impressed with his exploit that she knighted him while he was still at sea.

Chichester's trip must certainly stand as one of the greatest physical performances ever made by a man in his fifties.

The otter can dodge a rifle bullet

The otter, a member of the weasel family, makes his home on the banks of northern lakes and streams. This frisky fellow resembles a small seal, with a sleek, streamlined body, webbed hind feet, and a long, flat tail he uses as a rudder in swimming. An otter will often share a river bank with a beaver, but the two animals are as different as night and day: While the beaver is a hard-working, industrious sort, the otter is a fun loving fellow, one of the most playful of all animals—and one of the quickest!

Beavers spend a good deal of their day constructing dams, but otters prefer to spend their time building slides on the slopes of a snowy hill. Their favorite game is belly whopping. Their smooth stomachs are better to slide on than a toboggan, and their flat tails serve as steering gear. When the otters reach the bottom of the hill they wait for their playmates to take their slides. Then they all scurry back up to the top of the hill, take a short run, and belly whop down again. Best of all, otters love to slide down a hill right into the water!

For quickness, few animals can match the otter. In the water, this playboy of the animal world moves like greased lightning. He can poke his head out of a hole in the ice, disappear, and pop up through another hole yards away in a matter of seconds. And many hunters have reported that they've fired at an otter as he poked through an ice-hole, only to watch the creature disappear into the water again unharmed —*before* the bullet could reach the hole. The otter is indeed "faster than a speeding bullet"!

The Egyptian bean germinates while floating

The seeds of the Egyptian bean, or Indian lotus, enjoy a short river cruise before settling down to grow. This pink-blossomed plant, sacred to the Hindu and Buddhist alike, takes root in the silt of a river bottom, with its stalk extending upwards through the water. The fruits develop in large woody receptacles attached to the stalk at water level. Each receptacle normally contains from 20 to 25 individual sockets, with one fruit in each socket.

When the seeds are ripe, the receptacle breaks off from the stalk and the woody ark begins floating downstream. During their journey, the seeds begin to germinate, sending out shoots and leaves that give the water-borne seed pod the appearance of a floating flower pot. Eventually, the sprouted fruits are dislodged from the pod and sink to the bottom of the river, where the new plants will grow.

Grunions dance on the beach

Goldfish and tropical fish may keep you amused just by swimming around in their tanks, but there is another species of fish that puts these little entertainers to shame. Grunions, sardine-like fish about five inches long, stage a floor show on the beaches of southern California that might make you think you were watching trained animals in a circus!

Every year in the spring and summer, schools of grunions gather off California's beaches. When the moon and tides are just right, the grunions begin their show. Once carried onto shore by breaking waves, the female stands up on her tail and whirls around in a wild dance! As she dances, her tail digs a small hole in the wet sand. When the hole is deep enough, she deposits her eggs at the bottom.

The male grunion, also swept in by the waves, dances into the holes and fertilizes the eggs. Another wave then carries the male and female back into the ocean. The entire performance

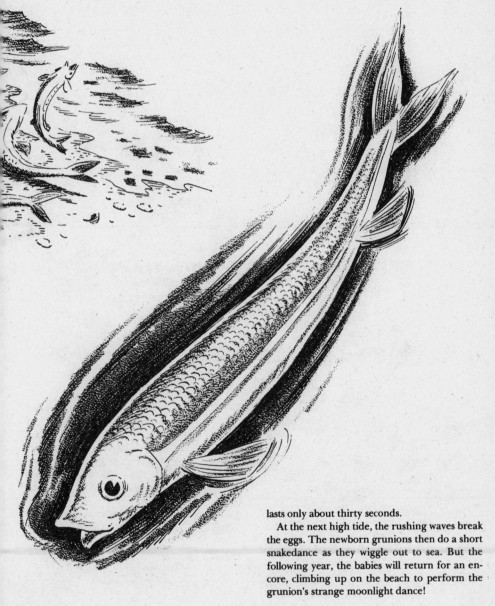

lasts only about thirty seconds.

At the next high tide, the rushing waves break the eggs. The newborn grunions then do a short snakedance as they wiggle out to sea. But the following year, the babies will return for an encore, climbing up on the beach to perform the grunion's strange moonlight dance!

Ross paddled across the English Channel in four hours and seven minutes

The kayak was invented by the Eskimos for hunting trips in the stilled icy seas of the Far North. Certainly this rather frail craft was not conceived to battle the churning swells and tidal currents of the English Channel. But civilized man, in order to evidence his mastery of nature, has always sought new ways to pit brain and muscle against seemingly unconquerable forces. And so the men of our day have taken to cross the Channel in kayaks. The fact is it's been done several times.

In this exercise, none was faster than one Henry Ross, an engineer from Surrey, England. Setting out from Gris Nez in France on a bright morning, August 10, 1950, Ross began to paddle toward Dover. It was the same 22-mile route taken by most Channel swimmers.

Aided by ideal weather and driven by furious determination, the 37-year-old Ross moved much faster than even he had planned. When he pulled into Dover only four hours and seven minutes after leaving France, he learned that he had bested the then existing record by a full 50 minutes.

The trap-door spider booby-traps its prey

Spiders have always been known as wily creatures, but the trap-door spider may be the slyest of them all. If you ever catch a glimpse of this crafty critter scurrying over the deserts of Mexico or the southwestern United States, don't be surprised if he disappears before your very eyes!

This amazing arachnid lives in upright tunnels he digs in the parched ground. The mouth of the tunnel is covered with a trapdoor that is made of sand and pebbles and hinged to the ground on one side. This door is so skillfully constructed that it's almost impossible to detect when closed. But the trap-door spider knows where the tunnels are, and in a split second he can open the door, slip inside, and close the door again—seemingly vanishing into thin air!

Equally clever is the way the trap-door spider booby-traps his prey. This creature has especially sensitive hearing, and when an unsuspecting insect wanders close to his trapdoor, the spider hears its tread, pops out of his tunnel, and carries his catch inside!

Cornflower fruits travel like airborne shuttlecocks

The cornflower, a common herb found throughout much of North America and Europe, has a curious way of dispersing its seeds. The fruits of the cornflower develop in shallow receptacles. Hairlike bristles project from each fruit. In damp weather, these bristles bunch together to form a sort of brush above the receptacle, with the fruits jammed in tightly underneath. In dry weather, the bristles fan out and raise their fruits to the top of the receptacle. Breezes swing the cornflower stalks, and the fruits are tossed into the air like tiny shuttlecocks!

Browning somersaulted seven feet and three inches

In 1954, the world's record for the high jump was six feet, eleven and one-half inches, held by Walt Davis who was almost that tall himself. But that year there was a little five-foot nine-inch gymnast who could leap even higher.

Dick Browning, a 20-year-old sophomore of the University of Illinois, was generally acknowledged to be the world's greatest tumbler at the time. His execution of the somersault was nonpareil. He was so good he could beat the best high jumper of his day.

On April 27, 1954, at an exhibition in Santa Barbara, California, Dick Browning, rounding off his routine, somersaulted over a bar which was seven feet, three inches high. When Browning's record was reported, track coaches all over the country scoffed. Track rules specifically insist that a high jump be executed from a one-foot take-off. If this five-foot nine-inch midget did in fact leap seven feet, then he must have, they claimed, pushed off with two feet. However, all who had been present and carefully watched the performance avowed that when Browning took off, he had turned his body slightly in order to get more spring, and that, in fact, one of his feet left the ground before the other. Dick's leap, witnesses insisted, complied with all the rules.

Whether the jump was or was not according to Hoyle is really beside the point. For the wonder still stands: how could a man execute a somersault so high that he indeed did clear a seven-foot three-inch bar?

The towers of the Shwe Dagon Pagoda are completely covered with gold

Each year, thousands of Burmese pilgrims journey to the capital city of Rangoon to visit the country's most sacred temple, the Shwe Dagon Pagoda. This 15th century temple-monastery, the center of all Burmese religious life, is most notable for its tall, cone-shaped towers, which are completely covered with gold.

Shwe Dagon is a complex of temples, reliquaries, towers, and gates, abounding in richly carved ornamentation. Surrounding the complex is a multi-colored tiled terrace 1,420 feet around. Towering above the terrace and gateways are the brick stupas, or sacred relic chambers, each of which is surmounted by a cone-shaped tower covered with gold leaf. The largest of these towers is 326 feet above the terrace, and its glittering gold pinnacle can be seen from virtually any part of Rangoon.

Through the ages, while Western churches have been pillaged, the Pyramids looted, and the Taj Mahal stripped of its gems, here in the center of a large city a fortune in gold has remained untouched. Neither an earthquake that ravaged the city, nor floods, nor heavy bombardment during the Second World War could destroy the fabulous golden cones of Shwe Dagon.

A pit viper finds its food by radar

Three poisonous snakes indigenous to the United States—the rattlesnake, copperhead, and water moccasin—all belong to a family of snakes known as the pit vipers. These creatures are probably the most recently evolved of all snakes, for they are equipped with not only venomous fangs, but a sort of radar system as well.

The pit vipers have a small hole, or *pit*, behind each nostril. This depression, which looks very much like a second nostril, is actually a sixth sense, a kind of radar organ sensitive to heat rays. By using this unusual organ a pit viper can find its prey—even in the dark—by following the body heat radiated by the victim's body!

Sigmund swam continuously for 89 hours and 48 minutes

At 7:22 p.m., July 25, 1940, John Sigmund lowered himself into the Mississippi River at St. Louis, Missouri, and set out on one of the most adventuresome swims ever attempted. The 30-year-old St. Louis butcher would swim for 89 hours and 48 minutes before being pulled out of the water on July 28, dazed and exhausted, at Caruthersville, Missouri.

The Mississippi River is so muddy that floating objects often can't be seen. During his stint, Sigmund injured a leg on a submerged log. Some time later, the waves of a passing barge washed him against his accompanying cabin cruiser and nearly knocked him unconscious. And to add to his travail, on the very last night of his journey, Sigmund wandered three miles off course when he mistakenly entered one of the Mississippi's tributaries.

For energy, his wife, Catherine, frequently furnished him with candy bars. It was only through her constant prodding during the final 25 miles that the exhausted Sigmund was prevented from falling asleep in the water. At the finish—292 miles from his starting point, an all-time distance record—hundreds of bystanders cheered. But Sigmund could not acknowledge their acclaim. Unable to either walk or talk, he was carried off by friends.

Nevertheless, the next day John showed no ill effects. The damage—a sun-blistered face, wobbly legs, and aching muscles—would quickly pass away.

The Lithops plant is a "living stone"

Camouflage is uncommon in the plant kingdom. The bizarre shapes and color arrangements displayed by many species serve mainly to attract pollinators, rarely to protect the plant from potential harm. However, there is one remarkable family of plants that has developed a highly effective form of camouflage. These plants resemble rocks and pebbles so closely that they are commonly called "living stones."

These stone mimics are found in the barren, rock-strewn wastes of southern Africa, where the paucity of vegetative life would make an undisguised plant an easy prey for the birds, baboons, and other creatures that feed in the area. The "living stones," however, blend in perfectly with this rocky landscape. One species resembles pieces of greenish granite; another mimics limestone; another, quartz. Perhaps the most remarkable members of the family are those of the Lithops group, which closely resemble small pebbles.

Lithops plants are stemless, and their leaves are buried in the soil so that only the tips are visible. These tips form a fleshy, roundish structure, which is flat on top and almost flush against the ground. Their mottled shades of gray, brown, and red mimic the coloration of the pebbles that surround them. Frequently, the plants spread sideways, so that one plant may appear to be several stones.

The Lithops are distinguished by a narrow slit which runs across the flat upper surface of the leaf. During the flowering season, tall flower stems rise from the slit. But when the dry season returns, the flowers disappear, and the mimics once again become indistinguishable from the stony landscape.

Some turtles live for more than 200 years

There is a great deal of truth in the old fable of the hare and the tortoise. The turtle may be one of the slowest creatures in the animal kingdom, but what he lacks in speed he makes up for in longevity. For not only was the turtle thriving long before most of today's animals came into existence, but this cousin of the early dinosaurs lives longer than any other creature on earth! Incredible as it may seem, giant tortoises have been known to attain an age of well over two hundred years, and scientists believe that some turtles may even reach the age of three centuries!

Why does this hard-shelled fellow live so long? Because he takes thing easy! A turtle eats slowly, moves slowly, grows slowly, even breathes slowly. It takes more than a year just for the sluggish reptile's shell to become hard. And some turtle eggs take as long as a year to hatch!

During his winter hibernation, the turtle's body functions so minimally he's practically in a state of suspended animation. When winter comes, the cold-blooded creature burrows deep into the mud at the bottom of some body of water—an ocean, lake, river, or pond. His ordinarily slow breathing ceases almost entirely. The tiny amount of oxygen he needs to stay alive is contained in the mud around him. And this mud is also just warm enough to keep him from freezing.

Turtles can be found living both on land and in fresh and salt water, and the marine and terrestrial forms both vary greatly in size. Marine turtles range from just an inch or so up to six feet in length. The Galapagos turtle, a terrestrial species, can weigh up to 500 pounds; but the average adult Leatherback—the largest marine turtle—measures six feet long and weighs 1,000 pounds!

Walcott won the heavyweight boxing title at age 37

A boxer is generally in his prime during his mid-twenties. By the time he has hit twenty-nine he is, as a rule, considered a has-been, ready for retirement.

But not Jersey Joe Walcott. On July 18, 1951, when he entered the ring against the faster, more agile Ezzard Charles, Jersey Joe was challenging the champ for the third time. Twice before, Walcott had tried and lost. Moreover, Walcott had twice lost to former champ Joe Louis. After a total of four failures—in itself a record for trying to take the heavyweight title—Walcott had resigned from the ring.

That Jersey Joe would venture a championship fight for the fifth time was astonishing; and the odds of six to one against him reflected how fistic experts regarded his chances.

Ezzard Charles had seemed a cinch to win. He had come to fight with a string of 24 straight wins behind him. Walcott, the "has-been" and father of six, had gone into the ring with a lot of bills to pay. He had come out of retirement because he needed the money.

The bout was held in Pittsburgh's Forbes Field. A goodly crowd of 28,000 attended and a television audience of 60 million watched. Walcott, 194 pounds, got off to a slow start. But in the third round he opened up a cut under Charles' eye. In the next three rounds, Joe racked up points, and in the seventh, the "old man" lured the champ into a trap. Feinting a body punch, Joe let go with a short, crisp hook—only about six inches—to Charles' jaw. Ezzard fell, tried to rise, then toppled again. The fight was over.

Thus Jersey Joe, a veteran of 21 years in the ring and thirty-seven years old, became the oldest man ever to win the world's heavyweight title.

A seal can swim steadily for eight months

Alaskan seals are the best long-distance swimmers in the world. In late spring and summer, they bear their young on the rocky islands off the Alaskan coast. Then they take to the water and swim south to avoid the frigid Arctic winter. For eight months these sleek mammals remain in the ocean, sometimes swimming as much as six thousand miles without once touching land before they return to Alaska in the spring.

Much of these eight months are spent underwater, but, unlike most mammals, seals do not have to hold their breaths to prevent themselves from drowning. Like beavers and hippopotamuses, seals have a ringlike muscle around each nostril that can be contracted to prevent water from entering their lungs.

The Cherry Sisters' terrible acting made them famous and rich

Perhaps the strangest success story in the theatrical world is that of the fabulous Cherry Sisters. Leaving their home in the Iowa corn country in 1893, the four girls made their debut in Cedar Rapids in a skit they wrote themselves. For three years, the Cherry Sisters performed to packed theaters throughout the Middle West; people came to see them just to find out if they really were *that* bad. Their unbelievably atrocious acting enraged critics and provoked spectators to throw vegetables at the "actresses." Wisely, the sisters thought to travel with an iron screen which they could erect on stage for self-defense.

By 1896, the girls were offered a thousand dollars a week to perform on Broadway.

Seven years later, after the Cherry Sisters had earned the then respectable fortune of $200,000, they retired from theatrical life for the more peaceful life down on the farm. Oddly

enough, these successful Broadway "stars" remained convinced to the end that they were truly the most talented actresses to grace the American stage.

Sinclair walked nearly 216 miles without stopping

John Sinclair is the marathon-walking champion of the world, and he has racked up an impressive series of walking records. He walked from John O'Groats in Scotland to Land's End in Cornwall, the length of the island of Britain, about 600 miles, in 19 days and 22 hours. In 1967, he walked from Cape Town to Pretoria, a distance of more than 900 miles, in only 23 days.

But John Sinclair's greatest walking feat was performed between April 21 and 23, 1969. The walk took place at the Wingfield Aerodrome, a facility of the South African Navy just outside Simonstown, and it was conducted under official Navy auspices.

The 50-year-old Sinclair began his record-breaking stroll at 5 p.m. on Tuesday, April 21st. Maintaining a steady pace of four miles an hour, and wearing sturdy leather boots that he had carefully broken in some weeks earlier in preparation for the event, he marched around the field's 5.25-mile perimeter, undaunted by the cold, windy rain that began to fall almost immediately after he started.

The rain continued for the next three days, and so did Sinclair. Officers and enlisted men of the South African Navy provided him with food and drink when needed, and served as official observers to ensure that he kept moving at all times and never varied from the measured course around the field.

John Sinclair made his last circuit around Wingfield Aerodrome at 3:42 p.m. on Thursday, April 23. In 47 hours and 42 minutes, he had walked 215 miles, 1,670 yards—the greatest feat of marathon walking ever recorded.

The resurrection plant moves in search of water

The resurrection plant, a desert growth found in arid regions of America and the Near East, owes its name to its extraordinary ability to come to life again from a seemingly dead and shriveled state. Of course, the plant does not really come back from the dead, but from a form of "hibernation" in which it is almost completely inactive. And unlike most other plants, which must wait for water, the resurrection plant can move over the land to search for needed moisture!

The name *resurrection plant* is applied to several species, including the Biblical rose of Jericho, which exhibit similar resurrective powers. In the presence of water, a resurrection plant will flourish, sporting green fernlike leaves. But when moisture is scarce, the plant pulls up its roots and withers into a dry, ball-like mass of apparently dead matter, completely devoid of green coloration. This withered mass is carried along the ground by the wind, and can remain in a dormant state *for years* if no water is found!

But once moisture is located, or after a rain, the plant sinks roots into the wet ground and springs to life again. Its leaves uncurl, again revealing green tissue on their undersides. The plant fares well until the moisture has evaporated, then curls up into a withered ball and roams again in search of water!

Kangaroos can't walk—but they can travel at 40 miles an hour

The kangaroo is undoubtedly the world's champion jumper. This curious-looking Australian mammal cannot walk at all—but he sure can leap! Moving along in fifteen-to twenty-foot bounds, a racing kangaroo can travel at close to forty miles an hour. And he can leap without stopping for hours at a time, sometimes covering a distance of twenty miles without a rest!

The kangaroo has a small head and large pointed ears, like a rabbit's. His front limbs are very short, but his hind quarters are the size of a mule's, with feet that sometimes measure ten inches from the heel to the longest toe. The kangaroo's thick tail is so strong that he can sit on it as if it were a stool. Big feet give the kangaroo a firm grounding, and his strong tail helps him

keep his balance during long leaps. Although he is no taller than five feet, this bouncy fellow can easily hop over a parked car!

The kangaroo is a marsupial, which means that the female has a pouch for transporting her offspring. After birth, an infant kangaroo—only an inch long—is immediately placed in this fur-lined pouch, outside his mother's stomach, where he nurses cozily for four to five months. This arrangement is convenient for the parent, too, because she can go about her business without taking time out to look after her baby. When the young kangaroo grows too large to fit into

the pouch, he leaves his snug retreat and learns to leap like his parents.

The kangaroo is a vegetarian, and will seldom harm another animal. But the big bouncers can be trained to box with boxing gloves, just like prizefighters. The kangaroo will use his two front paws to hit, swing, and deliver some surprisingly solid blows. His tail acts as a third leg, and gives him extra support. A trained kangaroo will stay on his feet long after his boxing partner is exhausted!

Pat Havener packed 90 cans of sardines in 10 minutes

Among the thousands of contests that take place each year, one of the most curious is the World Championship Sardine Packing Contest, which is held every August at Fishermen's Memorial Pier in Rockland, Maine. A regular part of the annual Maine Seafoods Festival, this contest, which reflects the importance of the sardine industry to Maine's economy, attracts numerous entrants from canneries throughout the state.

To pack a sardine, one must pick it up, deftly snip off its head and tail with razor-sharp scissors, and place it neatly in an open sardine can. Whoever packs the most sardines in a 10-minute period receives a cash prize and an engraved trophy from the governor of Maine.

The all-time champion sardine-packer is Mrs. Patricia Havener of Waldoboro, Maine, who, with her mother and sisters, works for the Port Clyde Packing Company in Rockland. In August 1971, when she was 24 years old, Pat Havener packed 90 cans of "number fives" (five sardines to the can) in 10 minutes.

With an overall total of 450 sardines, Pat processed an average of 45 of the shiny little fish each and every minute.

The cuckoo pint "tars-and-feathers" insects to assure pollination

Most plants that depend upon insects for pollination are gracious hosts, providing their visitors with a convenient passage to and from the nectary. But the cuckoo pint, an arum plant indigenous to Europe, is, on the contrary, quite inhospitable. To assure pollination, the cuckoo pint traps its helpful guests and "tars-and-feathers" the insects before permitting them to depart.

The cuckoo pint generates a fetid odor during the early evening hours, which attracts minute flies that normally breed in cow dung. Mistaking the flower for rotting meat, the flies enter its tubelike chamber and tumble down into the floral trap.

As a fly enters the flower, any pollen it may have picked up from another cuckoo pint is brushed off against the pistil at the bottom of the chamber, thereby pollinating the plant. The fly then gorges itself on a secretion found near the bottom of the pistil. When sated, the fly tries to leave the plant, but the slippery walls of the chamber prevent escape. The prisoner remains, "tarring" itself with the sticky nectar all night long.

In the morning, the stamen further up in the tube trembles lightly and "feathers" the fly with pollen. The flower then wilts and opens slightly, allowing the pollen-laden fly to emerge.

Mary Joyce traveled 1,000 miles by dog sled

The rigors of the frozen North are famed in song and story. A dog-sled trip of even 100 miles holds its terrors for even a strong man enured to the biting cold and fierce winds of the frigid zone.

Yet on Thursday, March 26, 1936, in the dead of the Arctic winter, one 27-year-old Alaskan girl drove her dog sled into Fairbanks, Alaska, from distant Taku—a trip of 1,000 miles. She had left her hunting lodge which was 40 miles from Juneau on December 22, 1935, heading into the treacherous mountains, the blizzards, and the loneliness which lay ahead. For about three months, without any human aid, she battled the elements, rarely encountering weather any mild-

cap and knee-length moccasins, Miss Joyce presented a striking picture as she swung down the home stretch of the Richardson Highway into Fairbanks, where standing exultantly in front of her team of five huskies, she was acclaimed by the town's notables.

er than 34 degrees below zero, and hitting days when the thermometer dropped to 60 below.

Neatly attired in dark blue hiking trousers, heavy blue woolen jacket, snug-fitting black fur

The frogfish catches its prey with rod and reel

Fishermen have nothing on the frogfish, for this peculiar sea creature catches its supper with a built-in hook and line. Long strands that resemble thin fishing lines are rooted to the top of the frogfish's head. Lying in ambush, the frogfish casts out the strands, and smaller fish, taking these dangling threads to be swimming worms, go for a nibble. Once caught on the barbed end of the strand, the would-be worm eaters are immediately gobbled up by the frogfish.

Victoria Zacchini traveled 200 feet as a human cannonball

Few circus events require the daring and poise of the stunt which has become to be known as "The Human Cannonball." This act employs lots of phony noise and smoke, and then jets a human being into space from the mouth of a cannon.

Despite the hoopla, the successful completion of this act depends on exact coordination between the person who is being shot, the huge spring that catapults him, and the assistants in charge of the mechanism. The "cannonball" must maintain his poise while traveling through the air—and he travels faster than a speeding automobile. He is supposed to land in a net some distance away, but if the propulsion is weak or there is some other flaw, he can fall short of that distance with disastrous results. Over 30 human "bullets" have died during the 20th century.

During April of 1943, in New York's Polo Grounds, Victoria Zacchini was shot from the barrel of the 22-foot silver cannon at a speed of well over 100 miles an hour. The 110-pound human projectile climbed to a height of over 100 feet and then fell safely into a net 200 feet away—a record shot!

A 40-pound wolverine can kill a 300-pound caribou

The wolverine is the largest and fiercest member of the weasel family. This furry resident of the northern regions is a savage hunter, stalking its prey and then leaping from a rock or tree for the kill. Although the wolverine is usually less than four feet long, and weighs only forty pounds or

An anaconda can swallow a pig

The gigantic anaconda snake of South America may make do with only one meal in several months, but what a meal it is! This monster of the boa family may range up to twenty-eight feet in length and weigh nearly two hundred pounds, and it is quite capable of swallowing an entire pig or deer.

The anaconda kills by coiling its body around its prey and applying terrific pressure, thereby stopping the victim's heart. Then the snake sets to work swallowing the animal whole, a job that may take several hours. Powerful digestive juices in the serpent's stomach can easily dissolve the largest bones.

The anaconda's huge meal forms a lump that swells the snake out of shape. A hunter who catches one of these snakes soon after a meal can kill the serpent, cut open its body, remove the pig that has just been swallowed, and rush it home to his own cooking pot!

so, this ravenous creature will attack almost any animal it meets—even a three-hundred-pound caribou!

The wolverine is as cunning as it is vicious, and will rob the most cleverly constructed traps. It can, in the words of one trapper, dig like a badger, climb like a squirrel, swim like an otter, and jump to the height of a man.

French-Canadians call the wolverine *carcajou*—glutton—because it will gorge itself on almost anything. But this fierce little fellow will never attack a man.

The aardvark "plants" and fertilizes the desert melon's seeds

The desert melon has a curious relationship with an animal that shares its South African habitat, the aardvark. The melon provides water for the aardvark, and in turn the insectivore helps spread the melon's seeds.

An aardvark will claw open a desert melon to drink the water inside the fruit. In so doing, it ingests a number of melon seeds. The undigested seeds are excreted with the animal's dung. Since the aardvark buries its dung, the desert melon seeds find a place in the soil, and a supply of nourishing manure as well!

William Northmore lost $850,000 on the turn of a card

William Northmore (1690-1735) of Okehampton, England, was an inveterate gambler. Cards were what he loved best, but he'd just as soon bet on the horses, or on votes in Parliament.

After several years of stunning success, he met his downfall in the form of an ace of diamonds. With the turn of that one card, his entire fortune of $850,000 was wiped out. Northmore vowed never to gamble another penny, but his promise was somewhat hollow, for he had nary a penny to gamble with.

Lady Luck soon smiled on the beggared young man, not at the gaming tables, but at the polls. The townspeople of Okehampton, in sympathy for Northmore's plight, elected him to Parliament in 1714, and in every election thereafter until his death 19 years later.

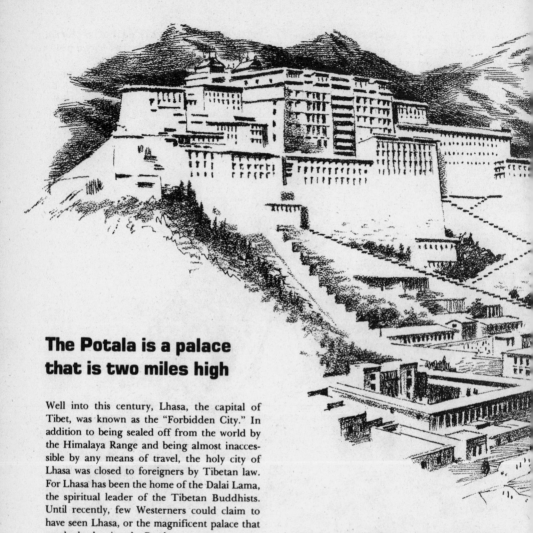

The Potala is a palace that is two miles high

Well into this century, Lhasa, the capital of Tibet, was known as the "Forbidden City." In addition to being sealed off from the world by the Himalaya Range and being almost inaccessible by any means of travel, the holy city of Lhasa was closed to foreigners by Tibetan law. For Lhasa has been the home of the Dalai Lama, the spiritual leader of the Tibetan Buddhists. Until recently, few Westerners could claim to have seen Lhasa, or the magnificent palace that overlooks the city: the Potala.

Begun in the year 700, the Potala has served through the centuries as the palace of the Dalai Lama, the seat of the Tibetan government, a college, a monastery, and a fort. Lhasa itself is 12,000 feet above sea level, an altitude at which even the hardiest foreigner will find physical activity extremely taxing; yet the Potala was built high above the city, straddling a steep hill just outside Lhasa. Long zig-zagging stairways provide the only access to the fortress.

The Potala—the "Palace of the Gods"—is a massive complex of buildings which extends for 1,000 feet across the side of the hill and rises nine stories over its lofty foundation. More than 1,400 windows look down over the city. Inside, over 1,000 monks can live and study in the Potala's 500 rooms. The quarters of the Dalai Lama are in a smaller palace within the Potala. For the most part, the fortress is white-washed and unornamented, built to withstand the bitter Tibetan winter—but the central portion of the

There is a fish that climbs trees

The Australian walking fish has the best of two worlds. In the water it swims like any other fish. But this unusual fish's fins are bent in such a way that they can be used for walking, too. And the walking fish often does take a stroll, right out of the water, climbing the lower branches of trees at the water's edge and roosting there for hours! This peculiar fish seems capable of surviving quite well out of water, and even snacks on insects it finds in the trees.

Potala is painted red, and its roof and towers are covered with glittering gold!

Since the Chinese invasion of Tibet in 1959, the Dalai Lama has lived in exile in India. The Potala has been shelled by Chinese troops, and many monks have fled to neighboring Himalayan countries. But in the minds of all Tibetans, the Potala, the palace that soars to the clouds, remains the most sacred building in the world.

Kittinger dropped 16 miles before opening his parachute

Inscribed on the cockpit door of the balloon was a legend that read: "The world's biggest step." And indeed it was! For the balloon carrying Joseph Kittinger, a United States Air Force captain, was 19 miles up in the sky, sailing along at a height of 102,000 feet over New Mexico, when on August 16, 1960, Kittinger took that step, and made history.

Falling freely through the air, Kittinger picked up speed each second. Mile after mile he fell, with his parachute firmly packed on his back. But though he encountered a pitiless wind as he reached a falling speed of over 600 miles an hour, the 32-year-old Kittinger maintained his composure. It wasn't easy to brook a temperature as low, at times, as 94 degrees below zero.

Yet, before releasing his chute, the dauntless captain dropped 84,700 feet—more than 16 miles! He had fallen through space for four minutes and 38 seconds, a world's record for a free fall.

After Kittinger opened his parachute, it took 13 minutes for him to float down the last three miles to terra firma.

The scarlet pimpernel can predict the weather

The next time you go camping in the woods and would like the weather forecast in the morning, don't turn on a transistor radio—try to find a scarlet pimpernel. The scarlet, white, or purplish flowers of this herb will close up in the morning if rain or cloudy weather is in store, and expand if the weather will be fair. This prophetic property has earned the scarlet pimpernel the nickname of "poor man's weatherglass."

Mosienko scored three goals in 21 seconds in a professional hockey game

In a lackluster professional hockey game in New York on March 23, 1952, the New York Rangers were pitted against the Chicago Black Hawks. The visitors were behind, 6 to 2, in the final period; some of the more than 3,000 fans who had come to see the game had already left the dreary spectacle. The Rangers had the game virtually won. What was there to stay for?

Then, with less than 14 minutes to play, right wing Bill Mosienko, thirty years old, picked up a pass from teammate Gus Bodnar and rapped in a goal.

On the ensuing face-off, Bodnar again got the puck to Mosienko, and the pint-sized 160-pounder smashed in goal No. 2. Only 11 seconds had separated the two tallies. The score now stood at 6 to 4.

On the next face-off, Mosienko skated into position. There was Bodnar again with another perfect pass. The Chicago player faked a defenseman out of position and blasted a long shot at the befuddled goalie, who stood helpless as the puck passed by him into the net for Mosienko's third score! This trio of tallies took all of 21 seconds—a record that is likely to hold for many a year.

Mosienko was done for the night, but his teammates were not. Infused with new life, they scored still another two goals against their now fog-eyed opponents to win an amazing 7 to 6 victory.

The honeybee's wings beat two hundred times per second

A honeybee hive is one of the busiest places in the world, a crowded city literally buzzing with activity. In the fifty thousand rooms, or cells, of an average beehive, more than 35,000 bees go about their never-ending labors, each performing a special job.

There is the queen, who lays her own weight in eggs daily; there are drones, male bees whose only task is to mate with newly hatched queens; there are workers, females who serve as nurses, guards, cell builders, and food gatherers for the insect metropolis. These bees leave the hive to seek the flower nectar with which they manufacture honey and wax for the colony. And it's hard work—it takes 37,000 trips from hive to flower and back again to produce just one pound of honey!

But bees are quick and thrive on constant work. Their frail wings beat at the incredible rate of two hundred times per second! That's so fast that the human eye perceives only a blur—and some cameras do, too!

The bee's rapid wing beat is put to another use when the insects are in their hive. Since it is difficult for fresh air to reach all the workers and young bees in the middle of a hive, the resident bees set up an air-conditioning system, beating their wings to create a draft. In the winter, this activity keeps the bees warm.

Incidentally, bees are unaware of the buzzing sound they're noted for. As far as anyone can tell, honeybees are completely deaf.